"A Truthful Impression of the Country"

"A Truthful Impression of the Country"

British and American Travel Writing in China, 1880–1949

Nicholas Clifford

Ann Arbor

THE UNIVERSITY OF MICHIGAN PRESS

2004   2003   2002   2001   4   3   2   1

A CIP catalog record for this book is available from the British Library.

Library of Congress Cataloging-in-Publication Data

Clifford, N. J. (Nicholas J.)
    "A truthful impression of the country" : British and American
travel writing in China, 1880–1949 / Nicholas Clifford.
        p.   cm.
    Includes bibliographical references and index.
    ISBN 0-472-11197-3 (acid-free)
    1. China—Description and travel. 2. Travelers' writings,
English—History and criticism. 3. British—Travel—China—History—
19th century. 4. British—Travel—China—History—20th century. 5.
Travelers' writings, American—History and criticism. 6. Americans—
Travel—China—History—19th century. 7. Americans—Travel—China—
History—20th century. I. Title.
DS709 .C634   2001
915.104'4—dc21   00-012313

For Deborah

I cannot hope to escape errors, but I have made a laborious effort to be accurate, and I trust and believe that they are not of material importance, and that in the main this volume will be found to convey a truthful impression of the country and its people.
  —Isabella Bird Bishop, *The Yangtze Valley and Beyond*

To travel is, as it were, to go to the play, to attend a spectacle; and there is something heartless in stepping forth into foreign streets to feast on "character" when character consists simply of the slightly different costume in which labour and want present themselves . . . Our observation in any foreign land is extremely superficial, and our remarks are happily not addressed to the inhabitants themselves, who would be sure to exclaim upon the impudence of the fancy-picture.
                    —Henry James, "Italy Revisited"

Contents

Illustrations

Note on Romanization

The chaos of all things Chinese is well illustrated in the
spelling or transliteration of the characters for place names.
One finds Chifu and Cheefoo used with equal authority;
Chili, Chihli, or Dsh-ly; Taku or Dagu; Kanlung or Kowloon.
—Eliza Scidmore, *China: The Long-Lived Empire*

Except in direct quotations, and for commonly used names and terms
(e.g., Chiang Kai-shek) I have used *pinyin* romanization. The following
list may be of some help for those unfamiliar with the system.

Pinyin	Conventional	*Pinyin*	Conventional
Baoan	Pao-an	Guo Songdao	Kuo Sung-tao
Beijing	Peking	Guomindang	Kuomintang
Beiping	Peiping	Hangzhou	Hangchow
Bo Gu	Po Ku	Hankou	Hankow
Cai Yuanpei	Ts'ai Yuan-p'ei	Hu Shi	Hu Shih
Cao Cao	Ts'ao Ts'ao	Hubei	Hupeh
Chengdu	Ch'eng-tu	Jiangsu	Kiangsu
Chongqing	Chungking	Jiangxi	Kiangsi
Deng Fa	Teng Fa	Kang Youwei	K'ang Yu-wei
Du Fu	Tu Fu	Kangxi	K'ang-hsi
Du Yuesheng	Tu Yueh-sheng	Kunshan	Quinsan
Feng Gueifen	Feng Kuei-fen	Laozi	Lao-tzu
Feng Yuxiang	Feng Yü-hsiang	Li Bo	Li Po
Guangdong	Kwangtung	Li Hongzhang	Li Hung-chang
Guangxi	Kwangsi	Lianda	Lien-ta
Guangzhou	Canton	Liang Qichao	Liang Ch'i-ch'ao
Guilin	Kweilin	Lin Biao	Lin Piao
Gulangyu	Kulangsu	Lin Boqu	Lin Po-chü
Guling	Kuling	Liuzhou	Liuchow

Pinyin	Conventional	Pinyin	Conventional
Luo Ruiqing	Lo Jui-ch'ing	Tan Sitong	T'an Ssu-t'ung
Lu Xun	Lu Hsun	Tianjin	Tientsin
Ma Haide	Ma Hai-teh,	Tongzhou	Tungchow
	George Hatem	Wanxian	Wanhsien
Ma Jianzhong	Ma Chien-chung	Wenzhou	Wenchow
Mao Zedong	Mao Tse-tung	Wuzhou	Wuchow
Nanjing	Nanking	Xi'an	Sian, Hsi-an
Nankou	Nankow	Xiamen	Amoy
Ningbo	Ningpo	Xinjiang	Sinkiang
Peng Dehuai	P'eng Te-huai	Xinjing	Hsinking,
Qianlong	Ch'ien-lung		Changchun
Qiantang	Ch'ien-t'ang	Xuzhou	Hsuchow,
Qing	Ch'ing (Manchu)		Hsuchowfu
	dynasty	Yan Fu	Yen Fu
Qingdao	Tsingtao	Yan Xishan	Yen Hsi-shan
Qiu Jin	Ch'iu Chin	Yan'an	Yenan
Qufu	Ch'ü-fu	Zhang Guotao	Chang Kuo-t'ao
Rehe	Jehol	Zhang Junmai	Chün-mai,
Shaanxi	Shensi	Chang	Carson Chang
Shamian	Shameen	Zhejiang	Chekiang
Shandong	Shantung	Zhengzhou	Chengchow
Shanhaiguan	Shanhaikuan	Zhili	Chih-li
Shanxi	Shansi	Zhou Enlai	Chou En-lai
Sichuan	Szechwan	Zhu De	Chu Teh
Su Dongbo	Su Tung-po	Zhuangzi	Chuang-tzu
Suzhou	Soochow	Zuo Zongtang	Tso Tsung-t'ang

List of Travelers

The following list is intended simply as a quick reference for the reader. In several cases virtually no biographical information is available.

Travelers from the British Empire and Commonwealth

Acton, Harold, 1904–94. Resident of Peking in the late 1930s, where he also taught English literature; resident of Florence and writer on Italian history and art.

Alec-Tweedie, Mrs. (Ethel Brillana Tweedie), ?–1940. A prolific travel writer and biographer, she was in China in the mid-1920s.

Auden, Wystan Hugh, 1907–73. With Christopher Isherwood in China in 1938 on commission from Random House.

Bigland, Eileen, 1898–1970. Traveler and writer of travel books as well as biographies, especially of women.

Bird, Isabella (Isabella Bird Bishop), 1831–1904. Perhaps the most notable of the late Victorian travelers in the Americas, Africa, Asia, and the Middle East. In China in the mid-1890s.

Chesterton, Mrs. Cecil (Ada Elizabeth Chesterton), 1888–?. Traveler and journalist in China in the mid-1930s.

Colquhoun, Archibald Ross, 1848–1914. Publicist, explorer, sometime correspondent for the *Times,* and protagonist of a "Greater Britain" policy, interested particularly in the project of a railway from Burma to southwest China. Sought to be the Cecil Rhodes of China.

Cressy-Marcks, Violet, ?–1970. Made six trips to China and was in Chongqing during war as correspondent for the *Daily Express.*

Dingle, Edwin J., ?–1972. A businessman at time of travels, lived in China, traveled to Tibet, and later founded the Institute of Mental-physics in Los Angeles.

Dundas, Lawrence John Lumley, 1876–1961. Earl of Ronaldshay, later second marquess of Zetland. Writer particularly on public affairs and biographies of statesmen, including Curzon.

Fleming, Peter, 1907–71. Journalist and traveler who made four trips to China before World War II, writing for the *Times;* also in China-Burma-India theater during the war.

Gaunt, Mary Eliza Bakewell, 1872–1942. Australian novelist and trav-eler who wrote of East Africa as well China, in which she traveled from 1913 to 1914.

Gordon Cumming, Constance Frederica, 1837–1924. Traveled exten-sively in India, Ceylon, the Fiji Islands, Japan, and China.

Hyde, Robin (Iris Wilkinson), 1906–39. New Zealand poet, journalist, and novelist who traveled in wartime China in 1938–39 on her way to England.

Isherwood, Christopher, 1904–86. In China in 1938 with Auden, on commission from Random House.

Jackson, Innes, 1911–. After a year of classical Chinese at London she went to China, 1936–37, spending much of her time as a student at the Nanjing University. She published some translations from Chi-nese and wrote also under the name Innes Herdan. After 1949 she was active in the Society for Anglo-Chinese Understanding.

Johnston, Reginald F., 1874–1938. British official in Hong Kong and Weihaiwei; in 1918 he became tutor to the deposed Xuantong emperor (Henry Pu-yi), the Manchu pretender after 1912.

Little, Alicia (Mrs. Archibald Little), 1835–1926, novelist (as Miss A. E. N. Bewicke), traveler, writer, and anti-footbinding activist.

Little, Archibald, 1838–1908. British businessman in China, made the first passage by steam to Chongqing through Yangtze Gorges. Later editor of the *North China Herald,* Shanghai, and protagonist of British activism in China.

Morrison, George Ernest, 1865–1920. Australian, China correspondent for the *Times;* he was in Beijing at time of Boxer siege in 1900; later advisor to Yuan Shikai's government in early Republic.

Purcell, Victor, 1896–1965. Civil servant in China and Malaysia, also scholar of China and overseas Chinese.

Russell, Bertrand, 1872–1970. Mathematician and philosopher. In China shortly after World War I.

Sitwell, Osbert, 1892–1969. Traveled to China in the mid-1930s.

Yorke, Gerald, 1901–83. In China in early 1930s as correspondent for Reuters; later associated with the Hermetic Order of the Golden Dawn.

Travelers from the United States

Ayscough, Florence Wheelock, 1878–1942. Born in Shanghai, educated in the United States before returning to China; wrote many works about the country and its culture.

Dewey, John, 1859–1952. American philosopher and educator. In China shortly after World War I, where he was observer of the May Fourth movement of 1919.

Enders, Elizabeth Crump, n.d. After serving as a nurse in France in World War I, she lived with her French husband in China in the early 1920s.

Franck, Harry, 1881–1962. In China in the early 1920s, Franck was a prolific travel writer, covering Europe, Latin America, and Southeast Asia, among other places.

Homer, Joy, 1915–46. Sent to China in the late 1930s to help with Christian relief work during the war with Japan; served with U.S. Office of Strategic Services (OSS) during the war.

Kates, George, 1895–1990. Resident of Peking in the 1930s; besides *The Years That Were Fat,* he also wrote on Chinese furniture.

Kendall, Elizabeth, 1864–1952. Historian, taught at Wellesley College. In China in 1911 and returned later to teach at Yenching University in the early 1920s.

Peck, Graham, 1914–70. An artist as well as a writer, Peck traveled in China in the late 1930s and again in the wartime years, when he worked for the U.S. Office of War Information.

Seton, Grace Gallatin, 1872–1959. In China in the early 1920s; traveled and wrote about other parts of the world, active in the suffrage campaign and other women's causes.

Smedley, Agnes, 1892–1950. Traveler in China from late 1920s, correspondent, active in Communist affairs.

Snow, Edgar, 1905–72. In China from the late 1920s to the late 1930s; revisited the country after 1949 to write admiringly of the Maoist years.

Speakman, Harold, 1888–1928. A painter, novelist, and travel writer, describing his journeys in the United States, Ireland, and the Middle East, as well as his trip to China in the early 1920s.

Sues, Ilona Ralf, n.d. Polish-born writer, worked in Geneva on opium suppression, before going to China in the mid-1930s.

Wilson, Gen. James Harrison, 1837–1925. Served in the Civil War, the Spanish War, and the Boxer Rising, which took him back to China in 1900, after an earlier trip in the 1870s.

Preface

For all the complaints today about the declining possibilities for real travel in a world crisscrossed by jets, overrun with tourists, and over-built with the kinds of hotels and resorts they demand, travel writing and the dissection of such writing both continue to flourish. Much of the dissection has been done by critics, literary and cultural, who examine the ways in which travelers have represented peoples, cultures, and geographies beyond their own, viewing them through lenses colored by race, gender, and culture, sometimes demonizing them, more often exoticizing them, and sometimes simply domesticating them into a familiarity comforting to Europe and North America. All too often, however, such studies simply add a new layer over this process of exoticization or familiarization, for, by focusing primarily on the textual representations as such, the objects of those representations seem almost denied their real existence, in danger of being turned into peoples, nations, and cultures without voices.

This study, like others of its sort, obviously owes an enormous debt to Edward Said for the clarity with which he put certain questions that some might prefer to leave unraised. Yet here I seek to go beyond a focus on textual representation pure and simple or an indication of the ways in which my subjects got China right or wrong. I argue here in the first place that the study of travel writing must pay attention not only to the representations and discursive strategies of travel texts themselves but also that it is time to return to considerations of the objective situations of the peoples and cultures they purport to describe as well as the changes taking place therein. The observed, after all, have their own history no less than the observers. Second, my study argues that, whether convincingly for their readers or not, travel writers claim a particular kind of veracity and ask for a peculiar kind of trust on the part of those readers, one that is different from that given to, say, journalists or scholars. Finally, it argues that for various reasons a particularly important focus of travel writing at least in the twentieth century has been a search for authenticity, the desire to discover what it is that constitutes the true heart of the culture and people under observation.

So, the book is to be read primarily as an essay on travel writing in a particular place at a particular time. I have chosen China as an object here, for it is a country that for some centuries has occupied an important place in the Western imagination, reflected in a large body of travel writing that goes back at least to the Franciscan missionaries who made their way to the country in the mid-thirteenth century, even before Marco Polo. Here I concentrate on what is roughly a sixty-year period, from the late nineteenth century through the first half of the twentieth, a time of considerable change both within China and within the countries from which its foreign observers came. My approach here is that of a historian, not a literary or cultural critic, and at times I will take issue with the findings and methods of such critics. Still, my hope is that the general method of looking at travel writing that I have taken toward the Chinese example may be helpful for other periods and other lands as well.

I am grateful to those who read the book in part or in whole, including Edward Knox and Peter Rand, and above all to my wife, Deborah, whose writer's eye saved me from calamity on more than one occasion. Sybille Fritzsche kindly offered me help from her own researches on travelers earlier than mine. Two anonymous readers provided many suggestions that were helpful to me in the final preparation of the manuscript. I am grateful, too, to Adam Sobek of the Middlebury College Department of Geography, who prepared the map of China, and to Matt Paul of the Middlebury Reprographics Department, who prepared the files from which the photographs were reproduced. I would like to thank those who participated in an electronic discussion on H-ASIA in March 1996 about the applicability of Edward Said's considerations on Orientalism to East Asia, a discussion that helped me clarify my own thoughts on the subject (the thread can be found at http://ww2.h-net.msu.edu/~asia/threads/thrdorientalism.html). Finally, my deep thanks go to Ingrid Erickson, who has been a most helpful editor at the Press, and to Marcia LaBrenz for seeing the book through the process of copyediting. They have been quick to respond to my many queries, and I could not have asked for a better working relationship. Needless to say, the book's shortcomings are mine, not theirs.

Part of chapter 6 first appeared in somewhat different form as an article in the *New England Review* 18, no. 2 (Spring 1997), and I am grateful to the editors of that journal for permission to use it.

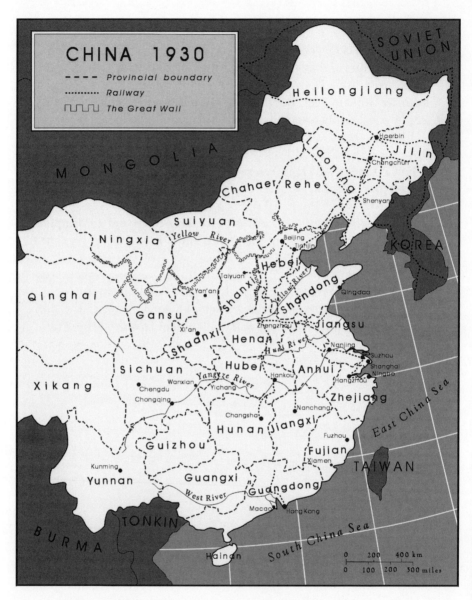

Map of China in early 1930s, showing major rivers, rail lines, and
the Great Wall.

Chapter 1

Introduction: China in Translation

In 1899 the sixty-eight-year-old Isabella Bird Bishop published an account of the journey to western China that she had undertaken some two years earlier, dedicating her book to the foreign secretary, Lord Salisbury, out of "the Author's Profound Respect, and Admiration of the Noble and Disinterested Services which he has Rendered to the British Empire." Originally, she'd had no intention of seeing the work into print (or so she said, at any rate) but gave way to the urging of others because, while recent events had turned the Yangtze Valley into a British sphere of interest, few people beyond China were aware of the vastness of the territory and its resources.[1]

Those recent events, of course, were what came to be called the "Scramble for Concessions," when after Japan's defeat of China in 1895 and its seizure of Taiwan, Western countries—Germany, Russia, France, Britain, and even the self-consciously anti-imperialist United States—presented their demands to the Qing government in Beijing to make certain they got their share of the spoils. Whether or not there was ever actually a British sphere in the Yangtze Valley is beside the point, and in any case spheres of interest, unlike leaseholds or concessions or settlements, had no standing in diplomacy or international law. In using the term, which she deplored, Bird was doing no more than participating in the popular political discourse of the day, though she warned that the greed implicit in the scramble would weaken the power of the government in Beijing and thus harm not only China but foreign interests in the country as well. A proponent of the Open Door, with its belief in equal commercial access for all comers, she may well have admired Salisbury for his opposition to some of the more vociferous China lobbyists in London. At the same time the idea that her country should be the one to take the lead in guiding China into a new international role seemed to her both a logical and laudable development.

Bird, of course, made no claims to be either diplomat or lawyer. She saw herself simply as a traveler and writer, a woman who had already published many accounts of her journeyings to various parts of the world. In that capacity she formed part of a larger company of men and women who visited and described China in those years, taken there sometimes by commerce, sometimes by evangelism, and sometimes by simple curiosity or scientific inquiry. Later generations, ready to believe that the power to know and to describe implies the power to control, might well consider her nonetheless as an agent of British imperialism, and her decision to publish the record of what she saw and heard as she made her way up the Great River to Sichuan, as undeniably contributing to the reach of Britain's informal empire in Asia—an empire of which she clearly approved and whose general aims she wished to forward.

In this book I propose to examine a number of records by British and American travelers to China, ranging from the late nineteenth through the first half of the twentieth century, and to place those accounts in the contexts of their times. That means examining not only the ways in which China was described for readerships back home but also the reasons why particular forms of representation were chosen and the ways in which those forms reflected changes taking place both in China itself and in the societies from which the travelers came. The choice of subject raises two questions: first, why this particular period, which might at first seem arbitrary and meaningless? And, second, why travelers rather than others who wrote about and described China in those years?

In China those years were anything but meaningless. The decline of the Qing dynasty, the overthrow of the empire, and the chaotic years of war and revolution that followed, as the country sought to reconstruct itself as a modern republic prior to the Communist victory of 1949, brought enormous changes to its political and social landscape. New institutions for a new nation were among them, as were China's attempts to redefine its international standing in the world, extricating itself from the weight of the unequal treaties imposed by the West and Japan after 1842. So too were the kinds of subjective changes evident in the political and cultural radicalism growing out of the May Fourth movement of 1919, with its scathing reassessment of China's past under the harsh glare of modernity. Indeed, as the legacy of communism fades, it may not be too much to argue that the China emerging into the twenty-first century owes at least as much to the transformations of these years as to those wrought by Mao Zedong before his death in 1976.

In the West the period began at the zenith of high imperialism, with all its cultural as well as military and diplomatic appurtenances. These included, notably, the idea of a civilizing mission and the assumption that the West had marked out the path of historical progress that others were destined to follow. It closed, however, with that imperialism and many of the myths on which it had been founded having been seriously wounded, if not yet quite dead. The transformation had something to do with the triumph of modernity and its views of impermanence and the contingent nature of truth. Perhaps more important was the injury done to the West by the enormous and bloody self-inflicted wounds of the two world wars. As far back as the 1920s, long before the ubiquity of postmodernism but after the slaughter of the Somme and Gallipoli, the old Enlightenment certainties of progress, with all their nineteenth-century accretions of Whig history, secularism, Darwinism (social and biological), and naive scientism, could never be so uncritically accepted again. Two decades later, despite the final Allied victory of 1945, the stunning military and political defeats inflicted on the Western nations by Japan a few years earlier ensured the end of the old empires.

Such changes acted upon the perceptions of those who traveled to the world beyond the West. China, which before 1914 had seemed mired in the swamp of an immutable conservatism, looking only to the past, by the 1920s began to appear in a more positive light, even a place from which the West might actually have something to learn. And, in a world succumbing to a blandly homogenizing modernity, certain aspects of its past, earlier dismissed as little more than obstacles to progress, began to seem worth preserving. Living in Beijing in the 1930s, for instance, men like George Kates, Harold Acton, and Osbert Sitwell undertook to observe and record what they feared might be the last remnants of a once great civilization before it was swept away by the tide of the new or before simple neglect should allow its monuments to crumble into dust. Nor were the forces of the new necessarily those made in London or Liverpool, New York or Chicago; others bore the imprint of Tokyo or Moscow, and the responses to those particular currents, whether fearful or hopeful, colored the attitudes of travelers.

As indeed they often colored the attitudes of others who took China in these years as their concern. Journalists, scholars, diplomats, missionaries, memoir-writing expatriates, politicians, novelists, photographers, filmmakers, all played and continue to play their parts in producing a China for Western audiences. The reports sent back by the Jesuit mission after its arrival in the seventeenth century helped color the Enlightenment's view of China, and the first Protestant missionary writings began even before the opening of the country's interior by the treaties of 1860; already in 1840 W. H. Medhurst's survey, *China: Its State and Prospects,* appeared, and other books followed, such as Samuel Wells Williams's *The Middle Kingdom* (1888) and Marshall Broomhall's *The Chinese Empire: A General and Missionary Survey* (1907). By the late nineteenth century the serious discipline of Sinology, already born on the European continent, had spread to the Anglo-American world, with the scholarly contributions of men like James Legge on the Confucian classics, and Max Müller, who began his publication of the *Sacred Books of the East* in 1879.

This book, however, emphatically makes no claim to be yet another study of Western images of China. Harold Isaacs, Raymond Dawson, and, most recently, Jonathan Spence,[2] among others, have done that job quite well, and much of what has appeared since they wrote has been a gloss on their work. Nor is it yet another study of Orientalism or another exercise in the analysis of colonial discourse, though it is informed by such studies which, once one unpacks their sometimes tendentious language, often have valuable things to say.[3]

Nor, finally, is it about the travelers themselves, in ways that would interest a biographer or a critic concerned more with the inner than the outer journeys. Some of the writers considered here have full-scale biographies (Agnes Smedley, Isabella Bird, Edgar Snow, to say nothing of such figures as John Dewey, Bertrand Russell, and W. H. Auden), some have shorter notices in biographical dictionaries, while about others virtually nothing of the sort is available. Moreover, travelers in this period were not particularly forthcoming in the kind of information, personal and otherwise, that our own confessional age has come to expect. The New Zealand poet, novelist, and journalist Robin Hyde (Iris Wilkinson), for example, who made her way from her homeland to England through a China torn apart by war, had earlier had two children, one of whom died in infancy, and in addition she herself had been permanently crippled in an accident. In 1939, shortly after arriving in London, overwhelmed by depression and ill health, she killed herself. It is a terrible story, a wrenching story, but it plays no part in *Dragon Rampant,* the record of China she left behind.

Anne-Marie Brady has recently suggested that homosexual Westerners may have been drawn to China because they found there a freedom denied to them in their own countries.[4] This may well explain one particular kind of reticence in some of the writers discussed here— Graham Peck, Harold Acton, Christopher Isherwood, and W. H. Auden, for example. But it won't explain others, including what is often a vagueness about dates, itineraries, and names. Grace Seton, for example, journeyed to China from a "Far Eastern Paradise," but precisely which one is unclear. Isabella Bird said little about her own good works in supporting hospitals and medical missionaries. The casual reader might well be several chapters into *China Only Yesterday* before realizing that Innes Jackson was a woman, not a man. From their writings one would never guess that Violet Cressey-Marcks's rather distantly described traveling companion was in fact her husband or that Osbert Sitwell took to Beijing with him his new companion, David Horner. Joy Homer was the daughter of the singer Louise Homer; Seton herself the wife of Ernest Thompson Seton, the naturalist; Edwin Dingle developed an interest in Tantrism and in 1927 founded the Institute of Mentalphysics and the First Sanctuary of Mystical Christianity in Los Angeles; while Gerald Yorke in later life became Frater Volo Intelligere of the Hermetic Order of the Golden Dawn.

All these facts are, of course, vital to the biographer. Here, however, I concentrate on the travelers' accounts, what it was they saw fit to publish, appealing to a general readership back home, and thus I have included biographical material only when it seems to me to have a direct bearing on the records they left behind. Obviously, there are times when considerations of nationality, social class, or political leanings (Harry Franck's Americanism, Isabella Bird's admiration for the British Empire, Agnes Smedley's communism, for example) have a direct bearing on the writers' representations of China and the Chinese, and to these I do refer.

Moreover, not all who traveled to China and wrote about what they found there describe their voyages, and again I have had to decide whom to include and whom to ignore. Some of the men and women discussed here were seasoned travelers and travel writers—none more so than Isabella Bird in the late nineteenth century. Others might seem less obvious, like Archibald and Alicia Little, for example, or Florence Ayscough, who were old China hands, having lived there for years. Eric Teichman was a British diplomat and Richard Dobson an agent for British-American Tobacco. Yet they and others like them wrote of their travels within the country and brought to their accounts perspectives different from those just off the boat from Britain or America. Some, like Kates and Acton, became temporary expatriates, learning to see beyond the often shuttered world of the foreign settlements. Others mixed journalism with their traveling, like Peter Fleming or Robin Hyde. Indeed, by the 1930s, as the shadows of war gathered over China, the line between the travel account and journalism became less and less clear, so that Christopher Isherwood and W. H. Auden, commissioned in early 1937 to do a book on China as travelers, arrived in 1938 to find themselves transformed into war correspondents instead. And, though it is not usually read that way, Edgar Snow's classic *Red Star over China* (1938) was one of the great travel accounts of its day. On the other hand, his wife, Nym Wales, and his contemporaries Emily Hahn, Colonel Evans Carlson, and Robert Payne, informative as their books may be about the China of their day, were not travel writers.

If the word *traveler* has an elastic definition, so too does *travel writing*. All too often, Peter Bishop reminds us, it's a form "conceived to be either a poor cousin of scientific observation, or else to fall short of the creativeness of 'pure' fiction."[5] Dennis Porter, in his brilliant study of European travel accounts of the eighteenth and nineteenth centuries, finds it necessary to offer a defense of his subject and reads *Empire of Signs,* Roland Barthes's vision of Japan, to imply that "we would all be better off, if the great majority of the world's travel books had never been written at all."[6] To Michael Kowalewski it is the preponderance of factual material about flora, fauna, topography, climate, foods, and local sexual customs that explains "why the genre has traditionally attracted the attention of historians and geographers rather than literary critics"[7] (one feels bound to think he means *mere* historians and geographers). Paul Fussell, writing of British "literary traveling" in the 1920s and 1930s, bars from consideration the great unwashed—not only those who were simply "tourists" rather than proper "travelers" but also those who, while they might be proper travelers, were not self-referentially literary. With a few exceptions he also excludes those who traveled east beyond the borders of the old Ottoman Empire.[8]

Historians, however, are apt to be sniffily suspicious of the artificiality of the frontiers implied by the word *literary*, and in any case there were comparatively few literary travelers to East Asia during those years. Henry James, Evelyn Waugh, Graham Greene, and D. H. Lawrence never made it, for example, though Osbert Sitwell, Harold Acton, W. H. Auden, and Christopher Isherwood did. So did Robert Byron, though he never wrote about China, because, according to Acton, he was so blinded by the glories of Beijing that, if he'd started, he would never have finished *The Road to Oxiana.*

This book thus takes a broad definition of travel writing and sweeps up into its net some men and women not usually thought of as travelers but whose various professions brought them to China and who left behind records of their voyages. What they all had in common was a direct experience with a country very different from the West and the need to communicate its strangeness and foreignness to audiences back home. In itself that quality hardly distinguished them from the journalists, experts, scholars, memoirists, and others who undertook the same task. Travelers, after all, inherited the same intellectual genealogy and carried with them the same baggage of conceptions, racial and social outlooks, images and memories drawn from earlier readings, that informed the work of other observers of the Chinese scene.

Why, then, choose travel writing? It is part of the argument of this book that travel writing—even when mixed with, say, journalism or scholarship—can be set off from such other descriptions and analyses and is of an order different from other accounts. Professional Sinologues, wrote the traveler Eliza Scidmore at the turn of the century, were not to be trusted, for they praised the Chinese as the fountain of all wisdom and virtue and were simply

> all in the clouds, lost in the fogs and mists of the Chinese language and the poetry of 2000 B.C. Something queer comes over the best of men when they get very far in the Chinese language and its classical literature. They become abnormal, impersonal, detached, dissociated from the living world, from the white-skinned, red-blooded human races of the West. Something in the climate, some mental microbe, gets into all of us here in China. The longer we stay here the less we see, the less we are fitted to judge.[9]

They go native, in other words. Journalists and analysts of China's condition faced other problems. Subject to the pressures of the contemporary passion for the actual, Victor Purcell complained in 1938, most of their books within a year had become "as stale to the public as yesterday's *Daily Blare*," and those on politics or the military "staler than a tipster's forecast on a race that has already been run."[10] Even the writings of the specialists—on China's railways, its land and labor problems, its government, its military capacity—while useful, also went too quickly out of date.

However exaggerated such characterizations might be, works by the experts or the journalists or the Old China Hands lacked the elements for which readers turned to travel literature. Travel writing has a strong claim on our imagination, promising, as Kowalewski remarks, "both adventure and return, escape and homecoming," and doing so through a recourse to the largest cluster of metaphors in the language.[11] As readers, we recognize a kinship with the traveler that we are likely to deny the scholarly expert or journalist—for several reasons. One is that the travel account is usually cast as a narrative, and, whatever may be the problems with that form, it is an age-old way of making sense out of otherwise inchoate experiences. Above all, there is about the travel account a directness, even a physicality, that is lacking in the work of the expert or the journalist. For the experts are bound by their academic sources, which are alien to us, and by the dry rationalism of their training, while the journalists are trained to see tomorrow's story, which too quickly becomes yesterday's. Moreover, such people too often speak down to us, as if they are instructing us, denying us that freshness of vision, the newness of sights seen for the first time, that sense of surprised innocence that we may draw from the traveler's view. Even if today we are wary enough to be on guard against the potentially spurious nature of that innocence, ready to discover lurking behind it what Mary Louise Pratt calls an "anti-conquest narrative," the device by which travelers, pretending to be no more than neutral observers, seek to distance themselves from an assumed guilt of domination.[12] Like such travelers, we too wish to hold ourselves apart from the oppressor, the enslaver, the opium merchant, the exploiter of cheap coolie labor.

So, while most of us find it difficult to recognize ourselves among conquerors, experts, expatriates, or journalists, we have traveled or at least someday may travel ourselves. Although the heroic journey no longer seems possible, travel can still allow us an opportunity to escape from our own condition into what Eric Leed calls "a domain of alternative realities, in which the self can assume its uniqueness and recover its freedom, in the climate of the new and unexpected."[13]

Yet most of us also find our voyages circumscribed by the constraints of the workaday world in which we live: practical ones, like the length of our vacations, the resources of our pocketbooks, the availability of transportation; and psychological ones, like the fear of danger and disease or simply of dirt and discomfort (like those who, according to a recent guidebook, "have given up eating . . . just to avoid having to use Chinese toilets").[14] Travelers—real travelers, that is—are those men and women who can cast away or ignore such constraints and thus do for the rest of us what we are unable or unwilling to do for ourselves. Travel carries with it a sense of adventure, of the new, of the unexpected, which many of us might prefer to encounter in the pages of a book rather than in the jungle, the desert, the mountains, or indeed in cities crowded with those who speak differently, dress differently, act differently, smell differently, and peer at us differently from those we are used to.

So, even when we stay at home, we can identify the travelers' curiosity with our own, we can understand their impressions, admire their courage as they encounter the unfamiliar, in a way not likely to be true of the expert or the expatriate, whose academic distance or sometimes bored familiarity with the subject we find less engaging than the travelers' openness to discovery. Travelers may well be transgressors and liars (think of Marco Milione, for instance)—and, in one conventional view at least, women even greater liars than men[15]—but travel texts nonetheless are charged with a kind of direct authority, emotional if not necessarily factual, that the texts of the experts and the others lack. "I have been induced to publish it," wrote Archibald Little in 1887 of his journal of a trip up the Yangtze to Chongqing, "in the belief that impressions formed and recorded day by day on the spot, give a better idea of the actual state of things in China than many of the elaborate and carefully compiled books which attempt a more exhaustive description of the country." "I have kept to the truth as I have seen and heard it," warned Violet Cressy-Marcks, recording her trip to western China and the Communist regions in the late 1930s.[16] "I have, as much as possible, kept from my matter frills and effects, though they might have made for more exciting reading." Such declarations are common and appeal for a particular kind of trust to be given by the reader, implying that, although we must forgo the pleasures of the literary imagination, we will find embedded in the travel account an authority that is of an altogether different order.

Thus we are apt to grant them the trust they ask for, keeping our awkward questions to ourselves. Were Little's observations really "recorded day by day on the spot," or were they, when the time came to prepare them for publication, filtered through a memory and ordered by what came to seem important only later? Should we believe that Constance Gordon Cumming really mailed off all those letters from China to people back home when she said she wrote them, or was the epistolary form in which she cast her book simply a quasifictional device for a later setting down of her record?[17] As readers, we put aside such questions, because the immediacy of these reports on the sights, sounds, and smells of the foreign promises a direct apprehension of reality. It is a trust strengthened by the travelers' readiness to experience loneliness, to see China directly for themselves, rather than insulated by a foreign community of like-minded men and women living abroad in a large city such as Shanghai or Hong Kong who might serve as a buffer against reality. We expect them to sort out for us the confusing and seemingly infinite number of new perceptions and assaults on the senses, tales told and explanations given and withheld, to order them and make sense of them. Granted that when travelers speculated on China's past or China's future they might drift over into the territories already staked out by the historians or the journalists or the anthropologists, lands for which their own passports carried visas of a doubtful validity. But when they stuck to their proper business they gave, and give, us a sense of place so that we might be able to imagine what a Chinese city and its people looked and smelled like, felt like, and sounded like.

The travelers' claim to directness also implies that we can expect from them a narration of the unfamiliar and exotic in a way that is accurate, dispassionate, and disinterested, largely unmediated by personal sensibilities or autobiographical excursions. Or at least so it used to be, when China was still a strange and impossibly far-off land. As familiarity increased, however, the expectations of readers changed. By the late nineteenth century, after all, no one wanted to be treated to yet another description of, say, St. Peter's or the Mont Blanc seen from the Mer-de-Glace; whatever interest such well-known sights might have now lay precisely in the ability of the writer to defamiliarize them, so that the reader might look on them with new eyes and new perspective. So too by the 1920s and 1930s the Shanghai Bund or the imperial palace of Beijing, though hardly as well-known as the cityscapes of the Place de la Concorde or the Grand Canal (the Venetian one, that is), had nevertheless become more recognizable, and that was one of the reasons why travel writing about China took a new turn in the years after World War I.

Travel writers share with historians a kind of kinship; both are mediators, their records putting into our language the strange, the exotic, the spatially or chronologically foreign, arranged within a conceptual and discursive framework that we can understand. In their journeys, whether geographical or chronological, are embedded elements both of new discovery and of revisitation, because even before the journeys begin the memories of earlier readings have already begun to form the pictures that their travels will ratify or confound. Both eighteenth-century Philadelphia and present-day China are foreign to us and must be made intelligible to a readership at home (at home in the West, at home in the early twenty-first century) in ways that do not violate the integrity and the reality of the peoples and cultures being represented.

Is the task even possible? Is an accurate representation of other countries and other times even worth trying? Edward Said and those who have followed him, concerned only with the geographically foreign, would seem to say that it is not possible, despite the guardedly optimistic note on which his *Orientalism* ends. Try as we may, we cannot escape the bounds of our colonialist or our Orientalist discourse. Such a view implies (as Porter points out) that "a knowledge—as opposed to an ideology—of the Other is impossible."[18] If that's true, then all attempts to write, say, a Chinese-centered Chinese history (as Paul Cohen asks us to do) or a liberated journalism (as David Spurr asks us to undertake) are bound to fail. So, we hedge, setting off those words like *fact, event, accuracy, objectivity,* and of course the big one, *truth,* with embarrassed little quotation marks, indicative of the close conspiracy into which we draw our audiences, taking the place of the figurative nudge of the elbow, the raised eyebrow: Reader, you and I both know that these accounts are not what they purport to be. Isabella Bird, making her way up the Yangtze toward southwestern China a century ago, expressed the hope "that in the main this volume will be found to convey a truthful impression of the country and its people."[19]

To us the phrase is interesting not only for its seeming ingenuousness but also for its unintended ambiguity. Are we to take the book simply as a truthful account of her own impressions? Or are we asked to believe that her impressions of China convey a truthful account of a particular social and natural landscape at a particular time?

Although on one level we may grant the travel writers our trust, willing to be drawn in because of the pleasure we take in reading their narratives, on another we have been taught to suspect the factual veracity of what they record, to wonder whether they are deceiving themselves or trying to deceive us. "Our observation in any foreign land is extremely superficial," wrote Henry James in 1878, "and our remarks are happily not addressed to the inhabitants themselves, who would be sure to exclaim upon the impudence of the fancy-picture."[20] However dispassionate and disinterested our travelers' accounts may claim to be, we want to search out their purposes, alert to the ways in which such narratives may be consciously or unconsciously constructed within particular bounds for particular purposes. Our own innocence lost, we have taught ourselves, as David Spurr points out, to ask how such writers go about constructing a coherent representation out of the often incomprehensible realities of an unfamiliar world and on what cultural, ideological, or literary suppositions and inheritances their works are based.[21]

This is not to say that the accounts of travelers are by the very nature of their directness more reliable than those of others. Nor does it simply imply that there are lots of different truths and the traveler's truth is simply one of them, jostling for our attention with all the others. There's a sense in which all artifacts—texts included—are truthful. Our task is to decide what they are truthful about and how to interrogate them if we expect truthful answers. We do not, for instance, turn to a speech by Joseph Goebbels in 1939 to get the straight facts on the Jewish question in central Europe or to the pronouncements of Chairman Mao in 1967 to discover how the seemingly patriotic Liu Shaoqi could become a capitalist roader deserving imprisonment and a lingering death. Yet as Goebbels's speech, properly questioned, can tell us something of the truth about Nazism, so Mao's accusations can tell us something of Chinese communism. It is our job as readers to decide which questions can legitimately be asked.

So, too, we must approach the travel account, understanding that it claims a special, or at least a different, kind of authority—"what I saw and heard with my own eyes and ears"—understanding that the traveler's task is then to translate that experience into an idiom that makes sense for the audience back home. Here the travel writer and the historian share the same territory. China is a hard fact; China really does exist, just as for the historian the American Civil War or the medieval European city or the eighteenth-century Japanese merchant guild really did exist—they are not simply the imaginative constructions of the writer. Just as literary translation demands a respect for the integrity of the original text, facing its executor with the sometimes all but unattainable task of preserving nuances of tone and idiom in an alien language ("a matter of conceiving what our language does not conceive," as Barthes says),[22] so the geographically or chronologically foreign must be put into an idiom that has meaning for an audience at home, without violating its integrity, either by privileging the West or by privileging the contemporary. *Traduttore, traditore:* the Other need not be China or Arabia; it can be America a century ago, for what the danger of ethnocentrism is to the travel writer, the danger of anachronism and present-mindedness is for the historian.

As it is also for those critics who restrict themselves to the study of texts as representations or to the analysis of particular kinds of Orientalist or colonial discourse. Of course, the factors that shape the discourse of the writers—intellectual, genealogical, social, religious, ideological, and so forth—are important, and of course they may be (as the critical theorists never tire of reminding us) limiting. But so, too, may be the boundaries within which our criticism takes place. Historians, knowing the outcomes of their stories, impose a shape on their pasts that participants in those pasts could not possibly have seen or understood. Travel writers also impose shapes on their experiences that might well have no meaning to the objects of their description (the natives) but which are supposed to have some meaning for their audiences (those other natives back home). Yet, as critics too, seemingly unconscious of our own positioning, we find ourselves also imposing upon other texts shapes that are conditioned by our own times, our own social and intellectual milieus, shapes that might well have seemed parochial and meaningless to the objects of our concern, who are the writers themselves. Subjecting their texts to our own particular form of imperial gaze, we claim the capacity to see in them what their own writers could not perceive. Like colonizers, who reconstitute the world they have "discovered," mapping, renaming, and reordering its peoples and landscapes without the messy obligation of having to study what the natives were up to before their arrival, we reorder and remap the textual landscapes we study, imposing upon them a taxonomy imported from other times and other climes.

Then, like the colonizers, once we have done so we can breathe a sigh of relief. Our problem has suddenly become much simpler, for, by divorcing those texts from what they purport to represent, the accuracy of that representation is almost beside the point, and so we are seemingly relieved of the burden of studying those other cultures and other peoples who were the writer's concern. Of course, the divorce is never complete, for the underlying reality of the thing described remains. But it is tempting to sidestep it, so that we concentrate on image rather than the object behind it. To David Spurr, for example, the interest of a figure like Idi Amin lies less in the horror he actually caused than in the way he chose to present himself and was in turn represented by a Western press seeking to satisfy a "traditional demand" for someone to play the savage African buffoon.[23] Why need we concern ourselves with the study of China or Japan or India or their languages or histories or cultures, if history and social analysis are no more than simply different forms of mythic representation,[24] if we are concerned only with a text as a production born within the boundaries we ourselves decide to impose on the author's own times and culture? There's a great paradox here: if the "Orient" or "China" becomes interesting to us as no more than a figure of Western imagining or invention, then in a perverse sense the project of Orientalism has achieved its ultimate victory, the critics of discourse have become complicit with the object of their criticism, and China or India have become artifices, denied any objective existence of their own, reduced simply to textual productions.

Hence, I've tried to steer away from the contemporary temptation—reflected in the titles of a flood of books and essays—of seeing the translations of the travel writers as no more than mere "inventions" or "imaginings," as if the object, once translated, existed only in the mind of the person representing it, no more real, say, than Roland Barthes's fictive Japan (he, of course, was beaten to the punch by Oscar Wilde's supposition that "the whole of Japan is a pure invention. There is no such country, there are no such people . . . the Japanese people are . . . simply a mode of style, an exquisite fancy of art").[25] Read sympathetically and historically, travel accounts also remind us that we must get behind any notion that there has been a single essentialized "Orient" or

"China" in the mind of the West and must be concerned with hetero-geneity, with the interplay between the subjective and the objective, between observer and observed, between things seen and heard and the ways they were recorded. The country observed by Agnes Smedley in 1940 was objectively quite different from the China observed by the Beijing Jesuits at the court of the Qianlong emperor in 1740 or the China encountered by the British traveler Robert Fortune in 1840. And Smed-ley herself was neither eighteenth-century Jesuit nor nineteenth-cen-tury British merchant. The relationship between observer and observed does not simply flow in one direction, with the observer in command. Rather, it is a complex transaction between the two, and the writings of the observer, while framed with a particular universe of discourse (or universes, since we all participate in more than one, and they wash over and join with one another), still must account for the objective reality of the observed in all its variety.

Moreover, China, and perhaps all of East Asia does not always fit neatly into the categories that we as critics might wish to devise for it. In particular, it does not fit well into the categories of Orientalism. The word, as Edward Said defines it, means more than simple European or American ethnocentrism but embraces a particular discourse with a long history that, by its statements and its descriptions, becomes a Western style for the domination of the Orient.[26] "All cultures tend to make representations of foreign cultures," he writes in *Culture and Imperialism*, "the better to master or in some way control them. Yet not all cultures make representations of foreign cultures and in fact master or control them. This is the distinction, I believe, of modern Western cultures" (a Chinese, reading such a sentence, might well wonder what has become of the Japanese imperialism that ravaged his country some sixty years ago).[27]

Said generally confines himself to Western representations of what he calls the "Near Orient," meaning the Arab world and Islam, and by and large the "Far Orient," or East Asia, is left to take care of itself. It's no accident, I think, that he and those who follow him, whether disci-ples or critics, have had little to say about the world beyond the Middle East or India.[28] In the Western mind (or at least in some Western minds) East Asia in general and China in particular were different—for several reasons. One was simply that, while China was certainly an object of *imperial* ambition in the nineteenth and twentieth centuries (Asian as well as Western, we must remember), it was far less the object of *colo-*

nial ambition than America, Africa, South Asia, or the Middle East have all been in various periods. Hong Kong island was acquired by Britain in 1842 after the Opium War, yet China's only substantial territorial loss was not to a Western country at all but to Japan, which took control of the entire island of Taiwan in 1895. Elsewhere foreigners for the most part contented themselves with simple footholds, reflected in the whole panoply of concessions, settlements, and leaseholds that were the fruit of the system of unequal treaties, embracing them all, to one degree or another, within the broad arms of the Open Door. Unlike India or the Philippines or Korea, China remained at least formally independent.

Another reason for China's difference has more to do with historical and cultural memory, for Western intercourse with that country lacked the long and often strife-torn history of Western intercourse with Islam. Hence, the legacy of earlier centuries was quite different and included recollections of the writings left by Marco Polo, for example, and those of the Beijing Jesuits in the late Ming and early Qing, whose often glowing descriptions of the Middle Kingdom, published in the *Lettres Édifiantes et curieuses,* had awakened so much interest in the Europe of the Enlightenment. Out of such views arose a kind of sympathetic Orientalism, which needs to be set against the imagination of Orientalism as a system of control. Although the reality travelers encountered in late Qing China was a severe comedown from these earlier pictures, still there remained among Westerners the memory of what Raymond Dawson calls "a homogeneous Confucian state of unrivalled moral and political excellence."[29] That memory defined China as a place apart not only from the West but from Islam and from Africa, the dark continent of negation and savagery, incapable of properly exploiting its own rich resources, or Latin America, where Iberian indolence had failed to awaken the native people from their torpor.[30]

For all its dirt, smells, and incomprehensible manners China could be seen as the home of an ancient and highly literate civilization and a complex and sophisticated polity. Not a Western polity, to be sure, but still one deserving Western respect and from which the West might even have something to learn. The commanding imperial gaze—"monarch-of-all-I-survey," as Pratt calls it—was less likely to be cast over the landscape of Zhili or Guangdong than over the West African coast or the Congo basin, and the note of newness, discovery, and penetration was muted, since it would sound far less convincing in a coun-

try so thickly peopled and where monuments to a past greatness, crumbling though they might be in the modern world, were so much in evidence. (There were exceptions, of course, like the common and misleading boast that Shanghai had been little more than a dingy mudflat
before the British arrived to put it to rights.) Elsewhere in the world the
naming of geographical features might imply domination and control
(the world's highest mountain called after a British surveyor) but not,
generally, in China. Europeans might corrupt Chinese sounds as they
transliterated them, but they did not usually impose new names on
cities, mountains, or rivers. As Venezia became Venice and München
Munich for English speakers, so Beijing became Peking; it was not
rechristened Sinopolis. Meanwhile, New York became and remains for
Chinese speakers *Niu Yue*, "knob appointment."[31]

Finally, perhaps Orientalism doesn't fit because an analysis of its
particular discourse simply does not leave enough room for the multiplicity of meanings that we meet in the Occidental responses, the het-
erogeneity that arose in part from the changes undergone by both
observer and observed through the years. Of course, such a statement
is not to deny the very real insights that the analysts of Orientalist or
colonial discourse have provided us. But it is important not to allow
theory to take command, remembering, as Sara Mills reminds us in a
charmingly ingenuous admission, "it is often difficult to find a theory
which will enable you to make interesting and insightful statements
about a text which you would not have been able to say without the
theory."[32] If travel writers sometimes found in foreign lands no more
than a visual ratification of their own prior ideas, the same might be
said of their critics as well: if they decide, for example, that the deter-
mining feature of a text is going to be its participation within a discourse of Orientalism or colonialism, then it too becomes no more than
a ratification of prior ideas, blinding its readers to what else may be
found there. In the late 1930s, for instance, certain writers—Agnes
Smedley and Edgar Snow among them—had recourse to a whole array
of Orientalist images and common Western stereotypes. They used
them, however, not to undergird but to subvert any Western domination of the Orient.

There is one more reason to look at the accounts of travel in these
particular years. Dennis Porter has argued that the European grand
tour of the eighteenth century was undertaken not only for self-cultiva-
tion but also to reaffirm the common and self-confident civilized her-

itage of the West. In this sense it complemented the great voyages of circumnavigation that were mapping, describing, and classifying unknown lands and peoples and so producing them as objects of European knowledge.[33] A hundred years later, while the original purposes both of the grand tour and the voyage of circumnavigation were vanishing, Asia remained an object of curiosity and China the center of another kind of self-confident cultural tradition whose interest lay precisely in the fact that it was not the travelers' own. Thanks to the steamship, the Suez Canal, and the transcontinental railways of North America, access to the Pacific had become a good deal easier than it had been earlier, but the combination of adventure and curiosity remained, even if you were not the first Westerner to gaze out over the mountains of Yunnan or make your way up through the Yangtze Gorges to the inner recesses of Sichuan.

So, even while Captain Cook was giving way to Thomas Cook, China remained open to travel, real travel. While the kind of distinction between travel and tourism that Paul Fussell insists upon in *Abroad* may always have been an artificial one, there is no doubt that the perception of difference has been with us for a long time. In the eighteenth century Edward Gibbon was already complaining about the English swarming through Lausanne's narrow streets, and by the first half of the nineteenth century the lament had swollen to a chorus: railways and hotels had made going abroad too easy, there were too many tourists, too many unwelcome changes brought about by their presence. Indeed, the very lightening of the burdens of tourism made travel more difficult for the discerning few who imagined themselves capable of discovering the authentic Italy or France or Switzerland rather than the shams offered by the writers of popular guidebooks.[34] And with Europe fallen to the tourists would they not soon conquer the rest of the world? Already in 1848 the newly founded *Punch* wrote of steam packet owners who had begun to "survey mankind with comprehensive view, / And manage trips to China and Peru," and almost thirty years earlier Thomas Moore had made a similar complaint.

> Why, then, farewell all hope to find
> A spot that's free of London-kind!
> Who knows, if to the West we roam,
> some Blue "at home"
> Among the Blacks of Carolina—

Or, flying to the Eastward, see
Some Mrs. Hopkins, taking tea
And toast upon the Wall of China.[35]

By the 1870s, in fact, the fictional Plantagenet Palliser, duke of Omnium, was considering "a lengthened visit to the cities of China" with his daughter, in order to break her infatuation with the unsuitable Francis Tregear (unfortunately for us, if not for Lady Mary, the trip never took place).[36] In 1894 the real Australian G. E. Morrison, though speaking no Chinese, made his way alone up the Yangtze and then overland to the Burmese frontier, showing his readers "how easily and pleasantly this journey, which a few years ago would have been regarded as a formidable undertaking, can now be done."[37] After a journey through Siberia to the Gulf of Tonkin in the late 1890s, Archibald Colquhoun predicted that soon a mere fifteen days would suffice to make the trip from Europe to central China by rail, and thus "the magnitude of the Asian continent will have become a mere tradition among travellers."[38] Archibald Little, journeying up the Great River above Yichang in 1883, rejoiced that he had been fortunate enough to see the Yangtze Gorges before European tourists and European innovations had destroyed their charm. In fact, getting there and getting about still wasn't quite that easy. As Little pointed out, while an American-style steamship would carry you the thousand miles from Shanghai to Yichang in a week, the last five hundred miles to Chongqing might take five or six weeks—longer than the time needed to get from London to Shanghai itself.[39] By the end of the nineteenth century Eliza Scidmore, one of the pioneers of Western tourism in East Asia, found Japan and India overflowing with tourists, railways, hotels, guides, couriers, and guidebooks. But China still lacked any such amenities. "Neither Murray nor Baedeker has penetrated the empire . . . and Cook has only touched the edge of it at Canton."[40]

Some years earlier, in fact, a firm in Hong Kong had brought out Archdeacon John Gray's *Walks in the City of Canton*, its 695 pages written presumably for the traveler with time on his hands. Scidmore herself had already published a slim guidebook for the Canadian Pacific Railway in 1892, taking the traveler by train from Montreal through Banff to Vancouver and thence to Japan and China on one of the new White Empresses ("Time and distance have been almost annihilated by modern machinery, and the trip from New York to Yokohama takes no longer now than did the trip from New York to Liverpool but a few years ago"). Alicia Little, or Mrs. Archibald Little, as she preferred to call herself, a longtime resident of Shanghai and western China, published a guide to Beijing in 1905, and in 1909 a guide to the West River appeared in Hong Kong, put out by a consortium of steamship companies. A year later the first volume from Thomas Cook could be bought.[41]

Even before the Great War, as tourism in its modern form was beginning, so there was also emerging a wish to distinguish travelers' China from tourists' China. Already it was becoming fashionable to dismiss the coastal cities of the east—Shanghai, Hong Kong, Guang-zhou, touched as they were by modernity and progress and foreign res-idence—as no more than counterfeits of the real China. Places through which one had to pass, no doubt, but hardly worth any more attention than Calais or Boulogne would demand of the traveler hurrying toward the real France of the Auvergne or the Dordogne. "Those of my readers who have followed me through all or any of my eleven vol-umes of travels must be aware that my chief wish on arriving at a for-eign settlement or treaty port in the East is to get out of it as soon as pos-sible," wrote Isabella Bird in 1898,[42] warning her audience to look elsewhere if it sought a detailed description of Shanghai. In 1911 real travel in China meant to Elizabeth Kendall having to "shun the half-Europeanized town and the treaty port . . . [to] leave behind the com-forts of hotel and railway, and [to] be ready to accept the rough and the smooth of unbeaten trails."[43] Twenty-odd years later Harold Acton found Canton "more Chinoiserie than Chinese," while George Kates, disembarking in Shanghai, put up there only for a single night before boarding a third-class train for Beijing, where he would live for seven years.[44] Such semi-Westernized cities might be alright for merchants or for those who demanded all the amenities (and then some) of Anglo-American family life, but, if the traveler must settle for any length of time in a city, the old northern capital, with its bracing climate and blue skies, its temples and palaces, its huge gray walls and gates, as well as its cultural memories reaching back beyond the Ming to Khubilai's Cambaluc, was the only place to live.

Finally, any study like this must set itself bounds. Frontiers may be artificial conventions, imposed regardless of cultural or chronological crossings, but they are necessary in work like this. Chronological fron-tiers first: I have stopped at 1949 simply because the foundation of the People's Republic raises all kinds of new questions whose engagement would make the work impossibly long. Geography next: for the most part I have restricted myself to China, culturally rather than geographically defined, and have avoided those excursions into Tibet and Central Asia that drew some of the greatest travelers of the period: Sir Aurel Stein, Owen Lattimore, and Alexandra David-Neel, among others. China might claim sovereignty over Tibet or Mongolia or Turkestan, may today even be Sinicizing those parts of the country, but culturally they still lay on the other side of the inner Asian frontier.

Within those limits I propose to examine these texts in a way that will try to understand the difficulties their writers faced: that is, their efforts to negotiate a frontier between the hard fact of what was seen and heard and the audiences for which they were writing. By *frontier* I mean not a clear line between two sovereignties, like the Rhine or the Pyrenees, but a frontier that is always uncertain and shifting, like the Inner Asian frontiers of China about which Owen Lattimore wrote or the American Pacific frontier recently described by Jean Heffer.[45] We are clearly on one side of it; they are clearly on the other. But in between there is a good deal of unclaimed territory, a region open to negotiation, and within this territory the authors of travel accounts work, trying not to lose sight of either side and conscious, to one degree or another, of the particular tints the spectacles of their times and their cultures impart to the landscapes over which they look. As we examine the works of these British and American travelers, we must try not to lose sight of China, the real China that existed beyond their and our imaginings, the better to understand their tasks and the problems they faced.

Chapter 2

China Left Behind

O Cina, O Cina . . . come dormivi lieta, gonfia dei tuoi set-
tantamila secoli . . . poi nacque Turandot!

Timelessness and the Absence of History

Sybille Fritzsche, writing of the perceptions of China among Western travelers in the nineteenth century, suggests two primary ways in which they framed the country.[1] The first was to peer at China through the glasses of Orientalism, viewing China as Other, its past and present shaped by a particular set of institutions, beliefs, and values that continued to order its society and produce a unique Chinese character bearing little or no resemblance to that of the West. Marx's rather offhand ascription to the Orient of an "Asiatic mode of production," unrelated to the familiar historical stages through which Europe's economic organization had passed, might stand as a model here. The second view, however, was predicated not on China's uniqueness but on its backwardness. For various reasons (geographic isolation and the dead hand of Confucianism were usually cited) the country remained mired in the past. The Beijing local, though enjoying an earlier start, now lay motionless with lights dimmed, shunted onto a siding while the London-Paris express roared through. Yet the tracks of social and historical evolution led in the same direction for everyone, and where the West now found itself China, though running late with frequent stops, would eventually reach. The abandonment of the Asiatic mode of production and the coopting by the Marxists (including Mao Zedong himself) of Marx's narrative of European historical development as a means of shaping the Chinese past can stand as an example.

Useful as the distinction is, it must not be overdone, for both kinds of representation might well appear within the traveler's text. The real

23

question, of course, was not whether China was different but why. Race, of course, might be adduced one factor, a kind of biological determinism inherited from the earlier classifications of the Enlightenment, now drawing a kind of spurious validity from what Said calls a second-order Darwinism, sanctioned by Darwin himself.[2] Yet the word *race*, heavily charged as it remains today, carries with it more than the usual dangers of anachronism when plucked out of the past. A century ago it was very loosely applied, cut to fit linguistic, national, or even religious or social groups (the Irish and Welsh races, the Italian and German races, even—in Anthony Trollope—the race of Tory squires who could never forgive Peel his abolition of the Corn Laws).

In any case we are dealing here with men and women whose views merely reflected the common and often contradictory ideas that filtered down from the anthropologists, the biologists, and the popularizers of Darwin and social Darwinism. As George Stocking points out, while the view of social evolutionism in the late nineteenth and early twentieth centuries was generally progressive, so that history as a whole was moving ahead toward the forms already achieved by northwestern Europe or North America, individual peoples, limited by their environments or their lower racial capacities, might stagnate or even slip back.[3] Were the Chinese among them? Although ideas of cultural and racial hierarchy were common, once one had placed Nordic Europeans at the top, there was no generally agreed-upon ranking of the lesser breeds. Nevertheless, wrote the anthropologist E. B. Tylor in 1871, "on the definite basis of compared facts, ethnographers are able to set up at least a rough scale of civilization. Few would dispute that the following races are arranged rightly in order of culture: Australian, Tahitian, Aztec, Chinese, Italian." To A. H. Keane of the University of London it was apparent that the Chinese "seem in some respects to be almost as incapable of progress as the Negroes themselves, the only essential difference being that the arrest of mental development comes later in life for the yellow than for the black man."[4] The difference, he suggested, might be due to cranial development.

Whatever the scientists might hold, however, many travelers reached different conclusions. R. F. Johnston, writing in 1908, scoffed at the popular European view that not only was Chinese civilization inferior to that of the West but that the Chinese themselves were less advanced on the evolutionary scale than Europeans. The Japanese, after all, might seem far more civilized in 1900 than they had been in

1850 before Perry's opening of the country, but it was hardly likely that fifty years could make a difference in their advance. "Evolution does not work quite so rapidly as that even in these days of 'hustle.'"[5]

Johnston's remark presumably grew out of his experiences with treaty port expatriates, whose peculiar narrowness of views later came to be tagged as the "Shanghai Mind." Among travelers, however, the biological inferiority of the Chinese was unlikely to be an issue. While their allusions to the Chinese as a race were frequent, they were as likely to be flattering as unflattering. Whatever else the Chinese might have been, they were not savages whose evolutionary backwardness consigned them forever to the lower rungs of the biological ladder and whose lot was simply to be pushed aside to make room for the higher races. They might well need to be Christianized, though by no means all travelers agreed on that, or brought the benefits of Western institutions and Western science. Unlike the "childish" Africans, however, they did not need to be civilized, for they had, if anything, too much civilization. Indeed, once freed from the cultural shackles of what one traveler called a "settled and inelastic system of civilization which came down from and is sanctified by antiquity,"[6] the Chinese might prove themselves not only the equals of Westerners but, indeed, their superiors.

Even when China was constructed as Other, locked into a different world, with different perceptions of reality, it did not follow that it was inferior. As Peter Bishop and Dennis Porter have shown, ideas of racial and cultural difference might coexist quite easily with a Western belief that the East, in its inheritance of an unchanging wisdom, knew how to draw on sources of knowledge that the West had never attained or, in its headlong rush toward material progress and bourgeois satisfactions, had lost.[7] Real racism, post-Darwinian scientific racism, with its views of biological determinism, the sort of racism that Patrick Brantlinger or Richard MacDonald find in Victorian writing about Africa, for example, was little in evidence, at least in these travelers' descriptions of China.[8]

"O China, O China," sings the mandarin Ping in act 2 of Puccini's opera *Turandot*, ". . . how peacefully you once drowsed, proud of your seventy thousand centuries! . . . until the birth of Turandot!" Although not even the most culture-proud Chinese would claim for his country's past the seven thousand millennia granted by the librettist Renato Simoni, well before the turn of the century China's drowsing had become a Western commonplace. As dynasty succeeded dynasty, nothing ever really changed, and the Chinese remained a people without a history—the people of eternal standstill, as Ranke, drawing on Hegel and Herder, had called them in a famous phrase. China had a far longer past than the West—no one would think of denying that—but the past and history are not the same thing. Here in China's past there was no narrative but only stories. One could always speak of China, all China, in the present tense, the generalizations applied to the country seen by travelers in the late Qing equally valid for the China they might have seen under the Ming five hundred years earlier or the Song or the Tang a thousand years back. Century after century rolled by, and the Chinese slept on, their dreams shaped by the deceptive security of a Great Wall that would protect them not only from external enemies but also from the ravages of chronology and change, little knowing that their iron house, to borrow Lu Xun's later metaphor, was already on fire.

So, as cycle succeeded cycle, China had known no Middle Ages, with its rise of trading cities and universities and parliaments, no Renaissance or Reformation, no Enlightenment, no American or French Revolutions. None of the familiar signposts that ordered the narrative of Western historical progress could be discerned by a study of China's past, nor could the physical evidence of change be glimpsed by the traveler journeying through China's natural and human landscape. "There is no history in Honan," wrote Richard Dobson in the 1930s, after living for some years in the north, where life gave no sign of having changed for thousands of years. Yet, as soon as he went south, he could make out the signs of progress and realized how much he had missed the historical landmarks he had grown used to in England. "In South China there was a *rapprochement:* the Chinese of the Coast, seafarers themselves, had adopted foreign notions and made them their own, meanwhile emigrating in their millions and exploiting the foreign enterprise on foreign soil."[9] But what he meant by history, of course, was the evidence of China's intercourse with the West, so much clearer in Guangdong than in the north.

Above all, there had been no scientific revolution, no Chinese Copernicus fundamentally changing the place of humanity and its little world in the cosmos. Up to the time of the Reformation the civilization of the Chinese had been at least as advanced as any in the world, wrote James Harrison Wilson in the 1880s, and their education, while different from that of the West, was its equal. Then, however, they had come to a stop. "They have stood absolutely still in knowledge since the middle ages. The discoveries of Galileo, Newton, and Laplace are a sealed book to them."[10] No Chinese Watt had appeared, no Stephenson, no inventors or engineers who, by joining the new science to technology, had given birth to the industrialism that by Wilson's day allowed Europe and North America to extend their sway over so much of the earth.

History, proper history, meant a record of change and progress, toward the spread of human freedom seen in Whig-Liberal terms and toward the emergence of the modern nation-state. No such purpose could be dug up, however, from the record of the Chinese past. Instead, it was, in the words of General Wilson,

> for the greater part an arid waste of intrigue, anarchy, and violence, varied with an almost endless series of internal and external wars. Here and there a great soldier or an honest and capable ruler emerges from the chaos and confusion, and governs the country wisely and well . . . but the great rulers of China can be counted on the fingers of one hand, while the essence of their history can be told in a few short chapters.

In thought and feeling the Chinese were at least five centuries behind the West, wrote Alicia Little, and Mary Gaunt went one step further, reading back the China she saw beyond the Middle Ages all the way to the ancient world: "Babylon come down to modern times, Babylon cumbrously adapting herself to the pressure of the nations who have raced ahead of the civilisation that was hers when they were barbarian hordes."[11]

The trope here, as Sara Mills reminds us, is typically Orientalist, casting the Chinese past in a framework devised by Europeans for Europe,[12] foregrounding the contrast between an activist energetic West and passive Eastern timelessness. For surely one of the chief aspects of that sort of Orientalism is the denial to other peoples, nations, and cultures of a history conceived in other than European and post-Enlightenment terms. Such a view, Said remarks, puts the European in command of Oriental history, time, and geography, ensuring that it becomes part of "world history" (a euphemism for the history of Europe); the Orient assumes its natural place as an appendage of Europe.[13] Nor was the view restricted to Europeans, for three decades after Mary Gaunt, when Mao Zedong appropriated the Marxist-Stalinist view of history for his own country, he became more protagonist than victim of Western Orientalism.[14]

Traveler after traveler noted China's tiredness, its fatigue, even its senility. The evidences of its former greatness might be visible, but in the modern age those monuments to a past glory were crumbling, visual metaphors starkly ratifying the Western commonplace that China was stagnant, indeed even declining. "China has been an old country for forty centuries," wrote the American Eliza Scidmore in 1900.

> It has been dying of old age and senile decay . . . its vitality running low, heart-stilling and soul-benumbing, slowly ossifying for this hundred years. During this wonderful century of Western progress it has swung slowly to a standstill, to a state of arrested existence, then retrograded, and the world watches now for the last symptoms and extinctions.[15]

The problem was neither race nor lack of civilization. Rather, it was one of overcivilization, for, as Mary Gaunt wrote, the Chinese had become "so civilised that they were decadent, effete, and every woman was helpless!"[16]

In this chapter and the one that follows I propose to examine the writings of several men and women, British, American, and Australian, who traveled in China during the closing years of the nineteenth century and the early years of the twentieth. Each was, to one degree or another, both witness of and participant in the greatest years of formal Western expansion, carrying the intellectual and ideological assumptions of the day as they were expressed through the rhetoric of imperialism and colonialism, and the discourses of race, progress, and historical change. Each, therefore, in writing about individual experiences, became part of that process that helped to "produce" another part of the world for a Western readership.[17]

Women and Men: The Observation of Change

To those whose views of Victorian women still see them relegated to the domestic sphere, trapped by home and hearth, the number of women represented here may seem surprising. Exceptional individuals they may have been, Isabella Bird, Mary Gaunt, Elizabeth Kendall, and the others. Yet there they were, tramping across the Middle Kingdom, not only traveling but writing and not only writing but publishing, hardly fitting into what Buzard calls the common colonialist stereotypes of "the Spinster Abroad or Memsahib, the eccentric traveler and the pampered Hill Station denizen."[18] Indeed, so much does their presence fly in the face of our received ideas about Victorian femininity today that we must, as Sara Mills suggests, resist the temptation to see them simply as "fun-loving, adventurous adolescent tomboys," their writings interesting primarily because of their autobiographical nature and republished in that spirit by feminist presses such as Virago[19] (or, as a trip to *www.isabellabird.com* shows, seeing their names borrowed a century later to sell "clothing for the adventurous woman").

Because of its very lack of an authoritative, scientific basis, Mills continues, travel writing, often cast in the form of journals or letters, was seen as particularly suited to women, who by nature were duplicitous, even liars, leaving to men the serious work of scientific description, classification, ethnography, and the like.[20] Nor has the notion that women have peculiar gifts or peculiar shortcomings in travel writing entirely left us. "Miss Gordon Cumming's books are," writes Dorothy Middleton, "alas, almost unreadable, so informative are they."[21] Perhaps. But perhaps also, to the historian at least, it is precisely the informative nature of her writings, as well as those of Isabella Bird, that gives them their interest. Bird might well have been making concessions to Victorian ideas of femininity in disclaiming any practical purpose for her journey. Yet the care with which she reported facts and figures and the dedication of her supposedly unplanned book (are we really meant to believe that a woman who had already written so widely about her travels would *not* succumb to the temptation to set down the record of her Chinese journey?) to Lord Salisbury would seem to undercut such statements. Men, after all, were also likely to claim that their journeys had no higher purpose than the enjoyment of travel for its own sake.

Mary Louise Pratt finds two kinds of narrator in travel writing: the largely impersonal "manners and customs" writer, whose narrator fades into the background, and the "sentimental" figure, in which the narrator is foregrounded.[22] Although she does not try to read a gendered significance into such a distinction, one might assume that, at least in the nineteenth century, men were more given to the former, and women to the latter. Isabella Bird, writing of her first trip to China in 1878, and Constance Gordon Cumming, the same year, both used an epistolary form, perhaps signifying a retreat into the personal that was uncharacteristic of men. Yet on the whole the writers considered here, men and women, fit no such easy mold. Both Isabella Bird and Eliza Scidmore, for example, surely spoke with the kind of authority popularly thought to be reserved to men, while others passed from one stance to another with ease.

Certainly, these writings give little warrant for the once popular interpretation that saw women as somehow less engaged in the imperialist enterprise, less "Orientalist," more sympathetic in their encounters with the Other than were men.[23] As Mills sensibly argues, not only must we avoid seeing such women simply as brave outlaws, fearlessly transgressing the constraints, physical, gendered, and textual, imposed on them by a Victorian patriarchy; we must also avoid seeing them as somehow proto-anti-imperialists, aligning themselves with the people in whose countries they traveled, devising strategies to subvert the colonialist discourse of the male world.[24] No less than men were they complicit in the project of imperialism, beneficiaries in China of the privileges conferred by the unequal treaties, and sharing a view of Western advance and Oriental backwardness. Certainly, a search for the ways in which women might have been ready to undercut male imperialism or male Orientalism turns up little. After all, there was nothing subversive in the views of Eliza Scidmore or Mary Gaunt that the Chinese would all be better off under foreign occupation.[25]

Indeed, as Dea Birkett has convincingly argued, Victorian women who traveled through distant lands adopted the persona of the White Male, precisely because it gave them the authority they needed to make their way safely. Conversely, one of the attractions of such travel through wild and occasionally dangerous country was that it enabled them to escape the restrictions of domestic social codes and to assume this posture of "temporary men." Thus, while the conditions under which they traveled, as well as the conditions under which they published their findings at home, might differ from those of men, in their representations of China, the common provenance of all these travelers—English-speaking Westerners, generally of the same class—was a good deal more important than any gendered differences. Race trumped gender, in other words, and in most cases these women looked on the lands and peoples through which they moved with eyes little different from those of white men.[26]

I am not arguing, of course, that women's writing is indistinguishable from that of men, and others, such as Sara Mills and Susan Morgan, have made persuasive cases for the need to read them differently.[27] But I do think that, if one looks not so much in the way they present themselves as the way they present China, then there is relatively little to distinguish them from men, little that can be construed as examples of feminine (or feminist) discourse. For example, while surely "counterhegemonic" notes antithetical to imperialism are to be found in travel writing, the important division lies not between women and men but between generations: those of both sexes who traveled before the Great War and those who came after. Political and ideological presuppositions might play an important role, too; in the 1930s, for example, Agnes Smedley's China was a good deal closer to that of Edgar Snow than to that of Joy Homer or Violet Cressy-Marcks.

Men or women, each of these travelers was also witness to a China itself undergoing prodigious changes. Those that came from the "impact of the West" were easy enough to see. The maiming of China's sovereignty (a term itself imported from the West) after Britain's victory in the Opium War of 1839–42 brought the unequal treaties and the first permanent Western settlements on Chinese soil. With them came new ideas and new technology, new business, management, and industrial practices in the cities of the east coast and the Yangtze Valley such as Shanghai, Tianjin, and Hankou. Less easy to make out were those changes, at least as important, that came from internal forces: the growth of population, the increasing pressure on land and resources, already upsetting the delicate human ecologies of the more crowded parts of the country, such as the Yellow River plain, the Yangtze Valley, and the Guangzhou hinterland in the southeast. Despite the earlier military glories of Chinese expansion into central Asia, the Qing armies had shown their weakness against the White Lotus risings in the late eighteenth century and proved almost completely ineffective in the face of the far greater challenges presented by the Taipings and the other rebellions of the mid-nineteenth century. Not only the rebellions themselves but also the means used to suppress them—the development of regional forces, seen in the armies built by leaders such as Zeng Guofan, Li Hongzhang, and Zuo Zongtang—meant a devolution of power from the capital to the provinces. After that, the self-strengthening movement—much admired by General Wilson—which saw China's first push toward modern industry, modern communications, and a modern military, only weakened the central government still further, since so much of its initiative and its financing came from the provinces rather than Beijing.

The limits of self-strengthening were finally made manifest in China's disastrous defeat by Japan in the war of 1894–95, which culminated in the loss of Taiwan and seemed an invitation to Western imperialism to join that of the Japanese in a division of China, if not into colonies, at least into a system of leaseholds and spheres of influence. The outbreak of the Boxer movement and the widespread killing of Western missionaries and their converts in 1900 not only sent a wave of fear through foreigners but also seemed to show that nothing fundamental had changed in China and that another wave of senseless superstition and antiforeign violence might break at any time. As the missionaries and their followers might see Boxerism as a reflection of satanic depravity, so the more secularly minded would the take movement as proof of China's willfully obstinate refusal to open its doors to progressivism and enlightenment. Meanwhile, though the United States' insistence on an Open Door might have helped to prevent a partition of China analogous to the contemporary partition of Africa, its purpose was to ease rather than restrict the further commercial penetration of China.

Simultaneously, however, the shock of defeat at Japan's hands helped bring further changes. Although the Hundred Days of reform, inspired by Kang Youwei in the summer of 1898, ended disastrously with some of the reformers killed, others on the run, and the young Guangxu emperor sequestrated by the dowager, the impetus was still there. Within a few years the so-called New Policies of the Manchu reform movement were taking hold. These saw, among other things, the end of the civil service examination system in 1905, the spread of modern education (including an increased number of students going to Japan and the West), the development of the New Armies, as well as initiatives to encourage the growth of Chinese entrepreneurship, particularly in the cities of the coast and the Yangtze Valley. On the political side, by 1909 the dynasty committed itself to the gradual development of a constitutional monarchy, inspired by the Japanese example and in October 1909 elected provincial assemblies met for the first time.

None of this was enough to save the dynasty, of course, particularly after the turn to reaction that took place following the death of the Guangxu emperor and the dowager within a day of each other in 1908. Indeed, the new organs of self-government, profiting from the long devolution of power since the mid-nineteenth century, were to become leaders in the republican revolution in late 1911, as province after province in effect seceded from allegiance to Beijing, and the infant emperor abdicated, giving way to a new republic headed briefly by Sun Yat-sen and then by Yuan Shikai.

Historians, of course, argue about how these and other such changes should be seen and which of them were more or less important. Certainly, most travelers of the time saw a country that seemed at last on the threshold of a great transformation. Of course, they did not see all that was taking place, nor did they necessarily agree on the importance of what they were looking at. Yet stagnant and immobile though China might earlier have appeared, by 1900 to most travelers it no longer reflected the kind of unchanging and essentialized Orient that we today perhaps take too easily as the object of colonial discourse. On the other hand, they reflected their times when they gave credit for that transformation to the generally beneficent impact of the West. Not surprisingly, too, their writings could be ambiguous, even contradictory. They could, for instance, take the Boxer Rising—a relatively short-lived single occurrence growing out of a particular set of political and ideological and environmental factors in North China at the end of the century—as emblematic of an atavistic Chinese cruelty and antiforeignism. As parts of the national or racial character, such qualities would forever make the Chinese threatening and incomprehensible (one might note ironically that, as the opening year of the twentieth century saw the siege of the Beijing legations, so in its closing year the world watched on television as angry crowds encircled the British and U.S. embassies, imprisoning the American ambassador in his office for several days). Yet almost in the next breath they could look with a guarded optimism on the progress of nationhood, science, Christianity, and industry, all encouraging proofs that China was following in Western footsteps.

Of course in all this travelers judged China by their own standards, and of course it's easy enough to argue that such "strategies of representation" masked a justification for continued Western power. Not surprisingly, the modes of the observers (their "strategies") themselves underwent changes, changes that reflected developments in the situation of the observed as well as in the mentalities of the observers themselves. Still, we also need to ask how far such representations might accurately have reflected the realities of the observed. As always, there was a continual negotiation between observer and observed, and it was a negotiation that had at least as much to do with objective reality as with preconceptions and inheritances, important as they were.

The Purposes and Conditions of Travel

Some travelers admitted to practical reasons for their journeys. The former Union general James Harrison Wilson was one, arriving in the wake of the depression of the 1870s to look for opportunities for American trade and investment, particularly in railway building. Archibald Colquhoun, in 1881, and Laurence John Dundas, the earl of Ronaldshay, a quarter-century later, traveled through southwestern China examining the prospects for a rail line from Burma and the possibilities for expanded trade through China's back door into Yunnan province, the same quest whose exploration had cost Vice-Consul Augustus Raymond Margary his life in 1875. In 1883 the merchant Archibald Little pushed up the river toward Chongqing, intent on opening the rich Sichuan basin to British enterprise, and in 1898 forced the first steamship through the rapids and whirlpools of the Three Gorges, leading to Chongqing's opening as a treaty port, sixteen hundred miles above the mouth of the Yangtze.

By then Little was convinced that the Open Door had been a failure, and, unlike Isabella Bird, he believed that, if Britain were to maintain its dominance in the Yangtze Valley, it must join in the coming partition of China into such spheres of interest.[28] Even though such a view never caught on in Whitehall, men and women like these represented the age-old dream of China as a vast market for Western manufacturers, a dream given a peculiar sharpness by the depression darkening the later years of the nineteenth century. Driven as they might be by curiosity and the desire for adventure, the prospects for trade were still on their minds. Bird, making her long trip through western China in 1897, protested that she only wanted "recreation and interest . . . after some months of severe travel in Korea." Yet for a merely recreational traveler she was extraordinarily conscientious in her setting down of geographic, demographic, and economic statistics. We learn, for example, that "2755 steam launches, owned and run by Chinese, towing 7889 passenger boats, carrying 605 foreign and 125,000 native passengers, entered and cleared in 1897 between Hangchow, Shanghai, and Soochow," while in the same year 200,000 fans were imported into steamy, torrid Chongqing.[29] Of course, it was no great trick to work up such figures by consulting consular reports or the returns on trade published by Sir Robert Hart's Imperial Chinese Maritime Customs. What counts is that she thought it necessary to do so rather than simply being content with recording her own observations.

Yet adventure and curiosity were more than a mere cover for economic investigation. "I am a savage at heart, and weary for the wilds," Bird wrote, resolutely stopping her ears against the siren calls of Hong Kong's creature comforts on her first trip to China.[30] As Dea Birkett points out, to a woman like Bird the journey into the wilds made possible the assumption of male powers and privileges, privileges that she would not enjoy at home and indeed would have to be shed in the sort of settled colonial society that had grown up in Hong Kong or in the larger treaty ports such as Shanghai.[31] Travel, moreover, gave proof of energy and a kind of atavistic virility—the word by no means restricted to men alone—at a time when civilization, or even decadence (of the kind exemplified by, say, Oscar Wilde and Aubrey Beardsley), might seem a danger sapping the strength of those left at home. Although the British and colonial chambers of commerce that helped underwrite Colquhoun's China journey in 1882 might not have been particularly interested in adventure, he certainly discovered an excitement in exploring a route some fifteen hundred miles, "of which two-thirds would be over untrodden ground, undescribed by European travellers."[32] His belief that such qualities set Englishmen off from others seemed confirmed when he was unable to convince a politely uncomprehending Chinese subprefect in western Guangxi that the object of his trip was to gain geographical knowledge.

These things were explained to him as could best be done. He seemed astonished when I told him the system of our learned societies at home, and that the greatest reward, which any private traveller, such as myself, could expect, was a gold medal. Much as he seemed interested, I fear the mandarin, in his inner heart, thought the game hardly worth the candle. Our restless curiosity in the matter of travel no Chinaman can understand.[33]

There was, of course, more than a hint of disingenuousness here, for Colquhoun's "restless curiosity" had as its object the possibility of a rail line from Burma. "It was not a scientific excursion," said William Spencer Percival of his trip up the Great River in 1887, for there were no new countries to discover or trade routes to open up but "simply an excursion for health and pleasure [to a] wild romantic country."[34] "My sole object in going to China was a personal desire to see China from the inside," wrote Edwin Dingle, a businessman and journalist who lived in Singapore, pointing out that he took no scientific instruments apart from an aneroid.[35] Yet, as he made his way from Shanghai up the Yangtze Valley to the Burmese border, spending a year in the southwest, he too freely offered his observations on the opportunities for British trade. He thought of writing an ethnology of the Miao in Yunnan province as well, and Reginald F. Johnston (who later became tutor to Henry Puyi, the deposed Xuantong emperor), while also disclaiming any governmental or scientific importance for his trip to the same regions in 1906, actually included a chapter on the non-Chinese peoples of the far west.[36] Eliza Scidmore, whose book was less an account of a particular journey than a composite of several, had already written guides to the cities of China and Japan for the Canadian Pacific, becoming one of the midwives at the birth of modern tourism in China. Travel was in her blood, the Australian Mary Gaunt claimed, and she set out to answer "the 'something calling—beyond the mountains,' the 'Come and find me' of Kipling"[37] (though it surely must have helped that she'd already contracted with a London publisher for one or two books on her voyages).

By the late nineteenth century steam navigation and the opening of the Suez Canal had made the passage out, whether from Britain or North America, far easier and more comfortable that it had been earlier. Steamers ran regularly scheduled trips along China's coast, up the Yangtze to Hankou and Yichang or up the West River above Guangzhou, and by the early twentieth century railway building had begun in earnest. But once off those particular beaten tracks, all the old difficulties rose up to present themselves to the traveler. "Travelling in China is a slow process, more often wearisome than otherwise,—a peculiar wearisomeness of its own," warned the American missionary Philip Pitcher, in his guide to the region around Xiamen. "The time of railroads is not yet, in this part of China."[38] Proper roads didn't exist, wrote Archibald Little, but simply narrow footpaths connecting towns and villages with one another.[39] From such paths, raised as they traversed the fields, a fall was always possible into the muck of the paddy below. "The sedan chair is an instrument of torture to the uninitiated," Pitcher decided,[40] while travelers in the north suffered the horrors of the springless Peking cart, with its round wooden wheels bumping over the rough and rutted roads. Boats, in which one could travel in comparative peace and comfort, were the preferred means of locomotion but were limited, of course, to rivers and canals.

And then, unless your boat were one on which you could sleep, you had to face the dreadful inns of China. Noise and dirt were everywhere, of course, and the mud, the refuse, the dust of the country, sometimes seemed to make its way onto almost every page of these writings. Even so, the inns deserved a place of their own. Traveler after traveler remarked on the indescribable filth of these tumble-down buildings, with their stinking cesspools, their vermin, their pigs rooting around the piles of garbage and offal. Faced with such quarters on her first night away from the comparative comfort of a boat drawn up the Great River, even Bird admitted having to fight down a "cowardly inclination to abbreviate my journey."[41] Stopping for a meal or for the night meant an almost complete lack of privacy, as villagers crowded round, poking holes in the paper windows to get a view of the foreigners eating, washing, preparing for bed, and the like, the whole mass pressing in for a closer view, its "unblinking, vacuous stare," as Dundas called it, wanting to make you "rush in and hit out right and left, and chance the consequences."[42] An interesting inversion—or subversion—of the traveler's own "imperial gaze," for it was now the foreigner who suddenly became object rather than subject of this particular means of appropriating the body and the landscape of the Other.[43] Worse yet was the occasional hostility of the crowds, the howling mobs, mannerless, brutal, coarse, conceited, and cowardly, as Bird called them (she had twice come under attack herself), "ignorant beyond all description, living in a state which is indescribable and incredible, in an inconceivable beastliness of dirt."[44] "I must ask the reader's pardon for again referring to Chinese inns," wrote Dingle, describing yet another fearful den, where man and beast lived in promiscuous and insupportable filth . . . Filth there was everywhere. It seemed inseparable from the people and a total apathy as regards matter in the wrong place pervaded all classes, from the highest to the lowest . . . I remember, however, that I am in China, and must not be disgusted.[45]

Country and City

Certainly, one unequivocal blessing China promised the traveler was the scenery. Not around dreary Tianjin perhaps or in the flat and featureless countryside of the Yangtze delta near Shanghai. But there were plenty of glowing descriptions of Beijing's setting, with the Western Hills rising beyond the city and the clear blue sky above it (except, of course, in those seasons when it seemed that the entire Ordos Desert was being deposited in one's lungs by the winds). The passage through the Yangtze Gorges invariably brought out a flood of descriptive adjectives. Watching a spring thunderstorm there, Dingle saw a

> vivid but broken flash of lightning, blazing in a flare of blue and amber, [which] poured livid reflections, and illuminated with dreadful distinctness, if only for one ghastly moment, the stupendous cliffs of Ichang Gorge, whose wall-like steepness suddenly became darkened as black as ink.
>
> Thus, with a grand impressiveness, this great gully in the mountains assumed hugely gigantic proportions, stretching interminably from east to west, up to heaven and down to earth, silhouetted to the north against a small remaining patch of golden purple, whose weird flames seemed awesomely to herald the coming of a new world into being, lasting but for a moment longer, until again the blue blaze quickly cut up the sky into a thousand shreds and tiny silver bars. And then, suddenly, with a vast down sweep, as if some colossal bird were taking the earth under her far-outstretching wings, dense darkness fell—impenetrable, sooty darkness, that in a moment shut out all light, all power of sight. Then from out the sombre heavens deep thunder boomed ominously as the reverberating roar of a pack of hunger-ridden lions, and the two men, aliens in an alien land, stood beneath the tattered

matting awning with a peculiar fear and some foreboding. We were tied in fast to the darkened sides of the great Ichang Gorge.[46]

We might almost be standing here before a painting by John Martin or gazing into the Wolf's Glen of Weber's *Freischütz*. After some pages of this, however, Dingle gave up, for the gorges had been described often enough. "Time and time again have they fallen to the imaginative pens of travellers—mostly bad or indifferent descriptions, few good; none better, perhaps, than Mrs. Bishop's."[47] Scidmore left the gorges to others; she did, however, swing down south of Shanghai, where she'd found little to detain the traveler, to see the famous Great Bore of the Qiantang river near Hangzhou, a column of water raised by the inrushing tide. Ghastly and sinister as it was, still the practical tourist guide in her could not help but feel that this kind of natural phenomenon had been wasted on the unimaginative Chinese, incapable of envisaging the virtues of a theme park. Some day, perhaps, excursion trains might carry tourists to the Bore View Hotel and chartered junks take them on wild rides up the river on the Bore's back. But for the moment it was a shame "that this money-coining, dividend-paying wonder could not have happened to a thrifty Swiss canton, instead of to the by-parts of Chekiang."[48]

On other occasions the Chinese landscape conjured up visions of the traveler's own land or at least of a familiar Europe. Charmed by the spring countryside outside Ningbo as her canal boat passed through rich fields of sugar cane and maize, Constance Gordon Cumming woke "at earliest dawn to greet as lovely a May-day as heart could desire . . . True to traditions of home, we washed our faces in the May dew which lay so abundantly on fields of the richest pink clover, and the banks of golden buttercups and celandine." Fragrant honeysuckle and snowy hawthorn bloomed as richly as on an English lane. "No wonder that happy birds here sing so joyously! and the cuckoo's note sounded so natural as almost to make us forget how far from home we were."[49]

The views of the upper West River above Guangzhou reminded Archibald Colquhoun of Highland lochs or the Swiss and Italian lakes.[50] For the few who got there, it was the scenery of southwestern China, of the far reaches of Sichuan and Yunnan provinces, that most enchanted the travelers, though they also noted the wasted fields and deserted villages, grim reminders of the great Muslim rebellion a few years earlier.[51] The Switzerland of China, Dingle called it (a name Bird had already appropriated), but even better, perhaps, combining a "truly Alpine magnificence with the minute sylvan beauty of Killarney or Devonshire."[52] Some thirty years later a British traveler making her way into Yunnan over the new Burma Road rejected the Alpine comparison suggested to her by her guide, insisting that the landscape be seen as Chinese, not European. But he, wiser perhaps than she in foreign ways, was convinced that after the war, only if they thought it like Switzerland would the Western tourists come.[53] Bird, admiring the graceful beauty of China's bridges, again made the Swiss comparison, while Elizabeth Kendall—born and raised in the Champlain Valley of western Vermont—found them far preferable to the "hideous, shed-like structures that disfigure many a beautiful stream in New England."[54]

To view scenery in this way is to aestheticize it, in Mary Louise Pratt's term, to tame it and see it as if in a museum, the appreciative observers acting as verbal painters who produce it for others (and thereby assert their control).[55] Moreover, some have suggested that the comparisons with the familiar—Devonshire, the Alps, the Italian lakes—are a way of bringing the complexities of the foreign under control, accepting what is observed into one's own mental horizons, through the selective remembrance of certain aspects and the negating or dismissing of others.[56] More important, I think, is that what the traveler found admirable was likely to be the natural rather than the human or the interplay between the two. Taking refuge from another thunderstorm, this time in Yunnan, Dingle was grateful for the undisturbed silence that allowed him "to feel the heart-beat of Nature and her beauty in perfect harmony with all that is best within us." When the clouds had passed, however,

> it seemed as if a silken cord had suddenly been severed, and I had been dragged from a world of sweet infinitude down to a sphere mundane and everyday, to something I had known before . . . I heard the crack of the bamboo and the patter of feet in the sodden, slippery pathway, and I knew my men were come. Crawling out from my rock, I descended again to common things, having to listen to the disgusting talk of my Chinese followers, though a very slender vocabulary saved me from losing entirely the memory of that great picture then passing away.[57]

People—the hordes and hordes of Chinese people, in other words—got in the way of the scenery, and there was no escaping them. Unlike Africa, the empty continent of darkness being opened to light and usefulness by Stanley, Kingsley, and other Victorian travelers, there were here in China no suggestions of new vistas suddenly revealed for the first time to the human eye. Humanity, unfortunately, was only too evident, and its presence kept spoiling the picture. "'Every prospect pleases,' as the hymn says," noted Gaunt, crossing the rich Shanxi plain under a cloudless sky, "and only man is vile. He wasn't vile; really I think he was a very good fellow in his own way, which was in a dimension into which I have never and am never likely to enter, but he was certainly unclean, ignorant, a serf, poverty-stricken with a poverty we hardly conceive of in the West."[58] While some nineteenth-century photographers such as John Thomson and Felice Beato recorded the rich variety of China's people, others turned their cameras away from a humanity that might get in the way of aestheticized landscapes or monuments. Shortly after the turn of the century, for example, the German Ernst Boerschmann produced for his readers a China strangely emptied of the men and women whose inconvenient presence might have challenged the European gaze. It was a feat even more startlingly replicated by the American Eliot Porter some seventy years later in a China roughly three times the size of Boerschmann's in its population.[59]

Yet, while the countryside could arouse a sense of aesthetic pleasure, as well as comforting memories of familiar Europe, human habitations played no such role. Indeed, cities, towns, and villages were best kept at a distance, framed by the larger landscape to retain their picturesque qualities. From a distance they might seem quite as romantic as those of Europe; it was only when you got closer that the illusion disappeared. Although the sparkling blue waters of a Yunnan lake reminded Colquhoun of sailing on Lugano, he found that the "artistic villages" lining the shores did not bear too close an inspection, with their pigs and peasantry.[60] So, too, Frances Trollope had preferred the Florence seen from Fiesole to Florence down the hill, where real Italians lived and walked the streets.[61] "Graceful and unique in appearance as is an inland mountain city when viewed from a distance," Archibald Little wrote of Chongqing. "I regret to say that, as with many a picturesque town in Southern Europe, the charm of a Chinese city vanishes entirely on closer acquaintance. Filth seems inseparable from Chinese humanity, and a total apathy in regard to matter in the wrong place, pervades all classes, from the highest to the lowest."[62] A walled town might look impressive (Bird noted one that reminded her of Mont-Saint-Michel),[63] a village set in the hills might conjure up images of bucolic loveliness. Once within them, however, the traveler realized that they were irredeemably Chinese, and the reality of humanity, with its dirt and strange noises, its poverty and the stenches of animal and human waste, took over to drive out the earlier aesthetic sensations.[64] In this aspect, as Archibald Colquhoun complained, the landscape simply mirrored its inhabitants, for "a Chinaman never looks so dirty as when trying to clean himself. Got up in his silk attire he bears inspection from the washing point of view, for his imperfections are hidden; but in *déshabille*, he is like many a pleasant or beautiful landscape or picture, a thing that does not bear looking into."[65]

> A city! [wrote Philip Pitcher of Xiamen]. But not the kind of city you have in mind. There are no wide avenues, beautiful private residences, magnificent public and mercantile buildings . . . All is directly opposite to this condition of things. The streets are narrow and crooked,—with the sewer underneath and plainly in sight thro [*sic*] the chinks of the uneven flagstones,—ever winding and twisting, descending and ascending, and finally ending in the great nowhere.[66]

In a Western city you could, if you so chose, avoid the slums. It was a characteristic of Chinese cities, however, that rich and poor lived close to one another. Wealth was hidden rather than publicly displayed, so that, even while the great houses existed, they lay behind high walls, invisible to the passerby, and it was easy to conclude that virtually the whole city was a slum. Visiting a mandarin in Guangzhou, Gordon Cumming and her companions were carried for miles through the densely crowded town with its foul and stinking streets, until they passed through the gates of the great man's house. "The sudden change from the dirt and squalor and dense population of the streets, to the large enclosure with luxurious houses and pleasure-grounds, which form a sort of patriarchal encampment for the family of a wealthy great man, is most startling."[67] The magnificence of some of these establishments, with their buildings, their courtyards, their gardens, was unmistakable. But they were not on public view, set in their own districts as were, say, the houses of the rich in Mayfair or Louisburg Square.

Still, however narrow the alleys, however repulsive their dirt and disorder might be, the life of the streets could still be fascinating. Gordon Cumming thought Guangzhou a wonderful city, better than Cairo or Benares in its busyness, and she carefully observed the different shops in the different districts, the work being done by lanternmakers, woodcarvers, tailors, glass blowers, artificial flower makers, and the like.[68] "My admiration and amazement never cease," wrote Bird on her first visit to the same "marvelous city."

> I grudge the hours that I am obliged to spend in sleep; a week has gone like half a day, each hour heightening any impressions of the fascination and interest of Canton, and of the singular force and importance of the Chinese. Canton is intoxicating from its picturesqueness, colour, novelty, and movement. To-day I have been carried eighteen miles through and round it, revelling the whole time in its enchantments, and drinking for the first time of that water of which it may truly be said that whoso drinks "shall thirst again"—true Orientalism.[69]

A good thing that the rattle of the carts, the shouting of the peddlers, and all the other noises of the streets must have drowned out the sound of Edward Said sharpening his critical pencils in the next century. Yet even in such cities, a few temples aside—usually in disrepair, their paint flaking, their grounds dirty (unlike those in clean, well-kempt Japan)[70]—there were in general few established sights of the sort the European traveler might expect, few great monuments like those to be found in English or French cathedral towns or the cities of Italy and Germany. No Chartres or St. Peter's to recall the ages of faith, no Roman Forum to encapsulate antiquity. Even the capital itself was disappointing. A dreary wilderness of dirt and dust, wrote Gordon Cumming, with its dull dead walls and one-storied houses, its general air of neglect and decay, its unswept streets, stagnant sewers, dirty crowds, and evil odors.[71] The "unspeakably filthy place of the world," wrote Wilson in the 1880s, dirtier than Constantinople, and nastier even than any other Chinese city—"and nothing worse can be said of it."[72]

Yet at least Beijing had its monuments. "City of dreadful dirt," though she called it, Eliza Scidmore also found it the most spectacular, picturesque, surprising, and interesting city in the country. Not because of its modern aspects, of course, but precisely because it lacked them, because, racked and ruined though it might be, it was still a virtually intact Central Asian city of the thirteenth century, almost untouched by the "demon progress" and the "dread monotony of the universal commonplace." Around it rose the greatest and most massive walls and gates in the world, not beautiful, perhaps, but overpowering by their sheer mass, their brute size.[73] And there were temples—the garish Lama Temple, with its ill-tempered monks and sinister rituals, and above all the great complex of the Temple of Heaven, with its circular white marble altar and blue tiled halls, where at the winter solstice the emperor's procession would repair for the sacrifices guaranteeing good harvests (Gordon Cumming, visiting the site, found there not the emperor but former president Ulysses Grant, yet, though she'd once met him, he snubbed her).[74] Alicia Little, in Beijing in 1901 after the imperial family had fled, leaving in occupation the Allied troops that had put down the Boxers, was able to enter the halls of the Forbidden City, normally closed off to all save those on the emperor's business. In the familiar comparison with the West, it was her own geography that came off second best. "St. James's seems like a baby plaything by comparison, the Tuileries confined"; only in the great days of papal Rome could anything analogous be imagined. The halls of the Forbidden City, lacking the ornament and decoration of European palaces, were nonetheless even more impressive than those.

> There is absolutely no frittering away on decoration as in so many European buildings. The great designers of the Chinese palace relied upon size and proportion to abase man's soul into his boots before he drew near his ruler, and even now it is difficult to traverse these great distances on foot without realising how small one is. To a Chinese drawing near to his Emperor, the feeling of smallness would have been overpowering.[75]

In more normal times, of course, the traveler had to be content with only occasional glimpses of the imperial palace, caught from outside the golden tiled archways and gates that led into it. Perhaps Beijing was best looked down on from above, rather like those late-nineteenth-century bird's-eye views of New England towns, which produced a whole neatly bounded community reduced to manageable size. You could count on nature to frame the picture atop the city's walls, thanks to the many trees adorning the private courtyards invisible to the pedestrian in the gray-walled *hutongs* below, which made the capital seem sometimes a city set in a forest. Illusive though such an impression might be, removed from the noise and the dust and the squalor of the streets, you could see, almost as if by magic, the harmonious gray roofs of the houses of mandarins, the yellow palace roofs rising above the trees, the pavilions on Coal Hill, with their shining green, gold, and peacock blue roofs, and beyond them the Western Hills standing clear against the deep blue sky. "Then you realise how many cool pleasant homes wealthy citizens contrive to reserve in the midst of these dingy, grey, densely, crowded streets, of which you only catch a glimpse here and there, just enough to give a suggestion of life to the whole scene."[76]

A few years ago Arthur Waldron suggested that the Great Wall of China has never in fact existed—or at least never existed in quite the way it has become imagined. To a certain extent at least, he argues, it is a Western invention, and those parts of the Wall customarily seen by tourists near Beijing are the symbol of a failed Ming dynasty foreign policy, rather than the edge of a two thousand–mile frontier dividing China from the barbarians.[77] Be that as it may, by the late nineteenth century the Wall had already become a required sight for travelers, approached either at Shanhaiguan, where it came down to meet the sea, or at Nankou Pass, which led west through the mountains to Kalgan. "The one artificial construction on the face of the earth that may be seen by the inhabitants of Mars,"[78] wrote Scidmore, greatly improving on the belief, still common today, that it is visible from the moon. "And it looks exactly like its picture in school geographies! One had half expected that it would not, could not, be so irrationally, impractically picturesque, so uselessly solid and stupendous . . . It is one of the few great sights of the world that is not disappointing."[79] General Wilson found it laid out "in total defiance of all the rules of military engineering" yet still so arranged that, with any effort made in its defense, a modern army would find it difficult to penetrate. Traveling in company with two members of the American legation (one of whom was the Tibetan traveler W. W. Rockhill), it had taken him about three days to get there, but by the time Mary Gaunt saw it, in 1913, she was able to go by train, in the private observation car of an American millionaire and his family. She was impressed by the number of lives its building must have cost, and in Nankou Pass she found a romantic setting that recalled "barbaric Italy or Provence of the Middle Ages."[80]

"Old wall, new railway," wrote Kendall, looking at it from the same place. "Which will serve China best? One sought to keep the world out, the other should help to create a Chinese nation that will not need to fear the world."[81] The Great Wall may be myth, and a myth that came to serve the purposes of a new twentieth-century nationalism for leaders such as Sun Yat-sen, Mao Zedong, and Deng Xiaoping. But it served the purposes of travelers too, in their own imaginings of China's past. Like the huge gray walls and gates of barbaric Beijing, the presence of the Great Wall ratified foreign preconceptions of the unchanging insularity of a nation that was only then, as Marx had earlier predicted, seeing its frontiers being beaten down by the determined power of Western capital, Western commerce, and Western evangelism, both sacred and secular.

Chinese Characteristics: Dirt, Dissimulation, and Depravity

"Oh, the filth, the unspeakable filth, of these people!" wrote Edward Dingle. "Would that the Chinese would emulate the cleanliness of the Japs, though even that I would question. In several years in the Orient I have not yet come across the cleanliness in any race of people to be compared with that cleanliness which in England is next to godliness."[82] "Soap and carbolic will do more than diplomacy or gunpowder" to regenerate China, an old foreign resident told Scidmore, though—echoing the tyrannical First Emperor of the Qin—he admitted that even more important would be to "burn the classics and behead the literati."[83]

Dirt was never far from the writings of these travelers, and not only in the wayside inns—for two reasons, perhaps. One was that the dirt of China was always there; it was not simply part of an imaginary mental construction of the Other. It was real, palpable; it got in your clothes, in your nostrils, in your mouth, on your skin. The other was that, particularly to the nineteenth-century Anglo-Saxon Protestant mind, dirt was proof of a moral failing, a standard signifier of degeneration and the uncivilized.[84] Still, there was an ambivalence about dirt,

European dirt, at any rate, if not Chinese dirt. As James Buzard points out, while the dirt and poverty of Rome reminded Frances Trollope only of the dirt and poverty of Manchester, for Henry James and other Americans it helped to create the picturesque, lending a chiaroscuro of color and tone.[85] An overlay of dirt thus helped to authenticate the city's antiquity in a way that would have been impossible for a clean Forum or Coliseum (think of Roman ruins in Switzerland) that might have been built yesterday, like Disneyland.

Dirt served one useful function in China and one only: it helped to validate the traveler's experience of the country. Passing the night between the clean sheets of Shanghai's Palace Hotel or the Wagons-Lits in Beijing was not experiencing real China; passing the night in a filthy smoke-begrimed Hubei inn, with the hogs snuffling outside, was. But there was nothing, absolutely nothing, picturesque about Chinese dirt, whether found in a village in the interior, a city like Guangzhou, or in the capital of Beijing itself. Not just because it betrayed the moral failings of the Chinese; also, I think, because it existed in a setting totally unfamiliar to the traveler. Roman or Venetian dirt was not only picturesque; it was also a reminder of the distance Europeans had come over the centuries, traveling from this sun-swept, messy, lazy, Catholic, and Mediterranean world toward the progressive, earnest, and antiseptic Protestantism of the advanced nations of the north. But in neither the Chinese landscape nor the cityscape were there familiar churches or fountains or ruins, acting as signposts that foreign travelers could read to remind them of their own past. Instead, they saw only the great gray barbaric walls and gates of Beijing rising over its filthy streets. China was dirty, China had always been dirty, and Chinese dirt was only the sign of a cultural vice crying out to be cured.

As was the uncertain attitude toward truth, good, clean, rational Western truth. Why, for instance, did one get all those different answers to questions about distance, about size, about production or trade, questions about matters that should have been so easily quantifiable? Told of a town where five thousand people had reportedly died from starvation in a year, G. E. Morrison found the numbers appalling but doubted their truth, a disregard of accuracy being common to all Orientals.[86] The complaint was echoed over and over again by others, so much so that Dingle could only conclude that "the Chinaman is a liar by nature."

That speech is the chief revelation of the mind, the first visible form that it takes, is undoubtedly true of the West: as the thought, so the speech. All social relations with us have their roots in mutual trust, and this trust is maintained by each man's sincerity of thought and speech. Not so in China. There is so much craft, so much diplomacy, so much subtle legerdemain that, if he chooses, the Chinaman may give you no end of trouble to inform you on the simplest subject. The Chinese, like so many cavilers and calumniators, all glib of tongue, who know better than any nation on earth how to turn voice and pen to account, have taken the utmost advantage of extended means of circulating thought, with the result that an Englishman such as myself, even if I were a deep scholar of their language, would have the greatest difficulty in getting at the truth about their affairs.[87]

As Isabella Bird complained, when traveling in China, a problem far greater than uncertain transport or filthy inns was

having to disinter all information about the route and the industries and customs of the people, through the medium of two languages, out of the capacities of persons who neither observed nor thought accurately, nor were accustomed to impart what they knew; who were used to telling lies, and to whom I could furnish no reasons for telling the truth, while they might have several for deceiving me on some points. This digging into obtuseness and cunning is the hardest part of the traveller's day.[88]

Moreover, in a country so badly mapped it never even seemed possible to get accurate statements about distance, and the length of the Chinese *li* seemed to vary as much as did region, dialect, and climate. Some travelers, however, were able to dismiss this particular problem with a shrug. As Agnes Smedley put it decades later on her travels through wartime China, "The Chinese are very realistic. When they march up a mountain, the *li* becomes longer; when they descend it is shorter."[89]

Cruelty seemed another characteristic of the Chinese; cruelty against the foreigner, cruelty against themselves. On her first trip to the country, in 1879, Isabella Bird had seen a prison in Guangzhou, and the dirt, filth, and savagery of the place had made a strong impression on her. Although at the execution ground she found nothing worse than a pool of blood and some heads being gnawed by dogs, she noted it was the practice to kill many condemned criminals at a single time: "My friend Mr. Bulkeley Johnson of Shanghai saw one hundred heads fall in one morning." The problem, however, was less a defect in the Chinese character than China's backwardness; heathen China, as Bird put it, was simply still practicing what Christian Europe had looked on with indifference for centuries.[90] Twenty years later, climbing over a pass in Szechwan, she was badly shaken by the horrifying sight of three criminals hanging from cages, their feet not quite touching the ground, being slowly strangled or starved to death, while nearby were two human heads in baskets, "with a ghastly look of inquisitive intelligence on their faces." The scene—common enough to be noted by other travelers—suddenly brought out a wave of near despair about the country in which she was traveling.

> At this time China, with its crowds, its poverty, its risks of absolute famine from droughts or floods, its untellable horrors, its filth, its brutality, its venality, its grasping, clutching, and pitiless greed, and its political and religious hopelessness, sat upon me like a nightmare. There are other and better aspects which dawn on the traveller more slowly, and there is even a certain lovableness about the people. I only put down what were my impressions at the time.[91]

Still, as G. E. Morrison noted, thanks to an arrested development of the sensory nervous system, the Chinese felt pain less than did Westerners, and that must have been some small comfort. Nor was he, for one, particularly upset by the condition of women, finding them far better off in China than in any other heathen country.[92] Here Morrison was an exception, however, for the kind of cruelty made visible by binding the feet of girls (a practice common to Han Chinese but not to Manchus or Hakka) aroused a widespread condemnation among Western travelers, men as well as women. It was, moreover, an irrational cruelty, for, by effectively crippling almost half the populace, footbinding became another block on the road to progress. Archibald Little linked the practice to Chinese dirtiness, noting that the inside of a Chinese house was properly cleaned only at the New Year. "What, however, can be expected of a race who cripple their women, and incapacitate the natural guardians of the home from all active exertion?"[93] His wife, Alicia Little, who in 1895 had founded a Natural Foot Association (Tianzu hui) to seek an end to the custom, was delighted to find in Kalgan an official who told her that his household had at least three pairs of unbound feet: those of his little daughter and his two slave girls.[94]

Such discoveries were unfortunately rare, and so footbinding came to be seen, by Mrs. Little and others, as qualitatively different from other Chinese characteristics. Unpleasant and regrettable as it was, Chinese dirt was a sign of poverty and backwardness that could be cured through enlightenment and education. The advance of rationalism would dispel the fogs of Chinese prevarication, insincerity, and just plain obfuscation. Even the barbaric treatment of criminals, in jails, at execution grounds, once common in the West, would change as China followed the road of progress. But foot binding simply made no sense. "Something sexual at the bottom of it, I believe," Mary Gaunt, who called herself an ardent suffragist, suggested, recalling the "swooning heroines of Dickens and Thackeray" as a Victorian ideal, though she was quick to dismiss the notion that it was no worse than the tightly laced-in waist of the Western woman, for it was an infinitely worse crime.[95] None of its eroticism was comprehensible to the Western mind, however, and it seemed to signify, almost as no other practice, the enduring nature of China's Otherness and a sign of its condition as Sick Man of Asia, whose illness apparently could be overcome, as one critic argues, only by the gospels of Christianity and progress.[96] Thus, the custom came to stand metonymically for the larger question of the subjection of women. "There seems to have been one great want in Confucius," Alicia Little wrote.

> Nowhere do we hear of his speaking of women with tenderness or reverence; and so through the centuries the great Chinese race has continued to treat woman as a necessary evil, a thorn in the side that cannot be dispensed with, a creature worthless save for the bearing of children . . . Confucius missed this great part of God's revelation of Himself in man.[97]

Chapter 3

Prescriptions for Change

Culture and Civilization

Europeans, Eric Leed suggests, tend to equate differences in space with differences in time. Nonconformity with Western ways and Western values easily became historicized and, because difference meant backwardness, was used to justify Europe's appropriation of the globe's resources as well as the domination of other peoples.[1] Or at least to justify a kind of Western hegemony by appealing to a *mission civilisatrice* that would bring the virtues of the modern to those unable to help themselves. Although Westerners might not arrogate to themselves the privilege of renaming China's cities or geographical features, they were quite ready to reserve the right to mark China's place in history. Like navigators, they fixed its position along a course already plotted by the West, assuming a single trajectory valid for all across the ocean of modernity. No less than the power to name, this power of chronological placement implied a form of control—not a physical control, like the direct imposition of colonialism, but a material and intellectual control, for it gave Westerners the right to decide what China needed and what prescriptions must be written to cure its ills. The mind-set of modernization was evident long before the flourishing of that theory among social scientists of the 1950s and 1960s or before its translation into Chinese as the *si xiandaihua* (Four Modernizations) of Mao Zedong and Zhou Enlai.

Yet Leed's generalization itself needs qualification. While the Orient has always signified difference, at times it has also implied wealth and luxury as well as an advanced commerce and industry. Late-nineteenth-century travelers to China were still heirs of earlier traditions of

51

representation, stretching back to Marco Polo, embracing the Jesuit fathers of the Ming and Qing and all the intellectual and material *chinoiserie* of the Enlightenment, to say nothing of the sober admiration of Adam Smith. A varied inheritance, in other words, with no unified set of figures or constructions waiting to be easily grouped together by the critic into a single essentialized Orientalist or other basket. Different as it might be, the West's China had by no means always been seen as backward or inferior. Yet by the late nineteenth century it was undeniably so. By then a trip to China, whether seen as a step back in time or a visit to a hopelessly alien and inexplicable people, helped to ratify a Western sense of superiority that had been far less evident a century and a half earlier. The relatively recent advantage of the West over the East had now become a fixed principle of history.

Had that enchanting Jesuit-Enlightenment China ever actually existed anywhere save in the Western mind? Eliza Scidmore, an unwitting postmodernist before her time, didn't think so; the West had only begun to discover the real China after its defeat by Japan in 1895. Before that only "an imaginary, fantastic, picturesque, spectacular and bizarre sort of a bogy China had haunted European minds."[2] Whatever may have been the respective levels of achievement—political, economic, technological—of China and the West in 1750 or 1800, by the time she wrote a significant distance had opened between them, and Europe's advance had gained it a substantial advantage over the rest of the globe. Not surprisingly, to travelers like Scidmore, China's backwardness was most apparent in precisely those spheres in which the West had recently made such enormous strides. The harnessing of technology, not only to industry and transport but also to social problems (the lighting and draining of cities), the growth of food production, the reform and rationalization of legal systems, the abolition of slavery, the growing emancipation of women—all these testified to the gospel of progress and proved that the problems men and women had created for themselves they could also solve.

If China had ceased to be a model for Europe, the problem was not simply one of Western perception. For, if the West had changed for the better over the last century, China had changed for the worse, and the country Scidmore and her contemporaries saw was a long way from the great nation that had so entranced the Enlightenment when the Qing was at its apogee. "That Chinese civilisation has for many years been allowed to get into a very bad state of repair is, of course, an undoubted fact," wrote Reginald Johnston in 1908. Still, he concluded, it was no worse than that of Europe in the days of the thumbscrew and the Holy Office, and he believed it quite possible that in the reign of the Kangxi emperor (1662–1722) China had been as civilized as most countries of Europe.[3] Today the evidence of the historians bears him out (indeed, their question may be how far Europe had caught up to China by Kangxi's day), and Johnston, unlike many others, knew something of the country's past.[4] Although it's unlikely that so fierce a critic as Scidmore would have been mollified had she known the grandeur of Kangxi's Beijing in 1690 rather than the decrepitude of Guangxu's in 1890, China at the height of the Qing was in fact much better administered and better governed than it would be a hundred years later. Its decline affected the objective China that travelers saw and represented for audiences at home, and helps to explain why Chinese difference now had come to mean backwardness in a way that had not been true a century earlier.

Race, civilization, and *culture*—Tylor had used all three terms when he placed the Chinese between the Aztec and the Italian on the ladder of development. In the eyes of our travelers, at an rate, race in the narrow scientific sense was not an important part of the problem of China's backwardness: that problem owed more to environment and history than biology. Geographical isolation and immunity from outside influences were largely at fault, for Western travelers generally confused the great inward turning that marked the late Ming dynasty in the sixteenth century with a permanent condition of China's long past. But there were other factors as well, and a word must be said about the terms *civilization* and *culture*.

Read in the context of a century ago, the words carry meanings rather different from those they have taken on today. At that point the modern anthropological sense of the word *culture* had not yet passed into common use. Rather, for most people the word would be taken in its humanist sense of "high culture," denoting the acceptance of a certain standard of manners and an intellectual development that carried with it, among other things, a respect for tradition, particularly a written, literary, and philosophical tradition. Obviously, that was a kind of culture that China—gentry China, at any rate, or what our travelers would have called mandarin China—had in full measure. *Civilization* is a more difficult word. For those who followed Matthew Arnold it might denote the external and the material, distinguished from the internal (culture properly speaking), but, in fact, the two words often meant the same. Indeed, it was precisely the overdevelopment of civilization in the cultural sense that had held China back on the road to Civilization, Civilization with a capital *C*, the kind of Civilization that the West now enjoyed, with its steam engines, its Christianity, and its public sanitation. Enlightenment Civilization, with its faith in the ideas and artifacts of progress, had to be distinguished from mere civilization, stagnant and grown meaningless after long since having lost its vitality.[5]

The opposites of *culture* and *civilization* might seem to be *savagery* and *barbarism*. Yet overcivilized China also had had its "barbarous" aspects. Again, taken in the context of its times, such a word had a multiplicity of meanings that we are apt to miss today. Putting criminals to death by starving them in wooden cages was barbarous in one sense of the word; the huge gray walls and gates of Beijing or the riot of color and statuary in a Guangdong temple were barbarous in another. Read in its nineteenth-century complexity, as John MacKenzie reminds us, the term *barbarous* is not simply the opposite of *civilized* but also carries "suggestions of the sublime, lack of restraint, an attractive, colourful and dramatic approach, liberating new sensations on a grand scale."[6] Much the same could be said of savagery, for, while in one sense it was a quality imputed to Africans or the half-naked and painted inhabitants of Tierra del Fuego whom Darwin observed, in another sense it was a virtue among Europeans. A red-blooded and forceful virility, exemplified through muscular Christianity, competition in games, and the strenuous life would keep Western Civilization from slowing to a halt, as mere civilization had done in effeminate and overrefined China.

Thus, Isabella Bird called herself "a savage at heart," and Mary Gaunt looked on approvingly while a

> European, an Englishman, or an American probably, comes hectoring down the street—no other word describes his attitude, when it is contrasted with that of the courteous Orientals round him. On the smallest provocation, far too small a provocation, he threatens to kick this coolie, he swings that one out of the way and, instead of being shocked, I am distinctly relieved. Here is exhibition of force, restrained force, that is welcome as a rude breeze, fresh from the sea or the mountains, is welcome in a heated, scented room. These people, even the poorer people of the streets,

are suffering from over-civilisation, from over-refinement. They need a touch of the primitive savage to make the red blood run in their veins.[7]

The inversion here of the civilized Other with the savage European was accordingly not as strange as it might sound to discourse analysts today. No empire was ever built by courtesy, as the British journalist Roger Pocock knew when he urged such manly actions on his countrymen to save themselves from the corruptions of an overbred and weakened civilization.[8] Behind such sentiments may well have lain the fin-de-siècle fears, conscious or unconscious, that the West itself was not immune to the kinds of decline evident in the recently discovered second law of thermodynamics. *Degeneration* (*Die Entartung*) was the title of Max Nordau's influential book of 1896, the phenomenon visible in the writings of Rimbaud, Mallarmé, Wilde, and Beardsley, in the painting of the Impressionists, and the music of Wagner. Others, like David Starr Jordan of Stanford, warned that war would kill off the best of the race, leaving the unfit behind to breed, thus ensuring biological as well as cultural and psychological degeneracy.[9]

Most travelers, of course, were not thinking in terms of a thermodynamic metaphor, and, while Elizah Scidmore might have found China beyond salvation, others thought that with a sufficient dose of Western activism the country could still be saved. Wherever civilization and savagery might lie in the picture of a European kicking a coolie, it still took the European to shock the Oriental out of his own degeneration and reverse the law of entropy. Above all, it was Confucianism, lying at the center of China's culture, that must assume much of the blame for China's sorry state. A hundred years earlier, thanks to the Jesuit reports and the enthusiasm of the philosophes, Confucius had become, in Adolf Reichwein's phrase, the patron saint of the Enlightenment, a man whose ideas had helped build a civilization not simply the equal of but often superior to that of the West.[10] The practical late nineteenth century, however, was more likely to find in him only the "wearisome sage," as Constance Gordon Cumming called him, "whose fossilised wisdom has petrified all original thought throughout the vast Empire ever since the sixth century before Christ." Like a vast, stifling, and none too clean blanket, the veneration of tradition lay over the country, preventing any new ideas, any innovations that might help meet modern problems. While earlier observers had admired the system of civil service examinations and the tradition of learning they embodied, Gordon Cumming and others were simply depressed by a view of the cells where the candidates were sequestered to write their formulaic essays, seeing only dilapidation, weeds, and a history of damaged brains and mental collapse.[11]

Traveler after traveler made the same point. The legacy of Confucianism had been, said Wilson, "to arrest all intellectual development and progress in China, and to mold the Chinese mind entirely upon one model. Nothing new or spontaneous can come of it.[12] Dingle saw in the pitiable condition of a Yunnan village evidence of an age-old cast of mind that led its inhabitants to "make no effort whatever to improve matters."[13] Bird complained of an "oppressive grooviness" in China and its people, and, though the last word rings strangely on the contemporary ear, for her it meant an obdurate reluctance to stray from the ruts of the past. "The ignorance which many men of the literary class show is wonderful," she remarked, after a military mandarin in the interior told her of a great vortex, opened by the gods in the Straits of Formosa, that had engulfed the combined navies of France, Britain, Japan, and Russia. "It is impossible to have patience with their ignorance because of their overweening self-conceit. It is passable in Africa, but not in these men with their literary degrees, and their elaborate culture 'of sorts,' and two thousand years of civilisation behind them."[14]

The duty of man, John Stuart Mill had taught, was to amend the course of nature, to control it so that it might conform to a higher standard. China's material life, incapable of advance, reflected its stultified intellectual life. For all the enormous aptitude, hard work, stamina, and even courage of its people, their crumbling dwellings and impassable roads testified to their primitive production and transport methods. Skillful and strong as were the trackers and the watermen who fought their junks upstream against the swift and dangerous flow of the Yangtze rapids, their methods were those of three thousand years earlier, and in all that time they had made no innovations, though in other parts of the world similar problems had been met and overcome. A burlesque of navigation, Scidmore called it, while Dundas, watching such men handle a junk in trouble in the gorges, reflected that even the most primitive hand winch would have enormously relieved their difficulties. The failure to have devised such a machine was a "striking example of that complete lack of imagination which has long doomed China to a perpetual back seat among the competing Powers in the present advanced stage of the progress of humanity."[15]

The lack of innovation, of progress, placed China outside history, its long past no more than a meaningless gray blur stretching dimly back over the ages. So, too, its vast population was simply a faceless mass of people with no singularity, and there is in most of these travel accounts no real record of the people as individuals. Certainly, the reader meets a Manchu princess here, a mandarin or merchant there, and, at the other end of the social scale, the boatmen and carrying coolies and personal servants ("Boys," like Isabella Bird's unsatisfactory Be-dien) who helped make the foreigner's trip possible. But they were types, not flesh-and-blood human beings. All Chinese were the same, Scidmore found, and all were hopeless: they and their qualities could be seen "seen everywhere in the unsavory empire, the same frightful monotony of life and character among this least attractive people of earth."[16] From one end of the empire to the other, from Siberia to Cochin China, they were all alike, three hundred million people, all

> cast in the same unvarying physical and mental mold, the same yellow skin, hard features, and harsh, mechanical voice; the same houses, graves, and clothes; the same prejudices, superstitions, and customs; the same selfish conservatism, blind worship of precedent and antiquity; a monotony, unambiguity, and repetition of life, character, and incident, that offend one almost to resentment . . . the same ignoble queue and the senseless cotton shoe are worn; everywhere this fifth of the human race is sunk in dirt and disorder, decadent, degenerate, indifferent to a fallen estate, consumed with conceit, selfish, vain, cowardly, and superstitious, without imagination, sentiment, chivalry, or sense of humor, combating with most zeal anything that would alter conditions even for the better, indifferent as to who rules or usurps the throne.[17]

As usual, she was far more scathing than most of her fellow travelers would have been. Yet the image was nothing new, for forty years earlier, in *On Liberty*, John Stuart Mill had cited China as a land characterized by a stultifying lack of individualism whose only hope for progress came from the outside, and Scidmore's fellow travelers would largely have agreed that this lack of distinctiveness, this suffocating uniformity, human no less than chronological, also inhibited change.

Travelers thus journeyed across a land whose main qualities appeared to be those of dirt, decay, cruelty, noise, and a cramped and apathetic conservatism that held men in bondage to a two thousand-year–old philosophy every bit as constraining as the tightly wrapped bandages that kept a girl's feet from growing normally. Could China—dirty, teeming China, fettered by its enfeebling conservatism—be saved? What possible hope could there be for this land of barbarism and decayed medieval splendor, this nation that juxtaposed a rich scenery and a rich heritage of learning with dirt, poverty, disease, and the degradation of women? It's all too easy to pick and choose excerpts from writers like these, leaving the modern reader with the impression that, on the one hand, they found nothing but a civilization found seriously wanting, a China sunk in backwardness and sloth, while, on the other hand, that they all exuded an unthinking and unquenchable Western ethnocentrism, if not outright racism. Such a view fits nicely into the Orientalist critique, of course, suggesting that such "strategies of representation," consciously or unconsciously undertaken, were designed to ensure that China be kept in subjection to the West until in some impossibly distant future it show itself worthy of equality.

Yet the view overlooks those aspects of China that travelers, sometimes to their surprise, found admirable. The Chinese capacity for industry and hard work was, of course, a commonplace. Their cities might be noisy, dirty, and stinking, but Gordon Cumming and Bird were impressed by the liveliness and apparent prosperity of the Guangzhou streets. Although their detractors considered the Chinese selfish, Bird devoted a chapter to Chinese charities, and Gaunt—after being convinced by R. F. Johnston that the Christian missionaries didn't deserve all the credit for introducing such ideas into China—praised the work being done by a Buddhist orphanage (though she also pointed out it was consciously modeled on Western lines).[18] Buddhism, Daoism, and demon worship might be extravagant and childishly superstitious, but Bird and Alicia Little, at least, found much to praise in Confucianism, with its "lofty ethics and profound agnosticism" and the reverence in which it held its classical literature.[19] Imperfect it might be, but China's old civilization, as yet undecayed, was admirably suited to the country and, despite its "tremendous infamies of practice," gave its people a high degree of individual liberty. Indeed, echoing Europe's earlier admiration for the civil service's meritocracy, which gave the peasant's son the opportunity to rise to high position, Bird saw China not only as comparable to America in its mingling of the classes but perhaps "the most truly democratic country in the world." Moreover, as the ironic Alicia Little pointed out, while the degree of master of arts could be obtained for money in superior England, its equivalent in "corruptible China . . . can only be gained by learning."[20]

Such sterling qualities had little to do with progress, of course, and many turn-of-the-century travelers would have agreed with Marx that the task of dragging China into real history, world history, was to be one of imperialism's highest functions. Praising the work of the Germans and Russians, only half-ironically did Scidmore approve another foreigner's prescription for a "good, hard European tyranny," followed by "a century or two of enlightened struggle for liberty, then united China and the millennium."[21] Some fifteen years later, after the overthrow of the dynasty, Mary Gaunt echoed such sentiments: "I cannot help thinking that it would be a great day for China, for the welfare of her toiling millions, millions toiling without hope, if she were partitioned up among the stable nations of the earth—that is to say, between Japan, Britain, and France."[22]

Few would have gone as far as these two women, and the Open Door policies of Britain and the United States—policies going back decades, even though not formally announced until John Hay did so in 1899—would not have permitted it. Foreign example, to be sure, foreign influence, yes, the work of missionaries and advisors—all these were needed, of course. So were enlightened policies by the Western nations. "China is certainly at the dawn of a new era," Bird concluded. "Whether the twentieth century shall place her where she ought to be, in the van of Oriental nations, or whether it shall witness her disintegration and decay, depends very largely on the statesmanship and influence of Great Britain."[23] Take away the reference to Britain, and the question of China's future could be posed much the same way in our day, a hundred years after Bird's houseboat had been drawn up through the lowering Yangtze Gorges and off into the mists of distant Sichuan.

Teaching by Example: Hong Kong and the Treaty Ports

Lacking any direct imposition of widespread foreign control, save in Japanese Taiwan, what remedies remained? Two paths suggested themselves: outsiders could help reform China by setting examples, or they could help reform it by the work and the preaching of missionaries, secular as well as sacred.

Scidmore pointed to Sir Robert Hart's administration of the Chinese Maritime Customs, with its network of foreign supervisors and collectors, as the one honest and hopeful feature of the government.[24] Such an institution, however, which had grown out of the chaos surrounding the Taiping Rebellion at midcentury, was less likely to be observed by most travelers. The most visible examples of progress, of course, were to be found in foreign-administered Hong Kong and the settlements and concessions in the larger treaty ports. Unlike Chinese cities, which so often seemed a wilderness of dirt and noise, here were cities instantly recognizable to the Western eye, with their well-delineated foreign quarters: on Hong Kong island, at Shamian (Shameen) in Guangzhou, Gulangyu (Kulangsu) in Xiamen, and, of course, the International Settlement and the French Concession of Shanghai, greatest of such outposts. Modern buildings, clean streets, a thriving international commerce visible in the busy wharves, godowns, and lighters—the view of Hong Kong or Shanghai provided the traveler with a visual testimony of foreign progress at work. Although it was already becoming common for the traveler to scorn such places as un-Chinese, it was also customary to compare their prosperity and order with the chaotic dilapidation of the "native cities" that lay next to them (a contrast that also shamed Chinese reformers such as Kang Youwei). Already by the 1880s General Wilson found in foreign Shanghai an advancement and refinement that would do credit to New York or Paris, while the city beyond the foreign settlements, with its struggling and sordid inhabitants, remained a typically Chinese collection of decaying ramshackle dwellings set amid dirty and slushy streets. "It is all inconceivably squalid and offensive to foreign eyes and nostrils, and fills the foreign soul with a sentiment of unutterable disgust."

Still, he took hope from the Settlement's example. "Progress has planted her foot firmly on the banks of the Wusung, and, from her safe abiding place in the foreign city, is sure, slowly but inevitably, to invade and overcome the whole vast empire."[25] Eliza Scidmore, with her characteristic disdain, was less optimistic, dismissing the un-Asian sounds of busy industry coming from the factories and textile mills along the Wusong outside Shanghai. The smell of bean oil, opium smoke, incense, and filthy humanity hung heavy in the air, and this, the true flavor of China, was enough to dispel any illusions; indeed, when the Chinese themselves moved into the foreign settlements, rather than taking advantage of the light and air or the gas, electricity, and modern water supply, they swarmed into the houses, overflowing them, and remained "Chinese to the last word."[26] Just as in the lovely countryside, here too in the modern cities, it was the people who got in the way and who spoiled the view. To her, at least, it was pure illusion to believe that anything—Western example, Western Christianity, or Western scientific education—could ever change these people at all.

Teaching by Preaching: Missionaries of the Secular and Sacred

Coming across the British-American Tobacco Company's placards advertising Rooster or Peacock or Purple Mountain cigarettes deep in the interior, Mary Gaunt admitted to a feeling of pride.

> I never saw the men who put them there, and I hate the blatant advertisement that spoils the scenery as a rule. Here I greeted them with a distinct thrill of pleasure. Here were men of my race and colour, doing pioneering work in the out-of-the-way corners of the earth, and I metaphorically made them a curtsy and wished them well, for no one knows better than I do the lonely lives they lead. But they are bringing China in touch with the outside world.[27]

So, too, Elizabeth Kendall, surprised to find kerosene for sale in the middle of Yunnan, reflected that, while one did not usually think of the Standard Oil Company as a missionary agency, it had done a great deal to light up China's darkness, morally as well as physically.[28]

Such missionaries of the secular were admirable, whether selling their wares in the Chinese countryside or bringing modern business methods to Shanghai and Hankou, though both Bird and Dingle faulted their own countrymen for devoting too much time to their clubs and their sports, leaving the field clear for the Germans or the French to move in.[29] It's less easy to generalize about the attitudes of these travelers toward the missionaries of the sacred. Not surprisingly, in the interior they were usually quite ready to accept the hospitality of the mission stations. Mary Gaunt, for example, arriving hot and exhausted in Rehe, had a momentary qualm about doing so because of her criticisms of the missions, but, faced with the choice between yet another filthy Chinese inn and a clean foreign compound, she capitulated and took the latter.[30] But the place of Christianity in China often seemed ambiguous. "The foreigner in China is divided into two camps," wrote Gaunt, sounding rather like E. M. Forster's nameless Anglo-Indian woman in the Chandrapore Club who announced that she was "all for Chaplains but all against Missionaries." "He is either missionary or he is anti-missionary. Both sides are keen on the matter." Others noted the general contempt of the treaty ports for such men and women—the "cheap sneers at missions and missionaries which often pass for wit in Anglo-Asiatic communities," as Bird called them.[31]

Not that the ambiguity stemmed from any particular admiration for Chinese religion. At best both Buddhism and Daoism seemed harmless superstitions, adding color to life and providing, as Alicia Little pointed out, a kind of social cement in the Chinese village (from where, she wondered, would such a function come in a Christianized China?).[32] At worst, in the Lamaism of Mongolia and the Tibetan borderlands, it was seen as a debased priestcraft, with all the resonances such a word had for the Anglo-American Protestant mind, playing on the abject credulity of its ignorant followers.[33] In the face of such backwardness Christianity could only be an improvement. The ambiguity toward the missionaries came, rather, for other reasons: a sense that their energies might better be spent among the poor of London or Liverpool or New York;[34] and a sense, particularly strong among those who had lived in China for some years, that the missionaries got in the way of good relations, particularly good trade relations, with the Chinese. Archibald Little praised the practical Dutch, who simply banned any religious propagandizing throughout the vast East Indian territories they controlled.[35]

Some travelers saw the missionaries as what General Wilson called "the advance guard of a higher and better civilization," their function at least as much secular as religious. To Gaunt they were pioneers of trade, forerunners of the merchants who would follow in their footsteps, though a few years earlier J. A. Hobson, in his classic dissection of imperialism, quoted the complaints of a British consul at Guangzhou that the missionaries were not doing enough to promote trade.[36] Elizabeth Kendall, introduced to a club founded by the Friends' mission in Chongqing where Christians and non-Christians, Europeans and Chinese, might meet one another as equals, praised it as a new departure

in mission work and a way "of presenting the best of Christian civilization to a class often repelled by missionary propaganda."[37]

Christian civilization and *missionary propaganda*—the words carry a
whole cargo of ideological freight deeply revealing of the period: Christianity seen as a civilization (meaning Anglo-American Protestant)
rather than as a structure of beliefs, and insofar as it had beliefs, dis-
missable as little better than "missionary propaganda." It was very
easy to confuse the roles of the missionary as advocate of modernization and as advocate of the Gospel, easy to confuse the distinction
between Christianity as a religion reflecting merely Western forms and
Christianity as a religion claiming a universal validity, easy to conflate
the largely Protestant Christianity the travelers had known at home
with nineteenth-century ideas of progress. At their best the missionaries could set an example to the Chinese more valuable than any preaching in their willingness to care for those whom Chinese society seemed
to have rejected: the poor, the women, the diseased, the orphans. In this
view what was really important was the medical, social, educational
work that such men and women did, and the message of the Gospel
was beside the point, except as it moved them to give up the comforts
of life at home for exile in a strange land (though some critics maintained that American Protestants, at least, appeared to live in much
greater comfort than they might have known at home). By the late nineteenth century the earlier enthusiasms of Evangelicalism in which
Isabella Bird, for example, had been raised and which had given rise to
the "faith missions" like the China Inland Mission were considered
quaint at best and embarrassing at worst by advanced circles, and a
writer like Gaunt was particularly anxious to reassure her readers that
she remained above such simple pieties.

In their purely religious aspect, however, the missionaries could
become a cause for concern. They squabbled with one another or cut
themselves off from one another because of their different beliefs.
Archibald Little quoted with approval the opinion of the Lazarist Père
David that the multiplicity of sects and churches with their different
terms for God only confused the Chinese and acted as a *seminarium
d'indifférence*, while Kendall noted the unwillingness of Protestants to
learn from the far longer Catholic experience in the country.[38] Some
missionaries allowed themselves to be drawn into lawsuits (particularly the Catholics but some American Protestants as well).[39] Finally,
there was the danger that they would adopt too many Chinese ways,

losing face not only for themselves but for all Westerners in the country. "It is so easy to sink to the level of the people, to become as Chinese as the Chinese themselves," observed Mary Gaunt. "Personally, I think it is a mistake to conform to Chinese customs. The missionaries are there to preach the better customs of the West, and there must be no lowering of the standard."[40]

If there was among foreigners in civilized China little of that fear of going native and descending to the level of the savages that Brantlinger finds in Victorian Africa,[41] there still could be no betrayal of the difference between Us and Them. Granted that Jesus preached a gospel of poverty, but too much poverty would be ineffective, for the Chinese were above all a practical people, and so Gaunt preferred the rich and well-equipped American Protestants to those who, like the China Inland Mission, followed the road of poverty or who, like the Catholics, adopted Chinese dress. "I dislike exceedingly that a European should be poor in an Oriental country."[42] Her view, however, was by no means universally shared. When her countryman G. E. Morrison professed to admire the way the American Protestants took over the best sites and built themselves the best houses, the irony was unmistakable. And an early guidebook to Guangdong needed no editorial comment to drive the same point home when it marked "the magnificent residences of the American missionaries [at Wuzhou in Guangxi], truly palatial when contrasted with the humble dwellings of the hard-working Catholic missionaries at this and other ports of the river."[43]

Still, few doubted that the Gospel—properly preached and properly lived—would have a beneficial effect on the Chinese character. The development of a Christian conscience, wrote Edwin Dingle, was crucial to China's greatness. "With it she will become perhaps the foremost empire of the world. But without it she is lost." By *it* he meant his own kind of English Protestant Christianity; a scornful appendix in his book excoriated French priests who adopted "the heathen rites of the Chinese," for in Shanghai he'd seen a Catholic church where the dragon and the cross were both exhibited.[44] Isabella Bird, more widely traveled, demonstrated a more sympathetic attitude to what Catholics call inculturation. Christianity, if it were to come to China, must wear a Chinese face. Although the Bible was an Oriental book, its imagery and thought enjoyed and understood by Orientals, the Book of Common Prayer was so thoroughly Western in its style and assumptions that it could not possibly be used for worship.[45] Christianity must arrive unflavored by the West and be presented by Chinese to Chinese, for no foreigners could ever know as well as the Chinese what arguments would appeal to their countrymen or, indeed, understand "their devious ways and crooked motives, and their unspeakable darkness and superstition."[46]

Changes Seen and Unseen

In some ways what these men and women did not report in their accounts was as important as what they did. They passed over lightly—or indeed were blind to—the new forms of society arising in and around the treaty ports, content with merely remarking on the striking differences they perceived between the backwards and dirty Chinese cities and the well-administered, progressive foreign settlements. On such phenomena as the formation of modern business and commercial associations they were silent or even scornful. Nor did they see the ways in which Chinese merchants were profiting both from Beijing's weakness and from the protection afforded by the foreign enclaves of such cities as Shanghai or Tianjin, ways that would lead to what Marie-Claire Bergère has called the "golden age" of the Chinese bourgeoisie in the early twentieth century. "Nothing so discourages one for the future of China and the chances of progress as this daily display of young China in its hours of ease," wrote Scidmore about what she found in Shanghai. "Combining all the domestic and imported depravity, these young Chinese of the merchant and comprador class, longest in contact with foreign ways, well entitle Shanghai to its repute in their world as the fastest and wickedest place in China."[47]

With rare exceptions—Alicia Little was one—they were oblivious to the influence of Meiji Japan, which had grown after its defeat of China in 1895 and became particularly strong after it overcame Russia in 1905. More surprisingly, apart from dutiful reports on occasional visits to mission-run schools in the interior, they said little about education. As travelers, it was unlikely, of course, that they would have been aware of the proliferation of reformist academies and study societies, like the missionary-inspired Society for the Diffusion of Christian and General Knowledge among the Chinese (Guangxuehui) in 1887 or the Society for the Study of Self-Strengthening (Qiangxuehui) of Kang Youwei and Liang Qichao in 1895. But they also ignored the first modern Chinese universities, like Shanghai's Nanyang (1896) and Beijing University (1898), whose first president had been the missionary Sinologue W. A. P. Martin. Nor did any of them apparently visit the missionary institutions such as St. John's University in Shanghai, which had been founded by the American Episcopalians in 1878, or Aurora (Zhendan) University, started in 1903 as a collaboration between the Catholic reformist scholar Ma Liang and the French Jesuits of Shanghai.

Not that they ignored China's initial attempts at change, the sorts of change being advocated by the leaders of the self-strengthening movement. In the mid-1980s General Wilson praised the policies of modernization set in train by Li Hongzhang ("the great hypnotizer," Scidmore called him, dismissing him with her characteristic contempt) and was convinced that Zuo Zongtang's conversion from antiforeignism to the cause of modern science and technology would prove "the very essence of progress and the death-knell of conservatism." Fifteen years later, however, after the Japanese war and after the Boxer Rising (which had taken him back to China), he had to admit his disillusionment, though he still professed his admiration for the aging Li, who had returned to Beijing to negotiate with the Allied occupiers of the capital.[48] About the dynasty's reforms in the last decade of its life—the raising and training of new armies, the emergence of chambers of commerce and similar associations, the birth of a modern press, for instance—they were, with a few exceptions, silent. None mentioned the abolition of the old civil service examinations in 1905 or the momentous political changes, such as the provincial assemblies (1909) and the first attempts at elections that grew out of the dynasty's decision to move toward a Japanese-inspired constitutionalism. Gaunt, in Beijing after the collapse of the Qing dynasty, was thoroughly scornful of the new republic. "The National Assembly was in an uproar, the Premier openly accused of murder, the Loan was in anything but a satisfactory state, everyone feared that the North and South would be at each other's throats before the month was out."[49] The assumptions about an ahistorical, unchanging China died hard; the clear implication was that China had not yet developed to the point where modern republicanism could govern it.

In general they reported little evidence of the kind of anti-imperialism that was already developing before the overthrow of the dynasty and which would be so central to the first decades of the new century, bringing protests against the unequal treaties, against extraterritoriality, against foreign industrial and railway investment, and foreign control over the Maritime Customs. Some travelers, particularly after the turn of the century, did sense a new spirit in the air. Dundas watched a day of races at a new college in Sichuan, where ten thousand onlookers cheered the victorious runners—"this, in the heart of a country in which but yesterday the ideal scholar was a literary fossil, with claws on his hands several inches long."[50] Although a few years later Dingle was apt to see in resistance to foreign encroachment a new form of Boxerism, he found an "air of progress" in Sichuan and saw troops in Yunnan undergoing modern training with modern weapons. In the same province Kendall watched a student play in which a stage Englishman kicked an Indian and a Frenchman beat an Annamese. "The teaching was plain. 'This will be your fate unless you are strong to resist.'"[51]

My purpose, however, is not to discover what such travelers got right or wrong about China, and of course it would be quite wrong to judge them by their inability to spot those aspects of the country that later historians have deemed important. Some of these men and women, after all, visited the country before such changes became evident. Moreover, they were primarily travelers, not journalists or investigators into China's prospects, even though some might have come at least in part to spy out the chances for foreign trade and investment. Nor is it surprising that they gave their own nations credit for the introduction of the reformist practices that they saw beginning. Unaware of the influence of such ideas as those coming from the late Qing school of statecraft or Kang Youwei's radical rereading of Confucius as a reformer, they assumed the Chinese were incapable of developing them by themselves. Such views, after all, in slightly different forms continued to dominate Western scholarship about modern China until well into the 1960s. As Paul Cohen has suggested, both those of an older tradition who stressed China's "reaction" to the "impact" of the West and those who more recently have pointed to the deleterious effects of imperialism have between them constructed a narrative of modern history in which, for good or ill, the foreign presence has become the dominant aspect in China's shaping. Unwitting Orientalists all, they have kept China subordinated to the West and, with an assist from China's own modern Nationalist and Communist historians, who also stressed the foreign impact, denied to that country the determination of its own history.

As Mill had said of China back in 1859, there was little question that any impetus for progress must come from the outside. Left to themselves, the Chinese simply were not up to it—they neither wanted change nor understood that it was needed.[52] In natural resources China might be rich, but, left to itself, the observations of these visitors suggested, China was capable of mobilizing neither the intellectual nor the social and economic resources to enter the twentieth century in a manner befitting its size and importance. Without Western influence "by force or persuasion," Archibald Little suggested, the recklessness of the people and the carelessness of the government would "allow the country to decay and become obliterated, like Nineveh and Babylon and the once flourishing cities of Asia Minor."[53]

Such a fear, of course, was very much on the minds of the new generation of Chinese reformers such as Liang Qichao and his colleagues, though they were apt to see their fate exemplified less by the dead cities of ancient Mesopotamia than by modern nations who, in their weakness, had allowed themselves to become swallowed up by the stronger—India, Poland, Turkey, Korea, Burma, Annam. By Liang's time Chinese reformers had moved from an early admission of Western superiority in weapons (by Feng Gueifen, Li Hongzhang, and the other Self-Strengtheners) to a later understanding that, as Guo Songdao wrote from London and Ma Jianzhong from Paris, European weapons were less important in explaining Western strength than European institutions. After China's traumatic loss to Japan in 1895, a popularized Darwinism, in the variants preached by Yan Fu and Liang Qichao, entered the reformist discourse: if struggle were the key to national survival, then Confucianism and Daoism, with their all too successful attempts to achieve harmony, had inhibited change and development.[54] Although the call of Tan Sitong, one of the martyred reformers of 1898, for a thoroughgoing Westernization was too radical for most, Kang Youwei found his own solution by reinventing Confucius as an apostle of progress.

Such Chinese reformers, and those who followed them, might well find in their country many of the same failings that Western critics did and might even believe that China had much to learn from the outside, not only in science, technology, and warfare but, increasingly, in political and social organization as well. Not that the Qing reformers and their revolutionary successors were likely to accept the criticisms of outsiders as either benevolent or constructive. The foreign presence remained a continual humiliation and a spur to the development of the kind of nationalism that informed so much of later Chinese thought and politics. While China might borrow from the outside, if the nation were to remain in charge of its own fate, change must come from the inside. Indeed, just as Mary Gaunt had wanted a touch of the primitive savage to strengthen the overrefined Chinese race, men like Yan and Liang (and, later, Mao Zedong) called on their compatriots to cultivate strong and healthy bodies, overcoming the humiliating image of China as Sick Man of Asia.[55]

It is tempting—incomplete but still tempting—to peer at the texts of Western travelers or Western publicists through Orientalist spectacles and find there little more than a rationalization for a continued foreign presence and foreign privilege in China. Perceptions of the country's shortcomings had always underlain the claims to the kinds of special status conferred by the unequal treaties: extraterritoriality, the virtually autonomous concessions and settlements of cities like Shanghai or Tianjin, the freedom of Christian missions to work in the hinterland, the artificially low tariff, and foreign administration of the Maritime Customs and salt revenues. It was a commonplace of treaty port and diplomatic circles to hold that before such privileges could be surrendered China must first achieve the rule of law, meaning, of course, a legal and judicial system on the Anglo-American model. It was in fact still true several decades later, for in 1931 that is what Sir Richard Feetham's investigations into the future of Shanghai's International Settlement argued, and even the radical Agnes Smedley jibbed at the thought of surrendering her extraterritorial rights if it meant subjecting herself to China's "medieval laws" and "barbarous prisons."[56]

Irony, perhaps, in her case. But was it also tinged with realism? Irony aside, today the studies of Said and his followers and the construction by historians on the left of the Open Door as a grand scheme for American imperialism have made us sensitive to the justifications for continued foreign hegemony that lie encoded in such statements. To the historian, however, it leaves the question of how, in analyzing the discourse of imperialism, one deals with the coincidences that arise between criticisms that come from the inside and those that are mounted from the outside. To take only one example: although the missionaries were not the first to criticize footbinding, they, and Alicia Little, did far more to spread the gospel of the natural foot than the few iconoclastic Qing scholars who had earlier inveighed against the practice. Are we to see them, then, as the protagonists of a new equality for

women? Or were they simply intolerant, ethnocentric, and culture
bound, ready to attack Confucianism by striking at the family system
that lay at its heart and which was built, to some extent at least, on the
subjection of women? And what of the Chinese critics, such as the Zhejiang revolutionary Qiu Jin, who thought footbinding the greatest
injustice in the world?[57] What of those new women who by the early
twentieth century were refusing to bind the feet of their daughters and
sometimes (like the mother of the writer Ding Ling) even unbinding
their own, a process apparently almost as painful as the original
destruction of the foot had been? Had they become the heralds of a new
age? Or were they no more than ideological compradors, unconsciously buying into colonialism's discursive universe, unwitting collaborators in a cultural imperialism imposed by a hegemonic West,
superbly confident of its own superiority?

Of course, it's always possible that the views of China's shortcomings held by foreign travelers such as Edwin Dingle or Isabella Bird and
by Chinese reformers such as Liang Qichao or Qiu Jin were both
wrong. Moreover, there's no doubt that criticisms coming from the
position of power and privilege enjoyed by extraterritorial foreigners in
China were morally quite different from criticisms made from a position of weakness in a country watching its own sovereignty draining
away from it. Still, the provenance of the criticism is immaterial to the
question of its validity, and there is no easy answer to the question of
how the historian or the critic should distinguish between such similarities when they come from different sources. Pratt uses the term
autoethnography to describe the ways in which colonized subjects
engage in a "partial collaboration" with the colonizers by appropriating the latter's idiom to represent themselves, though Arif Dirlik sees in
such "self-orientalization," as he calls it, an expression of power rather
than its reverse. Both these approaches argue for a more complex
understanding of such interrelationships than a simple retreat into a
stark binarity positing an ethnocentric and hegemonic West against a
powerless and colonized Other.[58]

Granted, the records of what these travelers saw and heard were
colored both by their intellectual inheritances and by the conceptions
and expectations of their day. But they were also colored by the objective reality on which they looked. The accounts they left cannot simply
be treated as no more than intellectual representations or "inventions"
molded by a single universe of colonial discourse. Nor can we ascribe

to them an imagined homogeneity as "Western" or "imperialist," forcing them into the Procrustean bed that we have devised from our own preconceptions and inheritances today. Of course, these men and women came to China when the assumptions on which imperialism and colonialism were based had permeated large parts of the Western intellectual universe and were accepted virtually without question. And, while race in the sense of biological inferiority was not usually an issue, one aspect of race, however, remained a concern at least to a few. Although Scidmore held that after Japan's defeat of China in 1895 no one could believe in the Yellow Peril any longer[59] (thus implicitly promoting the Japanese to honorary status as whites), others were less sure. Mary Gaunt, a firm believer in the separation of the races—she was horrified to meet a white woman who had ruined herself by marriage to an Oriental—echoed the fearful view of Australia and the American West that hordes of Chinese landing on foreign shores would lower the standard of living and reduce the people of those lands to "the hopeless condition of the toiling slaves of Babylon."[60] Dingle's fears of a racial struggle were a bit more complex; he had seen how Chinese in the Straits Settlements had abandoned their simple ways, seeking the luxuries of wealth and ease, and from such behavior the West had nothing to fear, for they would be competing with the West on an equal footing. If, on the other hand, the Chinese was not only to learn the ways of Western industry and production but also "to continue his present hardy frugality in living . . . then his advantage in entering upon the conflict among the nations for ultimate supremacy would be undoubted, immeasurable."[61] Isabella Bird, more optimistic, suggested that, while looked on from this point of view, the Chinese might well be a Yellow Peril, "surely looked at from another they constitute the Yellow Hope, and it may be possible that an empire genuinely Christianised, but not denationalised, may yet be the dominant power in Eastern Asia."[62] Substitute *Marxism* for *Christianity,* and you have here a view not so different from that of Mao Zedong's many Western admirers some sixty or seventy years later.

Chapter 4

The Search for the Authentic

China through New Eyes

In the early 1920s the American Elizabeth Enders found herself in a Beijing market watching tanks of goldfish exhibited for sale. "Fat, distorted ones," she noted,

> with little waving fins and bulging repulsive eyes bob slowly up and down. Their years of artificial breeding have brought them to these deformities, which the Chinese greatly admire. A little girl of eight or ten, with small bound feet, stood watching with the usual crowd of idlers, and plodded back and forth from tub to tub, in needle-pointed satin slippers. To us her feet seemed pitiably sad— but no doubt her husband is already chosen, and his family are content to know that the future little bride already has her "lilies" so well started—and thus her future is assured![1]

Standing on the heights of Coal Hill one day during those same years, another American—Florence Ayscough—gazed down on the Forbidden City, admiring

> the gleaming yellow roofs and soft rose-red walls of that enclosure where the Son of Heaven dwelt; a ruler who governed his domain by a system that glorified, not the strong man, the man of force, but the enlightened man, the man of virtue. A Ruler whose people have made their National Hero not a general victorious in war, but a sage who preached the ethics of peace. I speak of Confucius.[2]

Look at the change in tone that distinguished such passages from earlier writings. Enders here juxtaposed two images—the goldfish, to Western eyes deformed by a nature carefully manipulated, and the little girl, to Western eyes deformed by a nurture equally carefully manipulated. Yet she was reluctant to pass any direct judgment, reluctant in a way that would have been almost unthinkable ten or twenty years earlier, especially for a woman. The world had changed, and Enders, an observer of her time, let slip the opportunity to lecture the Chinese on the error of their ways, preaching neither to them nor to her readers.[3]

Ayscough's passage was equally revealing. Born in Shanghai and resident there for years, her accounts of travel within China were informed by a knowledge of history and culture most other writers lacked. Reading her here, however, we might almost be back with Voltaire gazing with awestruck wonder at the virtuous Chinese whom he'd never met or perhaps with one of those admiring Beijing Jesuits from whom the French philosopher drew his arguments. Her praise for the Chinese who elevated the arts of peace above the martial virtues admired in the West was all the more striking, since only a few pages earlier, with no apparent sense of contradiction, she had told her readers of the force, bloodshed, and treachery that had marked the rise to power of Zhu Yuanzhang, the tyrannical founder of the Ming dynasty, in the fourteenth century.

I cite these two passages because they reflect a new tone that one finds in the accounts of travelers after World War I and also because they serve to distinguish very clearly one of the qualities that set travel writing apart from other descriptions of China. Ten or twenty years earlier the country had been an object to be transformed by Western example and Western tutelage, and, while such a view persisted in the later analyses of China made by journalists and scholars, now at least among some travelers the older air of judgmentalism was muted, if not entirely gone.[4] In their writings there was now less certainty of Western superiority, either racial or institutional, and, even though they might still assume that Anglo-Saxon attitudes and Anglo-Saxon religions would cure China's ills, they began to find more good to say about its traditions, particularly its Confucianism. To a remarkable extent China had become now simply a nation to be taken on its own terms and indeed even a nation from which the West might have something to learn. The *mission civilisatrice* might live on, but no longer need its commerce be all one way.

Here Ayscough's Confucius had once again become the wise and revered lawgiver, rather than the ancient fossil whose crabbed doctrines had blocked all progress from China. The more skeptical Bertrand Russell, writing in the early 1920s after his visit to China, predictably enough found Confucius meritorious only by contrast with other traditional religious teachers.[5] Still, he too sounded for all the world like one of the *philosophe* admirers of the Qianlong emperor a century and a half earlier when he assured his readers that "the Chinese have discovered, and have practised for many centuries, a way of life which if it could be adopted by all the world, would make the world happy." Like Ayscough, he saw no apparent contradiction between such an assertion and his description a few pages later of the way the Taiping Rebellion had laid waste to central China and cost twenty million lives[6] (perhaps he blamed Taiping Christianity for the slaughter).

What's extraordinary is that this new leniency toward China's real and supposed failings came at a time when the country seemed in many ways at the nadir of its fortunes. For, while the decadent glories of the last dynasty might have passed, the present seemed to promise little improvement. The overthrow of the Manchus in 1911–12 and the foundation of the Republic, far from ushering in the new era of progress and peace that Sun Yat-sen and his fellow revolutionaries had promised, had only accelerated the trends already visible in the late Qing toward provincialism, separatism, and civil war. By the early 1920s, indeed, Sun himself had become no more than a local figure, ensconced in Guangzhou save when political conditions forced him to seek asylum in Shanghai's French Concession. Fighting became endemic by then as regional leaders—warlords—battled one another, and the writ of the republican government in Beijing ran no farther than it could be carried by the troops of whatever general happened to be occupying the Northern Capital at any particular time.[7] Not until 1924, after the founding of the Whampoa Military Academy, with Soviet help, did Sun's Nationalists begin to build up their own army and their own new officer corps. Yet, even after Chiang Kai-shek's National Revolutionary Army swept to victory in June 1928 and their leader proclaimed China once again united, large parts of the country remained outside the control of his Nationalist government.

As the observed had changed, so had the observers. The West of the 1920s was very different from the West of that last deceptively golden age before the onslaught of the Great War. Even in those years before the Holocaust and the practice of mass murder in the Soviet Union, the fresh memorials to the fallen appearing in the churches and cemeteries of Europe and America, to say nothing of Hong Kong and Shanghai, were a reminder of how the spiritual and emotional landscape of the metropole had altered. The four years of savage bloodletting that had taken the lives of millions on the Western and Eastern fronts and drained Europe's economic resources brought a shock to the confidence and self-esteem of European nations from which they would never recover. Just as the Peloponnesian War had led to the downfall of Greece, wrote the race publicist Lothrop Stoddard, so this civil war fought by whites against whites might become a prelude to Nordic racial suicide.[8] Meanwhile, although the formal boundaries of empire might be more far-flung than ever after Versailles, those very empires were facing new challenges both at home, from liberals, Socialists and Communists, and abroad, from new leaders such as Gandhi, Nehru, or Ho Chi Minh whose Western educations, far from making them collaborators with empire, had turned them against it. By the mid-1920s, too, the outbreak of revolution in China itself also brought the fear that Russian Bolshevism might be replacing the benign influences of Britain, the United States, and France as the chief carrier of modernization and the danger of revolution may have helped to enhance the reputation of Confucius and the ordered and stable society for which he stood.

Americans, whose country (like Japan) had emerged stronger rather than weaker from the war, might see themselves succeeding the British as the leading Western presence in China and take that as a sign of progress. So also Marxists and those whose perceptions of the course of history were colored, consciously or unconsciously, by Marxist formulations might still profess to see a world moving forward, though impelled by the kinds of social and economic forces to which the Whig historians, their eyes fixed on the grand narratives of Protestantism, the emergence of the nation, and the development of Anglo-Saxon parliamentarianism, had been largely blind.

Others, however, were less sure. While the inroads of science and the Darwinian tide had earlier subverted the claims of religion, now the very vision of a secular and rational progress inherited from the Enlightenment was called into question by the violence that modern Europe had done to itself. At least in some circles, what Mary Louise

Pratt calls the legitimating ideologies of nineteenth-century Euroimperialism—the civilizing mission, scientific racism, technology-based paradigms of progress[9]—suddenly began to seem spectral. "The 'civilized' nations of the world," wrote Bertrand Russell, "with their blockades, their poison gases, their bombs, submarines, and negro armies, will probably destroy each other within the next hundred years."[10] *Ex oriente lux:* once again, as in Enlightenment Europe two centuries earlier, China had a lesson to teach the West. "The Chinese are gentle, urbane, seeking only justice and freedom," Russell continued. "They have a civilization superior to ours in all respects that makes for human happiness."[11] Although China was falling into a new round of civil wars, compared to the barbarity of the wholesale European slaughter still fresh in Western memory, they seemed like little more than comic opera battles.[12]

To many young radical Chinese nationalists of the 1920s the depredations of warlordism were inextricably linked to foreign imperialism. Militarism and modernity were the poisoned gifts the West had forced on China, when all they had really wanted to learn, according to Russell, were those things that had an ethical, social, or intellectual interest.[13] The West, Graham Peck wrote in the 1930s, was bent on subduing the environment by constructing a mechanical civilization, air conditioned, sterilized, and soundproofed, smooth and featureless as the inside of a cocoon, all difficulties, mental, moral, and physical, eliminated. The Chinese, however, had long ago realized that true harmony was to be found simply by accepting the environment as it was. "A donkey or a litter was satisfactory transportation for a man who was not in a hurry; feather beds and upholstered furniture were unnecessary for those who had taught their bodies to sit or lie without restlessness on firm surfaces."[14] Technological backwardness, in short, was no longer the sign of a regrettable primitivism crying for reform but, rather, like Gandhi's spinning wheel, testimony to an admirably simple approach to life.

It would be too easy to classify such statements simply as examples of a new "counterhegemonic discourse." Ayscough's admiration for Confucius and Russell's view of the Chinese discovery of the roots of human happiness both owed much to an earlier tradition of idealizing China and using it as object lesson for Western shortcomings. It had been common in the eighteenth century, and Jackson Lears has pointed to Orientalism among American intellectuals as a response to the spiritual questions of the late nineteenth century.[15] After the war, however, it became diffused among a broader audience. It can be seen in the lionizing of Rabindranath Tagore (winner of the Nobel Prize for Literature in 1913), the early admiration for Gandhi, and in a new interest in Asian religions and philosophies (D. T. Suzuki's *Essays in Zen Buddhism* began to appear in 1927). It was there in the tumbling out of translations of the *Daode jing* (one of which rendered Laozi, the putative author, as "the Old Boy," which surely had a strange resonance in England), and in the translations of Chinese and Japanese literature by men such as Ezra Pound, whose *Cathay* came out in 1915, or the prolific Arthur Waley, whose first collection of Chinese poems appeared in 1916, or Witter Bynner, whose version of the *Three Hundred Poems of the Tang Dynasty* was published as *The Jade Mountain* in 1929.[16] It was there also in Pearl Buck's *The Good Earth* (1931), which, with its earthy yet idealized view of peasant life, did much to shape American views of China. It was also there in Puccini's reworking of Gozzi's eighteenth-century drama *Turandot,* first performed in 1926, in Lehar's *Land of Smiles* in 1929, and in the experiments with Asian music in the works of Granville Bantock, Benjamin Britten, Colin McPhee, and others. It was there, too, in the popularization of a Westernized Asian aesthetic, reflected in an admiration for, say, Japanese gardens or the interest in Chinese and Japanese scroll painting by such critics as Laurence Binyon and Roger Fry in the mid-1920s, in the Japanese exhibitions in London in 1911 and Boston in 1936, and the great Chinese show at London's Burlington House in 1935–36. At one end of the cultural scale Japanese architecture influenced Frank Lloyd Wright and the works of the Prairie School; at the other end Graumann's Chinese Theater stood for many of the movie palace exoticisms of the period.

Faddish it may have been, particularly on its popular level, easily dismissed as simply yet another enthusiasm for what Raymond Dawson calls the "willow pattern world."[17] Nonetheless, it signaled a greater degree of openness to the Orient than had been evident in the more self-assured Europe before the war. As Noel Annan suggests, Forster's India taught that truth could be more complex and odd than Greek rationalism[18] or, for that matter, than Enlightenment and Whig views of progress. No doubt, the new receptivity to the East also reflected the increasing influence of the new cultural anthropology that marked both a break with earlier categories of scientific racism and a willingness to embrace the realization that different people followed different paths.[19] Disillusion with the West and its failures could encourage a new respect for Asia and a sense that China's apparent headlong rush toward the modern risked losing something of value. So, too, in China itself, while the young men and women who helped launch the May Fourth movement in 1919 might be calling for *quanpan xihua,* "total Westernization," for some kinds of older Chinese intellectuals—Yan Fu and Liang Qichao among them—the killings on the battlefields of France and Flanders brought a sobering reassessment of the Western-inspired reform that they had championed a decade or two earlier. In the wake of May Fourth a battle broke out between those self-styled modernists who continued to believe that science (or scientism, properly speaking) held the key to truth and those who, like Zhang Junmai, argued for the continuing validity of an Asian spirit, thereby foreshadowing the debate at the end of the twentieth century over "Asian values."

Finally, another reason for the new leniency may simply have been that China no longer represented the kind of danger it once had. Of course, Chinese anarchy and civil war threatened Western interests in the country, as did the rise of Chinese communism on the one hand and Japanese imperialism on the other. But these were dangers less likely to exercise the traveler than the journalist or the policy maker in Washington and Whitehall. In particular, in this period one finds little mention of the Yellow Peril by travelers, and I use the term not in its crudely racist sense but in the belief that the Chinese, precisely because of their ability to work so hard for so little reward, would become threats to their Western counterparts. Of course, there were those who continued to see the white races in danger, and they also gave voice to the new fear of a Sino-Japanese entente against the West. The United States, after all, continued to exclude Chinese immigrants until 1943.[20] But the absence of the concern from travel accounts may simply have been a reflection of China's weakness and its apparent imperviousness to Western-prescribed self-improvement, which was evident in the dashed hopes after the revolution of 1911.

These postwar accounts differed from their predecessors in other ways as well. Sometimes the inner journey grew more important, personal impressions counting for more than the analyses of trade prospects or lists of facts and figures common to prewar writers. By the 1920s, Martin Green has suggested, the adventure stories of the nineteenth century were no longer taken as serious writing, particularly in

England, where there was a new revulsion against empire. In their place came, instead, a kind of "anti-adventure literature," humorous, ironic, and self-mocking, from such writers as Evelyn Waugh.[21] So, too, G. A. Henty's boys, who had earlier been *With Kitchener in the Soudan* or had gone *With the Allies to Pekin*, had now been joined by girls and, domesticated as Arthur Ransome's Swallows and Amazons, were imagining an untracked wilderness waiting to be opened in the safe confines of the Lake District. In *Missee Lee*, in fact, they reached China, only to find themselves held captive by a Cambridge-educated young woman pirate chief, who insisted on their doing Latin lessons every day.

Green may be distracted here by the intellectual opponents of empire such as E. M. Forster, Robert Graves, and George Orwell, and John MacKenzie reminds us that such writers did not speak for the nation, for in British popular culture little had actually changed. G. A. Henty remained in print, after all.[22] Still, at least among British and American travelers there was a new tone of self-deprecation, even disillusion, that would have been unthinkable in the confident years before 1914. And, though Americans were more apt to adopt a didactic tone in their writing, when Harold Speakman vowed to see China "Chinese fashion," he was poking fun at himself as much as at the tourist whose view of the country stopped at Shanghai. So was Richard Dobson, setting off for China in 1936 for British-American Tobacco, his mind "open and empty as an inverted colander" as far as the country was concerned.[23] The New Zealander Robin Hyde, depressed by the continual gray rain and gray crowds of Hong Kong in January 1938, said out loud that she was fed up. A Mr. Loo, who had befriended her, "waddled over and put his hand on my shoulder."

> "Everything must be Chinese, eh?"
> His little eyes were twinkling, I stare at him: in a flash the whole absurdity of wanting a foreign nation to be a sort of giant charade, a fancy-dress entertainment for the benefit of foreigners, came and went behind those perspicacious eyes.[24]

The new tone was also an apt one for an age in which the distinction between travel and tourism was becoming more blurred than ever. The mode might be one of ignorance, serious or lighthearted; Gerald Yorke, for example, pointed out he had lived in China only two years and must in no sense be considered an expert,[25] while Peter Fleming, at the start of *One's Company*, his first book on China, issued a "Warning to the Reader."

> The recorded history of Chinese civilization covers a period of four thousand years.
> The population of China is estimated at 450 millions.
> China is larger than Europe.
>
> The author of this book is twenty-six years old.
> He has spent, altogether, about seven months in China.
> He does not speak Chinese.[26]

"I, for one, had always thought of the Chinese as being a strange, grotesque people," wrote Harold Speakman, making an ironic joke of his own acceptance of common Western stereotypes.

> (The years have builded such a vast irrational barrier of trivial affairs like chopsticks and queues!) *Dah Sing, Quong Wong, Soo Chow*—there seemed to be something in their very names that made one think of phoenixes, cockatrices, griffins, and other infringements against the spirit of normalcy as we know it. True, the Chinese I had met at different places in the Occident had always been uniformly courteous and friendly. Yet I always had the feeling that they were "holding something back." "The Insidious Dr. Fu-Manchu" and all the rest had done their insidious work. At best (I used to think) they were a cold and reserved people; a people almost lacking in some of the characteristics which we have come to look upon as "human."
> *But when I went to China . . .* [the ellipses are his, suggesting his discovery that the truth lay somewhere else].[27]

At the start of *Roving through Southern China* the American travel writer Harry Franck dismissed any wish to make a literary or scientific contribution, saying that he had done no more than to go and look at what interested him.[28] Ten years later Osbert Sitwell not only denied all intent to write a book explaining China's social or political conditions but admitted that he had neither the ability nor the desire to divorce himself from a culture drawn from the shores of the Mediterranean rather than the China Sea. "I journeyed to China, for example, very largely to escape from Europe, but more especially in order to see China, and the wonderful beauty of the system of life it incorporated, before this should perish," he wrote, admitting that his judgments and impressions might well be "more *chinoiserie* than Chinese."[29] "I went to China totally unprepared," wrote the Polish-born Ilona Ralf Sues of her trip a few years later, claiming that her own ignorance of the country would make it easier to discover Chinese reality. "I do not believe I had read half a dozen books about it. I wanted to see things for myself, to be 'the eyes and ears of the man-in-the-street.'"[30] How, precisely, one was supposed to be the eyes and ears of the man-in-the-street when one neither spoke nor understood his language was a question she never engaged. Perhaps she thought, like Roland Barthes years later in Japan, that "the murmuring mass of an unknown language constitutes a delicious protection."[31]

Yet this belief that one might be better off without the advice of the so-called experts demonstrated more than simply a kind of democratic, damn-your-eyes approach to travel or an attempt to distance oneself from the authors of earlier accounts. The characterizations of these later writers were inherently subversive of the authority claimed by so many of the earlier Victorian traveler-discoverers. They were not, however, subversive of travel writing as a form, not parodies, like that produced by "Serena Livingston-Stanley" (Joan W. Lindsay) in her 1936 sendup of African adventure tales called *Through Darkest Pondelayo: An Account of the Adventures of Two English Ladies on a Cannibal Island.* Indeed, precisely because Fleming and his contemporaries knew they wrote for an audience that could no longer take seriously the gravity of their predecessors, their own confessed uncertainty paradoxically seemed to make them even more trustworthy guides to the unknown than those predecessors had ever been. In a day when more journalists and more experts were turning their attention to China, such writers made an uncompromisingly forceful appeal to the reader for faith in the peculiar authority of the travelers' experience and its recording. For, if the authority of the travel account comes from its directness, unmediated by the erudition of the scholar or the experience of the Old China Hand, then such writings, with their disavowal of any insider's special knowledge, only increased their claim to veracity. "You don't know anything about China," they said to the reader, "and I don't know much either. But I've been there, so let me tell you what I saw and heard."

Still, one wonders whether, had people like Fleming or Sues chosen to write about lands closer to home—the Balkans, say, or Egypt—they would have taken quite such a cavalier attitude to their history and culture. "I do not understand those blasé travelers who come to China boasting of their ignorance," wrote Harold Acton. "No doubt they have excellent eyes, but this dependence on a purely personal vision seldom accompanies a freedom from national prejudices, which Gibbon deemed indispensable, together with 'age, judgement, a competent knowledge of men and books'. Copious reading enhanced my enjoyment."[32] Still, like Eliza Scidmore, who deplored the queerness coming over those who devoted their time to the study of China, modern travelers such as Acton also sought to put a distance between themselves and the professional Sinologists. With their eyes firmly fixed on a distant past and blind to the reality of present-day China around them, such men became, in the words of George Kates, "wiser and wiser about matters ever more remote," convinced that Chinese history had ended long ago and that the study of the modern language "was beneath the dignity of higher learning."[33]

Conditions of Travel

In the years between the wars Beijing "pullulated" (Acton's word) with planners of romantic journeys, from the pompous and publicized Sven Hedin down to everyone who had slept in a Mongolian *yurt*. "The conventional Grand Tour of the eighteenth century produced scores of books more interesting than have travels in Turkestan and Tibet in the twentieth, despite—or is it because of?—our improved facilities."[34] Yet, while an experienced traveler such as the British consular officer Eric Teichman could recommend for the enterprising tourist the voyage by road from Beijing through Xi'an to Chengdu,[35] the trip was still one that might have tested the mettle even of an Isabella Bird, particularly if she had happened to find herself caught in the crossfire of competing warlord armies. Victor Purcell knew of a missionary who in 1926 had been transferred with his family from a small Sichuan town to one in Yunnan, only 560 miles away. He found it a good deal cheaper, however, a good deal quicker, and much, much safer to do a circuit of six thousand miles via Shanghai, Singapore, and Rangoon, coming back into China from Burma.[36] That same year, when Owen Lattimore tried to set off for Mongolia, he had to avoid the police and lay his plans in secret, though he suspected the reason was less the announced danger from bandits than the unwillingness of the "Christian" warlord Feng Yuxiang to have his missionary supporters learn of the shipments of weapons arriving at his headquarters from the godless Soviet Union.[37]

"Shanghai—gateway to the mystic temple cities of China. Or Hongkong—the Riviera of the East with the glamor of ancient Cathay," ran an advertisement for the Canadian Pacific steamers in 1925. "Summer Lasts All Year Long on the Southern Route . . . And all the way to Shanghai," boasted the Italian Line in 1936. Certainly, by the 1920s the voyage out—at least to the big cities of the coast—had become easier. From England the fortnightly services of the P & O, the Glen Line, the Ellerman Line, and Alfred Holt's Blue Funnel liners, with their classical names like *Ajax* and *Patroclus* and *Agammemnon,* reached China in six or seven weeks, and two weeks was enough to bring the traveler from San Francisco or Seattle or Vancouver by the Dollar Line or the Pacific Mail Line or the Canadian Pacific. By the 1920s, too, round-the-world cruises occasionally put in at Hong Kong or Shanghai, giving passengers a chance to disembark long enough to see the strange sights and, occasionally to hear the distant rumblings of civil war (though in February 1927, as Chiang Kai-shek's revolutionary armies closed in on Shanghai, the *Belgenland* skipped the city and steered directly for Hong Kong instead).[38] For the traveler in a hurry the Trans-Siberian promised an even quicker passage, although through-services were infrequent, and by 1936 Pan-American's new China Clipper reached Hong Kong only eight days out from the west coast, while Imperial Airways took some eight to nine days to cover the route from London to Hong Kong.[39]

A growing number of guidebooks made it at least somewhat easier to plan a trip. The Rev. C. E. Darwent's *Shanghai: A Handbook for Travellers and Residents to the Chief Objects of Interest in and around the Foreign Settlements and Native City,* its second edition published in 1920, made that city of vice sound rather more placid than the one described some fifteen years later in *All about Shanghai and Environs: A Standard Guidebook.* New and enlarged guides to Beijing and several other major cities appeared from Thomas Cook after the war. But most complete of all was the Japanese Government Railways' *Guide to China,* which came out in a second revised edition in 1924, looking and reading for all the world like an eastern Baedeker, with its pocket size and dark-red binding, its layout, its detailed brown, white, and blue city maps, its descriptions of sights and directions telling where to find accommodations, restaurants, silk, and curio shops as well as post offices, banks, and consulates.[40]

Having landed, the traveler could put up at any one of a number of Western hotels in Shanghai, such as the Astor or the Park or later the Cathay, while in Beijing could be found the Hôtel des Wagons-Lits, the Grand Hôtel de Pékin, and the Metropole. Graham Peck, arriving in the old capital in the mid-1930s, found himself facing a "glacier of virgin linen" in the chilly magnificence of his hotel's dining room, while a Russian quartet "sawed out the lugubriously dainty music heard in hotel dining-rooms all over the world."[41] Even in the smaller ports, and sometimes indeed in the interior, suitable accommodation and Western meals of a sort were available for those unwilling to chance a Chinese inn or Chinese cooking. "Life in a Chinese hotel begins with the movements of the earliest riser," wrote Victor Purcell.

> He is about his business long before dawn, and he thinks that it would be a shame if you did not share his health, wealth, and wisdom. He always has feet as big and clumsy as a pair of sea-lions and shod in hundred-league boots.[42]

"Nessun dorma," sung by Turandot's herald, would seem a superfluous injunction in such places. The shiny new exterior of the Grand Hôtel du Lac in Yunnanfu, Richard Dobson found, belied the dirty interior, and, thanks to the bone-idle servants, "the early mornings were made hideous by the screams and vituperation of an old French gorgon of a manageress who strove by whips and scorpions to induce an industry that was simply not there."[43] So, too, Peter Fleming's Grand Hotel de Kiangsi in Nanchang had "about six storeys, built round a dark courtyard which served as entrance-hall, airshaft, and urinal," noisy, smelly, and infested with soldiers and coolies who had no business being there. "It was not a bad hotel, but I would not choose it for a quiet week-end."[44]

From Shanghai Chinese and foreign steamships made regular runs up the Great River to cities such as Nanjing and Hankou, the Western ones at least offering almost the comfort of cruise liners, though, during these years of civil war, rifle fire or even worse from the banks was not uncommon. At Yichang the more adventurous could change to one of the smaller vessels that now made the passage through the rapids and whirlpools of the gorges all the way to Chongqing. Even with the coming of steam, that journey remained perilous, as Elizabeth Enders discovered in 1924, when the *Robert Dollar II* was wrecked, leaving her swimming for her life.[45] By 1930 the traveler could go by rail from Beijing to Harbin and the Trans-Siberian in the north, or west as far as Xi'an, or south as far as Changsha in Hunan, though the linking of the northern network to Guangzhou and Hong Kong did not open until 1936. Plans for the construction of a bridge across the Yangtze River at Hankou were stopped by the Japanese invasion the next year; otherwise, the *China Year Book* predicted, it would have been possible to travel by train from Hong Kong to the cities of Europe.[46] Timetables often reflected more optimism than reality, however, and the rail lines were by no means immune to war or even banditry; in a famous case in 1923 the crack Blue Train from Nanjing to Beijing was hijacked and its passengers, foreign and Chinese alike, held for ransom. Trains varied enormously in their levels of service, and rail travel could mean anything from riding an ancient freight car packed with soldiers to the kind of *wagon-lit* that reminded the young Denton Welch of France or Switzerland until he began to notice the differences.

> There were sinister newspaper parcels left under seats, and small jelly-fish of spittle quivering on the floors in the passages and compartments. In the dining-car, the waiters seemed to be serving dirty grey rags and string out of cracked, steaming puddingbasins. I suppose it must have been some sort of spaghetti. We paid no attention to it, but waited till Boy had heated some of our tinned food.[47]

Chinese passengers "spat emphatically," noted Ada Chesterton, on her way from Shanghai to Nanjing, "—a habit they share with the citizens of the United States."[48]

By the 1930s air travel had become a possibility, thanks to the foundation of the China National Aviation Corporation, a Sino-American joint venture, and the Eurasia Air Service, opened in partnership with Lufthansa. A few years earlier, Victor Purcell noted, a traveler in the interior of Guangdong or Guangxi did well if he covered fifteen to twenty miles a day—not very different from the time of Khubilai Khan—but one early autumn day in 1937 he flew the 460 miles from Hong Kong to Changsha in three hours and was able to look down on the Chinese landscape in a radically new way.

With a half turn of our eye we traversed a section of country, including a mountain pass, which had taken the conquering Manchu armies months to cover; in a casual look round over the wing when we turned from the morning paper we took in many square miles of historic ground, and of earth which had spewed up millions of yellow men from her womb and, when they were dead, had sucked their bodies back again to nourish her with their salts.[49]

"How neat the Chinese are!" wrote Peter Fleming, observing Manchuria from a Japanese aircraft in the early 1930s, finding in the symmetrical patterns of the farmland a dignity lacking in English garden suburbs or small American towns.[50] In the late 1930s Violet Cressy-Marcks saved eleven days of trekking by making a two-hour flight from Yunnanfu to Chongqing. So did Eileen Bigland in 1939, though she was terrified by the aerobatics of a pilot who flew with more enthusiasm than skill and by the report of a German fellow passenger that five such aircraft had been shot down by the Japanese within the past month.[51]

Still, there were not many trains or airplanes, and the only steamships to journey any distance were those that plied the coasts or sailed up the Yangtze. Highways remained primitive, and the over-crowded buses or trucks in which travelers rode severely tested whatever notions of a placid and unchanging China they might still have held. Peter Fleming was convinced his driver had constituted himself president of a suicide club with his passengers as members, and Graham Peck noted the gutted and crumpled carcasses of buses already lying by the side of a Sichuan road only recently opened to traffic.[52] The older forms of locomotion, of course, were still available. Houseboats remained a favorite way to travel in places like the Yangtze delta, with its intricate system of waterways.[53] Elsewhere travelers could still take to the mule litter or the wheelbarrow, the latter being, in the view of Harry Franck, the most comfortable form of land travel, in which two men, propelled by another and stretched out in relative comfort, "may discuss religion, philosophy, and the natural equality of man without straining the ears or losing a word."[54]

Yet, while modern industry and transport, modern education and fashion, might be changing the face of the land and the faces of its inhabitants (at least in the larger treaty ports), China was not Europe, and real travel was more readily available than in the Italy or Austria of

Baedeker, Cook, and American Express. In those years, wrote Graham Peck, a trip to the interior meant

> a slow farewell to Western-style comforts and the sophistications of urban Chinese life. From the great, complete metropolitan centers near the ocean you went inland by gradual stages, first to the end of the railway, then to the end of the motor road, then to the end of the telegraph line. Typical landmarks would be the last city rich enough for theatres, the last town with a clean hotel, the last village with a roofed restaurant. Out beyond the last little pathside stall which sold Shanghai cigarettes, you could feel you had really arrived in the archaic, impoverished interior.[55]

The worst of travel in such places, Peter Fleming complained, was that you could never safely get anything cold to drink, though he demonstrated a knack for unearthing amusing and hospitable Catholic missionaries, one of whose virtues was to have on hand quantities of iced beer. Meals were another problem; when Ada Chesterton met Pearl Buck in Shanghai (on her way home to receive the Pulitzer Prize for *The Good Earth*) the writer warned her about the dangers of unsanitary food and drink in the interior, and indeed Chesterton's traveling companion later had to be hospitalized for dysentery in Hankou.[56]

Finally, in one significant aspect, assumed but rarely mentioned, the conditions of travel went largely unchanged in these years. The whole structure of foreign privilege had not only survived the end of the dynasty and the Great War but, thanks to the collapse of central authority, emerged in the 1920s in some ways actually stronger than it had been before. Even bandits were affected; though one of them was killed, the other twenty-odd foreigners kidnaped from the Blue Train in 1923 were probably released sooner and in better health because of their nationality than might otherwise have been the case. And, though by the late 1920s the treaty powers might be willing to negotiate away some of the privileges they had obtained in the nineteenth century (in 1928, for instance, China won the right to set its own tariffs for the first time in almost a century), extraterritoriality—that great gift of the unequal treaties to the foreigner—was not on the bargaining table, or at least not on that table where the places were set by Britain and the United States. It's true that Chiang Kai-shek's Northern Expedition, driving up from Guangzhou to Beijing from 1926 to 1928, led to the evacuation of thousands of foreigners from the interior and the dispatch of thousands of British and American troops to Shanghai in early 1927. Six foreigners were shot to death that March when the Nationalist troops swept into Nanjing. They were, however, the only foreign casualties of those revolutionary years. Although some travelers might not care to dwell on it, the possession of a white skin in a brown-skinned land still carried with it considerable authority and protective power.

Four Roads to Chinese Reality

"I find in reading books that the Awakening of China has been announced a dozen or more times by foreign travelers in the last ten years, so I hesitate to announce it again," wrote John Dewey in the wake of the May Fourth movement of 1919. He did, however, convinced by the actions of the students and their allies that this time it really was happening.[57] Yet the awakening and the changes that followed brought an ambivalent response, if not among the journalists and the scholars, then at least among the travelers, and this is yet another reason why travel writing on China took a new turn in these years. Change was good, of course, as it seemed to promise a nation transformed by science, modern medicine, Protestant Christianity (or, for some observers, communism), higher education, better plumbing, and transportation into a land more like the familiar West. As the books and articles of the more optimistic testified, with the progress of modernization and Westernization in China, They would benefit by becoming more like Us.

For travelers, however, such changes sometimes came at a cost. In a time of easier access the country's backwardness could seem almost picturesque; the petrified conservatism that had so upset nineteenth-century travelers now became an admirable respect for tradition. As the world became increasingly homogenized through rapid communications, China, at least behind the facade of the treaty ports and their foreign settlements, remained different, and the differences—the country's "Chinese" characteristics—were now qualities to be valued rather than derided. What had seemed twenty or thirty years earlier evidences of China's hopeless imperviousness to modern ideas now became, like Confucius the revered lawgiver, aspects to be saved in a world in which modernity was bringing a spirit-numbing uniformity. Two decades earlier even the acid Eliza Scidmore had admired Beijing as a place where the "demon of progress has not brought down the dread monotony of the universal commonplace."[58] So, too, in the early 1920s, as he tramped about China, Harry Franck contrasted the innumerable differences in the details of life that he observed with the standardized sameness of the United States, where, thanks to mass production and mass advertising and mass marketing, Portland, Maine, had become practically indistinguishable from San Diego, California.[59]

As far back as Flaubert's day, Dennis Porter suggests, the lands beyond Europe had attracted those who were drawn to Otherness and the "uncivilized" (particularly as manifested in the Orient), not for scientific reasons, as in the eighteenth century, but simply for their own sake.[60] For such travelers a China easily accessible by railroads and modern highways and airplanes, with modern hotels in its inland cities, would no longer be China. Thus, the travel accounts written after the war show a new concern with what it was that constituted Chinese reality and a search for the real China, which could be distinguished from the counterfeit modernity evident in the larger cities. It was a quest for authenticity that had been largely absent from the accounts of the prewar travelers. Exotic and Oriental though it might be, China was for them simply there and needed no searching; the point, for a traveler like Dundas or Colquhoun or Little, was to experience it, to observe it, and to describe it as accurately as possible, as if one were a cartographer or an ethnologist.

Except, of course, that cartographers, at least, do not pass the same kinds of judgments that travelers did. Still, after about 1920 this relatively innocent approach seemed no longer possible. China's progress toward a Western-defined modernity and the endangering of its "Chinese" qualities, was only part of the problem. Just as important, perhaps, was a growing self-consciousness about tourism, about the ready-made packaging of sights and sites, which, common enough for decades in Europe, seemed now to be spreading to distant Asia as well, as the advertisements for cruises showed. "Tourists dislike tourists," Dean McCannell writes. "God is dead, but man's need to appear holier than his fellows lives."[61]

To the travelers' traditional appeal to the reader's trust, based on the directness of their own experience, was now added a new one. In an age of spreading global tourism the traveler often claimed an ability to discriminate between the real and the sham, just as a collector would discriminate between "authentic" artifacts of craft and material culture and the "inauthentic" curios offered to tourists.[62] In this way the construction of an authentic China for a readership back home became linked to a process of self-production, so that one's own authenticity as traveler was validated by one's ability to find the genuine article, in places off the beaten track, beyond the grasp of the tourist. This sort of a search for authenticity, James Buzard suggests, lies behind what he calls "anti-tourism," a way of seeing one's own cultural experience as authentic and unique, distinguished from the tourist's acceptance of vulgarity, repetition, and ignorance. (Although becoming an anti-tourist, Fussell points out, is not enough to make you a traveler; it may simply make you a snob.)[63]

For some the effort at self-authentication could lead to a kind of Pharisaicism, nudging readers to remind them what set the traveler apart from others—"Lord, I thank you that I am not as this mere tourist"—while for others it might take the form of a humorous self-irony. "It was my sincerest wish not only to see the country which lay back of Shanghai, but it see it *Chinese-fashion*," wrote Harold Speakman in the early 1920s. "The fact that I did not know just what Chinese-fashion meant—no stranger does until he tries it—only added the zest of experiment to an already well-developed enthusiasm."[64] Yet, if they'd had the choice, not many travelers a few decades earlier would have chosen to see China "Chinese-fashion"; the filthy inns, the slippery, muddy roads along cliffs or beside rice paddies, the uncertainties of transport, were all factors to be mitigated, even avoided, if possible. Isabella Bird, for example, appears to have subsisted for five months on a diet of chicken or eggs disguised by the copious stocks of curry she had brought from the coast, rather than trusting herself to Chinese food.[65]

In China, in any case, the distinction was not so much between traveler and tourist as between travelers or tourists, on the one hand, and treaty port residents, on the other, the sorts of people whose ideas of the country embraced only the view through the windows of the Shanghai Club or the orderly streets of Beijing's Legation Quarter and whose long residence in the country left them still mouthing the easy platitudes about China and the Chinese character they'd learned on their arrival decades earlier. Such Old China Hands, ignorant of China's past, oblivious to the signs of regeneration in the future yet pretending to know the real country, now became a favorite target of travel writers. The journalist Arthur Ransome skewered them with a famous chapter on the Shanghai mind when he covered the revolutionary events of 1927, and, though his picture was a caricature, for there was in fact more than one Shanghai mind, it had enough truth in it to be effective.[66]

The traveler's search for a real China was in one sense a subversive undertaking, contesting the popular notion of journalists, missionaries, and diplomats that a modernized nation in the Western image was somehow the inevitable goal of historical change. In another sense, however, it also risked reducing China to an exotic object that reflected Western fantasies, turning it almost into a kind of theme park, much as is happening to Tibet today (and, as Peter Bishop and Donald Lopez show, has happened for a great many years). It was a search that had both chronological and spatial dimensions and so might lead the traveler down four different roads. One carried the traveler back in time, making a journey into the past; another meant a journey into the interior, away from the Westernizing treaty ports of the coast; a third, dismissing the past, might find reality in the changing and modernizing China of the day; and yet a fourth demanded an imaginative foray into the China of the future.

Most texts, of course, shared more than one of these attributes. Moreover, particularly during these years, when the shadows of war were lengthening over the country, it was becoming difficult to draw a line between the travel account pure and simple and the book purporting to explain China, perhaps even to predict its future. Unlike, say, Italy or Greece, where the traveler moved among familiar monuments in a familiar landscape, China remained enough of an unknown quantity that travel books had to prove their utility to the world of the present by explaining things rather than simply setting forth the writer's impressions. Yet the search for authenticity bound them together. How could you analyze China, after all, or predict its future or even simply describe it to your audience if you did not know where the real China lay?

Chapter 5

Journeys to the Past and Journeys to the Heartland

Beijing: The Journey to Antiquity

"Own a piece of history," suggests an advertisement for a company in Nantucket, offering for sale an "authentic replica . . . branded to certify authenticity" of a deck chair from the *Titanic*. Elsewhere the notes to a recent recording of the *Messiah* inform us that the work is performed on "original, authentic, period instruments," the three adjectives almost bumping into one another in their anxiety to assure listeners that what they hear differs little from the sounds that would have struck Handel's audience two and a half centuries ago. Yet suppose the recording does in fact replicate precisely what the composer would have recognized as his own, managing to ignore two hundred years of changes in performance practice, different editions, and the like. It would become a perfect copy of a historical event and presumably achieve thereby a certain kind of timelessness.

But places, peoples, cultures, are not events taking place at a particular time in history, and for them the old is not always the authentic. Few would argue that Washington Square of the 1830s or the Chrysler Building of the 1930s is somehow the authentic New York. Whatever our views of the city, it is still a place that is living, growing, and changing, and it is the process itself that makes New York real, as opposed to a particular scene or a building that we might isolate in order to encapsulate the city of Henry James or Edith Wharton or Berenice Abbott. Faced with the foreign and the unfamiliar, however, we are less certain of where to look, and, when we go to the time, the expense, and the hardship of travel, we need some reassurance that what we have before

93

our eyes is really what we have paid to see. We may not demand a Florence eternally frozen in the quattrocento, but San Lorenzo or Santa Maria Novella still are likely to signify the real to us in a way that the city's ugly industrial suburbs do not.

Imperialist nostalgia is the term one critic uses to describe the way in which, after a form of life is deliberately changed, those responsible for the change then regret that things have not remained as they had been earlier.[1] Travelers to unfamiliar lands, however, often seek the past not so much because they mourn the passing of old ways as out of the belief that the old is the signifier of authenticity. Already in the 1870s Henry James had noted the passing of old Italy, real Italy, and by the 1920s modernity, Mussolini, and the tourists flocking to Capri and the Lido were finishing up what was left.[2] But in timeless Asia might still be found what Europe had lost, just as today trekking in Nepal or Sikkim is a way of escaping the steel and glass skyscrapers of Hong Kong and Shanghai, Kuala Lumpur and Bangkok. If Henry James had lived two or three decades later, he might have gone to China like Harold Acton, and his Isabel Archer, a flapper in short skirts and bobbed hair, would have wandered through the dim red and gold palaces of the Forbidden City rather than the winter-chilled galleries of the Uffizi. Although by that time some had already decided it was already too late and their Chinese traveling was restricted to journeys of scholarship and the imagination, like those of the great Hungarian historian Étienne Balazs or of Arthur Waley, of whom a friend reported that he already knew what China looked like and had no wish to go there. His China—real China—was the glorious land of the Han and the Tang, the China of Luoyang and Chang'an, and he preferred not to have his illusions shattered by the grimy and decaying realities of the present. Langdon Warner's outlook was similar, for, when he did make the trip on behalf of the Fogg Museum, he found the glories of old China long since dead, and the country of his day, with its misery, its cruelty, its bandits, its hardships, had little to recommend it.[3]

Robert Bickers has suggested that the nationalistic demands being made by an emerging modern Chinese bourgeoisie in the early twentieth century threatened the old stereotypes of Chinese subordination to the West and brought on the part of foreigners a dislike of modernized urban China and a new concern for the peasantry.[4] Be that as it may, this particular Western valorization of antiquity and tradition came at a time when in China itself the May Fourth generation was engaged in questioning what, if indeed anything, in their country's past might be worth keeping. Many of their strictures against that tradition, in fact, only echoed what foreigners had earlier been saying. "Our vaunted Chinese civilization is only a feast of human flesh prepared for the rich and the mighty," wrote Lu Xun in early 1925, echoing the theme of China's cannibalistic history that he'd set forth six years earlier in his "Diary of a Madman." "Those who praise China because they do not know this are excusable, but the rest deserve to be condemned forever." Two kinds of foreigners called forth his wrath.

> One considers the Chinese an inferior race which deserve to be no better off than it is, so they deliberately commend all that is old in China. The other likes every country in the world to look different in order to make travelling more interesting. In China they expect to see pigtails, in Japan wooden shoes, in Korea bamboo hats. If everyone looked alike they would find it boring; hence they oppose the Westernization of Asia. Both these types are detestable. As for Mr. Bertrand Russell, who praised the Chinese when some sedan-chair-bearers smiled at him at the West Lake, he may have been actuated by other motives. But if chair-bearers could stop smiling at their fares, China would long since have stopped being the China she is.[5]

This because Russell had admired those servants who, carrying the philosopher and his party over a steep pass on a hot day, were laughing among themselves, "as if they had not a care in the world," rather than complaining of the heat to get a bigger tip, as his own countrymen presumably would have done.[6] Perhaps Lu Xun would have been happier if he'd known that some years earlier Emily de Burgh Daly, being carried up a mountain path near Ningbo, had to deal with bearers who had claimed both her weight and the day's heat as reasons for demanding higher pay.[7]

In any case Lu Xun's strictures against his own society again raise the question of how we should handle "Orientalist" criticisms that are mounted by insiders rather than outsiders. Here, however, the characterization of autoethnography, with its collaborationist overtones,[8] seems to miss the point of the essayist's acerbic pen. Nevertheless, on 30 May 1925, a month after Lu Xun's piece was written, a British officer in Shanghai's International Settlement ordered his Chinese and Indian police to fire on a crowd of demonstrators in Nanking Road, killing eleven people, and the national outcry that swept across the country in the next few weeks—the May Thirtieth movement, it was called—gave heart to those who, like the writer, wanted China to stop "being the China she is." Foreigners might well wish to preserve the old, as long as they lived in their own settlements or, surrounded by servants, in houses that had once belonged to Manchu grandees. But many of the young men and women shaped by May Fourth and May Thirtieth saw little in China's culture of cannibalism that could or should be saved, and foreigners like Bertrand Russell—*even* the Russell they otherwise so respected—ran into trouble when they advised China not to throw out its past. Thus, Agnes Smedley, passing through Beijing in the late 1920s, was struck by the intellectuals she found who admired Russell's "superlatively keen analyses of society and his crystal-clear atheism" but who nonetheless opposed his book because it praised China's evils and made the young people arrogant.[9] While the May Fourth generation might not like criticisms coming from foreigners, they would have found even the earlier condemnations of Confucianism made by travelers like Scidmore and Gordon Cumming (the fossilized wisdom of a wearisome sage) wanting because they did not go far enough.

For the outsider, however, images drawn from the past could provide a firm anchor in an uncertain present, a way of recognizing the real China when you met it—the place where men wore pigtails, as Lu Xun called it. The morning after her arrival in Nanjing in the mid-1930s, Innes Jackson went for a walk, discovering a landscape whose authenticity was certified by its similarity to paintings she'd seen in the British Museum: "those pictures of queer rocks, trees, mountains, huts, ferryboats, fisherman, land and water scenes . . . were now presenting themselves in fact, hardly modified at all."[10] Harold Acton, after his assiduous reading in the translations of Waley, Giles, and Wieger, knew what to expect when he first saw Beijing in 1932 and felt himself like Gibbon entering the Eternal City.[11] On the other hand, ten years earlier Grace Seton found something clearly inauthentic in the modern young Miss Chen of Shanghai whom she met and whose favorite poet turned out to be Wordsworth—"Wordsworth, when the verse of her countrymen, Tu Fu, Li T'ai-po and Po Chü-i, is in the world!"[12] All very well, no doubt, for Americans to be open-minded toward Chinese poets, in other words, but no real Chinese ought to prefer English poetry. So, too, Peter Fleming was unimpressed by his interpreter Mr. Chen, whose

Harvard education had destroyed his faith in the ancient values of his culture and left him so profoundly out of sympathy for his country that he chose to live in the Nanchang YMCA for the foreign bathrooms and foreign cooking.[13]

If the earlier figure of pity or of fun had been the native obdurately attached to his old ways in the face of superior foreign learning, it had now become the native who was too Westernized—the wog, in short. Here was another sign of the change in sensibility after the war. Real Chinese, admirable Chinese, were now those who maintained the old traditions, and the China many travelers sought was one not yet invaded by the modern world, not yet become a Shanghai with its streetcars, traffic lights, department stores, night clubs, and skyscrapers. Elizabeth Enders, entering a sedan chair to be carried through the narrow streets of Suzhou—the Venice of China, as she and countless others called it because of its canals—felt as though she were stepping back into the Middle Ages, the town's noise, squalor, and beehive existence utterly unchanged over the centuries. "Now we are glimpsing China as it really is and has been through the centuries—in the mass, an unchanged civilization—working, living, and dying exactly as its forbears have for scores of generations."[14] Harold Speakman, exploring the hinterland of Shanghai from his houseboat, admired the "medieval battlements" of Kunshan and stepped ashore into the "Arabian Nights" on his arrival in Suzhou.[15] Later he heard two coolies in a village singing with great accuracy a theme from *Madame Butterfly*, noting that, since Japanese music comes from China, Puccini must have traced it to its source. The song of a watchman at Hangzhou (the ellipses are his) brought "a sense of the nearness of ancient, forgotten things.

"Thebes . . . Carthage . . . Babylon. Dusky, bearded men . . . These stars . . . *these* . . . over the Euphrates!

"The hills of Moab . . . David . . ."[16]

In 1927, four years after his book's publication, would come the first performance of *Turandot*, set in a timeless China with its mandarins Ping, Pang, and Pong.

In the 1930s Osbert Sitwell warned that his book was meant to be *escapist*, since he went to China not out of a pure love of wandering nor to see social struggle "nor, alas! in response to a request from my publishers to write a strong left-wing book about that country" but, rather, that he might examine "the wonderful beauty of the system of life it incorporated before this should perish."[17] As change threatened to engulf this half-real, half-imagined China, age became one of the confirming and comforting marks of authenticity, just as it once had in a Europe of chateaux and churches or even in its untouched poor living in cheerful squalor among the monuments of the past in a city like Venice (the Suzhou of Europe).[18] While some travelers made China familiar by references to a Western history (the Middle Ages, Venice, Rome), others drew on the Chinese past itself. Florence Ayscough's voyage up the Yangtze brought back a flood of historical and literary memories: the defeat of Cao Cao's forces at the battle of the Red Cliff, immortalized by Su Dongbo, the founding of the Ming dynasty at Nanjing, the poems of Li Bo and Du Fu describing the geography passing before her eyes, even though she was disappointed that the traveler could no longer hear the cries of their gibbons echoing high across the dark walls of the Qutang gorge.[19]

Traveling for Reuters in the early 1930s, Gerald Yorke spent much of his time looking at flood relief along the Yangtze and the Huai, at Japanese activities in Manchuria, and the struggle between Chiang Kai-shek and the Communists. Yet to find war and rebellion alone was to miss the point, for they did not represent the country's heart. Hence, he too went in search of an older reality, carrying his translations of the classics as he left the bustle of Shanghai, and sought a hospitable temple in Zhejiang, where he could retire for a while and devote himself to study. In a barge being drawn slowly down to Hangzhou, he lay back and watched the life along the waterway, the peasants transplanting young rice shoots, half-naked children on the backs of water buffalo, the lovely high-arched stone bridges under which he passed, the houses and pagodas that lined the banks. "All who have beautified China in this way have earned their seat on a lotus in the Western Paradise."[20]

Although Hangzhou, with its new buildings, was "a model of bad taste," the view of the West Lake was enough to make him forget it, and there in the hills overlooking the water he took two rooms in a temple, settling down to study Daoist meditation.[21] Contemporary annoyances persisted, however: the noisy spitting of a priest, the stench of night soil filling his room as it was poured on a nearby vegetable garden. So he decided to move on to yet another temple, and—like Bertrand Russell with his chair bearers—had nothing but praise for the boatmen, who were content to work fifteen hours at a stretch.

They are the most perfectly formed and most cheerful animals imaginable. The world will be the loser when their type has been eliminated by competition from train, motor bus, and launch. The genius of the Chinese lies in their capacity to bear cheerfully the burdens of the day. They do not appreciate the point of view which once prompted a Labour Government in England to inquire of its consular officials whether the Chinese work an eight-hour day in accordance with the agreement signed by their representative at Geneva.[22]

Nowhere did this search for authenticity in the past emerge more clearly than in the travelers' changing responses to Beijing. Granted that for some memories of the old barbarisms persisted. Grace Thompson Seton, having wangled an invitation to one of the ceremonies surrounding the wedding of the young Manchu pretender Puyi in 1922, found herself calling up memories of the old dowager and the Boxers as she passed the walls of the Imperial Palace on a frosty December night.

What tales of anguish, or torture, of horrid delight could they reveal to the psychic reader of the past! A sudden icy chill trickled down my spine as I slipped by the last crafty-eyed sentry, whose face, lighted by a flickering lantern above, bore that expression peculiar to eunuchs. I was glad that the press correspondent beside me was a perfectly good American.[23]

Even Graham Peck, a very different sort of traveler indeed, described his arrival in north China fifteen years later in terms freighted with the sort of menace that might have been drawn from a Hollywood thriller (or Franco Zeffirelli's setting of Puccini's opera). Landing under a "scarred moon" that showed through the mist, his ship docked "at a torchlit pier on the edge of a marsh, beside the neglected corpse of a railway station. Here the faint menace of the Asiatic night crystallized in a horde of giant porters in tattered coats and barbaric fur hats." Disembarking from his train on a winter night in Beijing, he found the "unmechanized city" filled with an "ominous hush," where "at the corners stood slit-eyed soldiers muffled in huge fur coats and hats, armed like bandits with pistols and curving swords on which the moonlight glittered."[24]

Yet, despite such echoes of past fears, by the 1920s for most travelers Scidmore's city of dreadful dust had become picturesque, its antiquity and genteel (if regrettable) decay charming, the very incompetence of the faceless puppets who succeeded one another as putative heads of the new Republic of China a guarantee of changelessness. By 1928, of course, it was no longer even the nominal capital of China, for Chiang Kai-shek, like the founder of the Ming dynasty over five hundred years earlier, had moved the headquarters of his Nationalist government down to Nanjing, leaving the old northern capital to its placid dreams of the past. "Peking is the one city in China where the traveller sees native life untouched and uninfluenced by foreign discipline and regulation," advised Thomas Cook's guide of 1917,

> and at the same time lives and moves in comfort, in good hotels, good streets, and first-class conveyances. Every phase of Chinese existence in the interior that is worthy of study is presented in Peking among surroundings where cleanliness is attainable, and the trying hardships of the primitive hinterland are unknown . . . Peking is all that is characteristically Chinese in the superlative degree, and it goes along with its life in its own high tenor, oblivious to the little foreign colony in the Legation Quarter, and indifferent to the thoughts and ways of the Occidentals who come and go.[25]

Although Nankou Pass, where one went to see the Great Wall, was overcome with tourists, grumbled a writer for the *National Geographic,*[26] Beijing was still real China (as Hong Kong and Shanghai decidedly were not) at its best, with all modern conveniences. "That's the wonder and marvel of it," remarks Mrs. Mascot in *Peonies and Ponies,* Acton's novel about the city in the 1930s. "Here you may taste the Middle Ages as your daily diet, with all the comforts of the twentieth century thrown in."[27] What Rome had been to Europe, wrote Elizabeth Enders, tossing chronology to the winds, Beijing had been to the East—"an eternal city, shrouded in antiquity, founded long before the days of Romulus and Remus, the great capital of a vast and complex nation." Here, the centuries falling away, she found the permanence she sought, in the city's street life, its temples and bazaars, its customs, in which Western influence had no more than scratched the surface.[28] Her Beijing, of course, reflected centuries of earlier Western imaginings, and it would be pedantic to point out that the city she saw was younger than Paris or

London, let alone the Rome founded by the wolf's twins (to say nothing of Aeneas). Still, the very timelessness that travelers had deplored a few decades earlier now testified to Beijing's reality. Here was a China admirably resistant to the modern world, where the heart of the people still kept time to the rhythms of the old calendar, resisting the tawdry gimcrackery of Chicago and Manchester or, for that matter, Osaka and Shanghai. Modern journalists and entrepreneurs might continue to find the old capital hopelessly backward and resistant to the new currents moving the nation; the directness of the travelers' experiences, however, put them in touch with a reality that analysts of China's contemporary condition could never grasp.

In Search of Old Peking was the title of a work by the American L. C. Arlington and the British William Lewisohn, published by Henry Vetch in 1935. More than a conventional guidebook, it described not only the city's sights but also monuments and buildings that by then were vanishing or had already disappeared. Vandalism, neglect, and the utter indifference of the authorities toward the city's rich heritage of historical monuments, as well as the cutting down of its groves of cedar and silver pine for lumber, were to blame.

> To all of us who have lived long in Peking and love it, this neglect is closely related to tragedy. Nothing can be more painful than to be the unwilling witness of the slow, but sure death, of a place one has learned to love for its quiet beauty and for the wonderful tradition that it holds.[29]

The complaint was a common one among travelers: the city was in decay, no one cared or took any responsibility for repair and restoration, and before long imperial Beijing would become another Baalbek or Nineveh.[30]

This fear of old Beijing's passing brought travelers like Acton and Sitwell and Kates to the city before, like Tokyo and Baghdad and Bombay, it should have been turned into another Manchester or Detroit, before the old civilized ways of its life changed. Nor was Chinese apathy the only villain, for beyond the city's walls waited barbarian forces, Japanese and Communist, each plotting in their own ways the old capital's destruction.[31] No one tried so self-consciously to recapture the sense of Beijing as it had been than the American George Kates, who lived there from 1933 to 1941. Although he traveled through north

China, for him Beijing was less a base for the geographical discovery of China than for an imaginative exploration of another culture before it vanished, and *The Years That Were Fat* is a long affectionate love song to a way of life already passing. Settling into a former palace, he sought— first unconsciously and then consciously—to recreate, as far as an American might, the existence of the old Chinese scholar. Yet he made no pretensions to the kind of dusty Sinology that, he wrote, tended "to make men learned rather than wise."[32] His particular reality was to be found in the daily *life* of old Beijing, with its streets and neighborhoods, rather than in the kind of academic study that would be no more than a pallid reflection of that life or in a concern with the nation's contemporary political and social problems.

Harold Acton arrived shortly after the Manchurian incident of 1931, having passed quickly through Japan, which he disliked intensely, not least because of what it was doing to China.[33] Arriving at Tanggu aboard a rusty steamer, he was elated by his first view, through clouds of dust, of the country and "awed and stupefied," as he fully expected to be, by the perfection of Beijing's imperial palaces. A trip to Shanghai, Guangzhou, and southeast Asia convinced him to return to the north, and there, overjoyed to be back in the old capital, he settled down to learn the language. Yet he never sought to detach himself so completely from the twentieth century as did Kates; for him there was "a sharp difference between Cathay and China, and with all due respect to Cathay, it was China I wished to know."[34]

"Perhaps," wrote Graham Peck—an artist as well as a writer—of Beijing, where he idled away six months after first arriving in China, "there has never been another locality so perfectly constructed for man's pleasure."[35] The city's outward appearance might be unprepossessing, with its low houses crowded together behind the drably uniform gray walls of the hutongs. But once inside the gates the scene changed; there were bright red or blue decorations on the roofs, a tree in the courtyard, and the brilliant blue northern sky overhead. Although the city was laid out according to a grand design centered on the Imperial Palace, the maze of little streets and alleys gave it a sense of life and a human dimension that Osbert Sitwell found quite different from the impersonal quality of Berlin or Hausmann's Paris. From his hotel room he could look down on a sea of gray roofs spread below him, surrounding the tall vivid islands of the Palace and the Imperial City, while beyond them the Western Hills rose blue in the distance. As the seasons changed, what had been a "bare, Breughel-like world of brown lanes, squat and narrow" became in the hot weather, "a sighing young summer forest," its gardens full of blossoms and trees, "and large earthenware bowls of goggling goldfish, engaged in their eternal skirt-dance of flowing fins and veils, while figures in the thinnest silk gowns fanned themselves beneath the tender, quivering shadow of young leaves."[36]

During those years Beijing was home not only to the usual collection of foreigners whose treaty port minds reflected their scorn for China but also to a more eccentric group of outsiders. "A rare collection," Graham Peck called them, "of diplomats, scholars, journalists, artists, fragments of defunct European and Asiatic aristocracies, traveling celebrities and celebrated travelers, semi-missionaries and ex-missionaries, curio-dealers, adventurers, and so on—." They reminded Acton of the foreigners he'd known in Florence, left free to wallow in their pet eccentricities, while the serious German Sinologists formed a set of rivalries that were "almost a repetition of those between art-historians in the valley of the Arno." Something about the city's atmosphere brought these characteristics out, wrote Peck, but eccentricity was demanding work after all, and after a while such people would sit back and relax in their tree-filled courtyards between the high gray walls of the hutongs, listening to the doves, tiny whistles attached to their wings, singing high through the air above them.[37]

Such men, at any rate, Acton found preferable to his own "intellectually constipated" compatriots, who believed that Beijing insidiously rotted the mind and spread sinister rumors about his going native (though another traveler in the 1920s noted that, while foreigners kept their distance from Chinese in the treaty ports, this was less true in Beijing). Meanwhile, he was charmed by the city's Chinese inhabitants, whose courtesy and good humor also reminded him of the Florentines. Teaching English literature at Beijing University, he admired the modern intellectuals who maintained their respect for tradition, though he suspected that Miss K'uai Chu-ping, a Somerville graduate who kept her impeccable Oxford accent, her college blazer and college slang, her dogs and her tennis racket, was more English even than he, and no doubt thought of him "if not as a mandarin in disguise, at any rate as a dago."[38] For him, as for men like Peck and Sitwell and Kates, the life of the streets held a continual fascination, and the city, with its palaces and old temples, became almost an entire country in itself to be explored. Acton even developed an enthusiasm for Chinese opera rare among foreigners, discovering in it parallels with the *commedia dell'arte* and the Elizabethan stage, "an ideal synthesis of the arts which I had always been seeking, a synthesis which only the Russian Ballet had approached in Europe." A more common view was the one expressed by his contemporary Violet Cressy-Marcks: "I believe one has to hear this music often, as with Wagner, to really love it and to understand it."[39] Wandering through the Western Hills, Osbert Sitwell came across a temple that served as haven for a group of aging eunuchs who had once been attached to the imperial palace. Together with him (and presumably David Horner, his companion on the trip) they bemoaned the dying out of true civilization in their respective lands.

> There was so much, they averred, that they wanted to ask us, and, not having expected our visit, they had not been given time to think out all their questions . . . But, did they drink tea in England? And were there still eunuchs in the Palace? No? . . . Everywhere it was the same; true civilization was dying out. Very sad . . . but they had heard that they had been recently abolished. Two years ago, an Englishman had visited them and said so: but they still survived, he had told them, in one place in London . . . in . . . a difficult word for them . . . Bloomsbury. It was, he had said, a Refuge for Eunuchs, like their own . . . How they longed to visit it, and see for themselves English ways of life.[40]

Put aside the rather heavy irony here, and there remains a sadness about these accounts, these laments for a dying civilization, reminiscent of Rosaldo's imperialist nostalgia, or Henry James's meetings with those who remembered "the blest reflection of sweetness and mildness and cheapness and ease" that had been Florence under the Grand Dukes, before its Hausmannization after Cavour.[41] It is all too easy to see them as insufferably precious, to reflect that these men, travelers and expatriates, were able to pick and choose precisely those aspects of old Beijing that appealed to them, renting their former Manchu palaces, their wants attended to by their hardworking servants. As foreigners still enjoying the old protections of the unequal treaties, they could pretend that China without cannibalism was real China, just as their English and American contemporaries, settling down in Tuscany and Umbria, could cast a selective vision over Italy, stripping the country of the less pleasant aspects of Mussolini and his Blackshirts. Their sadness remained the melancholy of outsiders, of those who, however much they sought to immerse themselves in the old life of the city, knew that it was not theirs, so that, when trouble came, they could take passage on a ship and go home.

Such a view is not entirely fair, of course. Not only because Acton, at least, spent several years teaching at Beijing University, imparting knowledge as well as learning, as he put it. But also because the audiences for which they were writing (Acton's book appeared in 1948 and Kates's a few years later) needed few reminders, after World War II, of the miseries of Chinese existence. In any case their readiness to take a selective view was hardly unique to them or people like them. Nobody would accuse Edgar Snow or Agnes Smedley of nostalgia or preciousness in their reporting on the Communists, but they too enjoyed the advantages of white skins and foreign passports, and they too could pick and choose those aspects of China they wished to see.

By the late 1930s Beijing might well seem a city that time had passed by like Florence or Venice, while Chiang Kai-shek tried to build a modern China in the Yangtze Valley. It was clear that its days of old glories were coming to an end, and not just because it was no longer the capital or because its buildings were crumbling from Chinese neglect or because of the imposition of tramcars and light poles. The real threat to Beijing's existence came from another group of foreigners, this time neither nostalgic travelers nor scholars nor expatriates. By the mid-1930s Japan's influence was growing, as Tokyo tried to detach the provinces of northern China from their already shaky allegiance to Nanjing and the Nationalists, the better to protect its new imperial holding in Manchuria. Then, in July 1937, war broke out, and within days Beijing was an occupied city. The Japanese flag, wrote Acton, "spread out like a vast wet stain of blood and pus, dripping from wherever it dangled, transforming buildings into charnel houses," and while he admired those who remained, he soon left.[42] George Kates stayed longer, and only just before Pearl Harbor did he pack up his own belongings and sail home to the United States.

Back of the Treaty Ports: The Journey to the Interior

Wherever real China might lie in the 1920s and 1930s, it was quite clear to most travelers where it did not. There was no point looking for it in Hong Kong or Hankou, Tianjin or Shanghai, or in the other large ports, where substantial foreign settlements clustered around buildings that would have hardly have seemed out of place in London or Chicago. If few travelers were apt to make the claim in so many words that they had discovered the real China, the implication of those who traveled into the interior was nonetheless clear, so that in a sense it was "not-Shanghai" or "not-Hankou" that defined this particular kind of authenticity.

Real China lay off the beaten track, and in China then it was still easier to get off the beaten track than it was in Europe. Even though you could now reach the interior without giving up Western creature comforts, by taking passage on one of the Yangtze steamers to Chongqing, for example, generally you went there precisely because you wanted to get beyond the superficial modernity of the larger treaty ports. "Behind the Veil," Elizabeth Enders called her chapter about the grim backwardness of life in Yichang as she rode the ill-fated *Robert Dollar II* up the Yangtze in the spring of 1924.[43] The interior came to represent the kind of back region Dean McCannell describes, a place behind the front put up for the tourist, a place where real truth lies, a place where the inner life and workings of the people may be found.[44] Your journey up the river took you not, as Marlow's did, away from the relative civilization of the Outer Station into the heart of darkness but, rather, away from the false civilization of the treaty ports into the heart of the land and the people. There and only there could you find the real Chinese you wouldn't meet in Shanghai, "the teeming millions," as Dundas had written a few years earlier, "who live the immemorial life of China, as distinct from the men of the coast, who rub shoulders daily with peoples thinking other thoughts."[45] Or the sorts of people you wouldn't read about in the newspapers either, whose perpetual accounts of killings and uprisings, Harry Franck complained, ignored the placid, everyday existence characteristic of most Chinese lives.[46] Even though you might be disappointed by the paucity of monuments compared with Europe or the shores of the Mediterranean, in the interior you could at least be reasonably sure of finding a life that was—or seemed to be—still unchanged. Philip Kerby called his book *Beyond the Bund,* Harold Speakman called his *Beyond Shanghai,* and after he first landed it didn't take him long to find a houseboat to carry him through the waterways of the Yangtze delta into the hinterland of eternal China.

Innes Jackson, riding the train on the eight-hour trip to Nanjing while she read Peter Fleming's *One's Company* and peered through steamed-up windows at the wintry landscape outside, found that it

The Imperial Palace at Beijing, shortly after the turn of the
century. Boerschmann, *Picturesque China,* 3.

Isabella Bird photographed the trackers who drew her boat
upstream through the Yangtze Gorges. Reprinted from Isabella
Bird Bishop, *The Yangtze Valley and Beyond,* facing 159. Grateful
acknowledgment is made to John Murray (Publishers), Ltd.

A junk in the Bellows Gorge of the Yangtze Gorges, about 1908.
Boerschmann, *Picturesque China*, 182.

A Chinese inn, typical of those described by travelers at the turn
of the century. Reprinted from Isabella Bird Bishop, *The Yangtze
Valley and Beyond,* facing 302. Grateful acknowledgment is made
to John Murray (Publishers), Ltd.

A bridge in Sichuan. Travelers greatly admired such structures. Reprinted from Isabella Bird Bishop, *The Yangtze Valley and Beyond,* facing 329. Grateful acknowledgment is made to John Murray (Publishers), Ltd.

Edwin J. Dingle surveys the Sichuan landscape from a mountaintop in 1909. Dingle, *Across China on Foot*, facing 256.

A part of the city wall of Guangzhou, about 1908. Boerschmann,
Picturesque China, 233.

Camel caravan passing a corner of the Beijing city wall in winter in the 1930s. Reprinted from Hedda Morrison, *A Photographer in Old Peking*, 21 (Hong Kong: Oxford University Press, 1985), with the kind permission of Claire Roberts.

Beijing: The Qianmen in the 1920s or 1930s, after a snowstorm. Reprinted with the kind permission of the Peace Book Company, Ltd., from Qi Fang and Qi Jiran, *Old Peking: the City and its People*, 5.

Beijing: The Qianmen in the mid-1930s. This was the city of travelers such as Harold Acton and George Kates. Reprinted from Hedda Morrison, *A Photographer in Old Peking*, 24 (Hong Kong: Oxford University Press, 1985), with the kind permission of Claire Roberts.

A *pailou* (memorial arch) at the east end of Changan Avenue in Beijing. Reprinted with the kind permission of the Peace Book Company, Ltd., from Qi Fang and Qi Jiran, *Old Peking: the City and its People*, 36.

The Shanghai Bund about 1930—to some, a sign of progress and hope; to others, no more than a piece of Western dreariness grafted onto China. Reprinted with the kind permission of Kelly & Walsh, Ltd., from *Shanghai of Today*, pl. 6.

Owen Lattimore photographed the marching Red Army in Yan'an in 1938. Reprinted with the kind permission of Professor David Lattimore, Courtesy of the Lattimore Collection, Peabody Museum, Harvard University.

was there her first real experience of China began, quite different from that she'd seen in Shanghai.⁴⁷ Only when he reached Suiyuan, after pleasantly idling away six months in Beijing, did Graham Peck feel that he'd at last come into contact with ordinary Chinese.⁴⁸ Although even in the interior the signs of change could be only too evident, and later in Chongqing he was distressed to find the stores full of imitation Western sleaze—tin thermos bottles, flimsy alarm clocks, shoddy clothes, dubious patent medicines, and the like—manufactured in Shanghai or Japan, to say nothing of a sign that promised in English, "FALSE EYES AND DENTAL PLUMBING INSERTED BY THE LATEST METHODISTS." The gadget belt, he called it.

> Just as the modern West has so far taken from China only puzzles, lanterns, and similar bric-à brac, quite ignoring those methods in the common arts of life—cooking, architecture, dress, recreation— which could be translated to good effect, so most of pre-war China had taken from the technical civilization of the West chiefly novelties of a varying degree of uselessness . . . To a Westerner it was startling enough to run across tawdry fragments of his own civilization isolated in a Chinese environment, but when the familiar objects were used as exotic details in a setting that was to the Westerner richly exotic, they gained a strikingly surrealist aspect.⁴⁹

A kind of made-in-China defamiliarization, in other words, not unlike the experience of Elizabeth Enders, who discovered a fair-haired, blue-eyed child—presumably the progeny of a foreign sailor—playing in a filthy gutter in Yichang.⁵⁰

The most prolific recorder of these explorations into the interior was the American Harry Franck. A man who had already written much about his travels in Europe and Latin America, he arrived in China in the early 1920s with his wife and child. Leaving them settled in Beijing, and, unfazed by fears of banditry or civil war, he tramped from Manchuria, Gansu, and Mongolia in the north to Sichuan, Yunnan, and the borderlands of Burma and French Indochina in the south, recording his impressions in two long books of over five hundred pages each. A plain American with plain tastes, he styled himself, "more interested in setting down a record of plain fact than of producing 'literature.'"⁵¹ Not for him the old fables of an idealized Middle Kingdom with its willow pattern world nor the more contemporary imaginings, drawn from the translations of the anachronistic profundities of Zen Buddhism, Laozi, and Zhuangzi, which promised an immediate antidote to the sterile rationality of Western thought. Franck made, instead, the traveler's classic appeal for credibility—here is what I have experienced myself, here is what I have seen and heard—and claimed for his record far more worth than all the writings of the self-styled experts or the overoptimistic missionaries and Westernized Chinese, who were hopelessly out of touch with their own country.[52]

Franck claimed to see the land and its people without sentimentality, his observer's mind uncluttered by any particular knowledge of the country's history or culture, unimpeded by the sort of intellectual or emotional baggage that might get in the way of the direct apprehension of reality. The plain facts he set forth were, of course, very much those a self-defined practical American of the 1920s might collect, just as the facts that earlier had made up Isabella Bird's truthful impression were those of a late-nineteenth-century Briton bent on spreading the gospel of progress and Christianity. But thirty years separated him from Bird. So did all the sweep of the Atlantic Ocean and all the differences between the consciously civilizing mission of the British Empire that she had represented and the assumed innocence of the isolationist and anti-imperialist America that he represented. The more than eleven hundred pages of his two volumes not only made no claims of literary merit; they were also devoid of self-reflection and pretended to make no social and political commentary or give any commercial advice. No doubt, he would have considered the desire to immerse oneself in a vanishing way of life, as George Kates did a decade later, as no more than an affected sentimentality. Yet, despite the almost unconscious acceptance of many of the easy prejudices of the day—in favor of white supremacy, suspicious of grasping Jews and superstitious Catholics—his Chinese were far from being the drab, unattractive, and undifferentiated mass that his countrywoman Eliza Scidmore had earlier found them. Indeed, their very diversity made a sharp contrast with the bland sameness of his own modern country back home.

Still, his two books had a certain preachiness to them, reminding one of Bertrand Russell's generalization that every American he met in the Far East save one "was a missionary for American Kultur, whether nominally connected with Christian Missions or not."[53] Franck was full of suggestions about how the Chinese might improve their lot, paying less attention to the ways of the ancestors, cleaning themselves up, getting rid of dirt and disease, reforesting the country (a point also made by John Dewey in his letters home from China), and wasting less good farm land on elaborate graves. "This worshipping of ancestors is all very well, if only the living could also be given a fair deal."[54] Chinese religion he found little more than a mix of idolatry and dirt, mumbo jumbo and hocus-pocus, its rituals mere pious antics, its monks hypocrites who vowed chastity but copulated with childless women. For all that, it was preferable to the unedifying, degenerate, and repulsive practices of the Mongol and Tibetan Buddhists. It was impossible, he wrote,

> to conceive of a priesthood—to use the word loosely—more deeply sunk in degradation. Not merely do the lamas live in filth and sloth, engaged only in the pursuit of their own salvation, in no way serving their fellow-men, but they are notorious libertines, moralless panderers, in many cases beggars of the lowest type . . . The higher ranks [of lamas] are in theory celibates, but no such rule actually cramps their personal desires, and the "Living Buddha" himself has led anything but a life of lonely bachelorhood. Among the rank and file of red-robed roughnecks, much the same standard of sexual morals seems to prevail as that reached by the lecherous touts of large cities.[55]

His language in such passages, with its insistence on meaningless mystification and its disbelief that celibacy might be practiced as well as preached, along with its sometimes direct comparisons with Catholicism, carried a clear echo of popular American nativism, fearful and repelled by what it perceived as superstitious priestcraft.[56]

Nowhere did Franck claim to have discovered the real China, not being given to that sort of open posturing. The clear inference was there, however, and the China he found in the interior was a China of the people (if not a People's China), a China that had been standing still for hundreds of years and showed few signs of movement. Several centuries below the West on the ladder of social evolution, his Chinese were a highly intelligent people in a state of arrested development, their ancient civilization like a frozen waterfall.[57] Yet he almost willfully ignored what evidences of modernity and change were to be found in the China of the early 1920s. He visited no schools or universities, save the Shanghai American School, which he castigated for its failure to teach either Chinese history or the Chinese language,[58] sought out none of the leading intellectual lights like Cai Yuanpei or the American-educated Hu Shi, and ignored the political leaders. His view of Sun Yat-sen's new government in Guangzhou was scathing; all that republicanism had brought was an enormous increase in the number of soldiers in the country, a curse every bit as destructive as flood or famine. Nor was sending several hundred students from the superficially Westernized treaty ports to places such as Harvard or Oxford going to make any difference.

Franck neither promised nor provided any sweeping solution to the country's ills. Nor was that his purpose, for China should be left alone to get on with its own life, hopeless as that life might seem to others. In that sense he not only drew a distinct line to separate himself from the modernizing apostles of progress among the missionaries, the journalists, the publicists, and the entrepreneurs of the treaty ports. They might join John Dewey in heralding the awakening of China, but Franck's readers would find little evidence of it in his books. Perhaps, in fact, they should take comfort from its absence.

Chinese Characteristics: Misfortune, Cruelty, and Authenticity

In Lu Xun's story of 1919, "Diary of a Madman," the protagonist, reading a book of history, finds that the words *virtue* and *righteousness* on every page act as a screen, a false front, behind which lies the stark truth that others refuse to see: China is a land of cannibalism, a land where for thousands of years men have devoured one another. Travelers like Acton and Kates might prefer not to read between the lines, taking at face value the high principles of Chinese philosophy and Chinese literature. To others, however, the dark side of the country they visited was not only evident but also served a very real purpose in their accounts. That was because it too became a proof that the traveler had penetrated to a particular kind of reality.

For the country remained a land of cruelty and misfortune (*China: Land of Famine* was the title of an American book of the 1920s).[59] Moreover, just as Chinese cities and towns might best be seen from a distance that aestheticized them, so too might misfortune become picturesque, when kept at a distance, as if a safety screen like the asbestos curtain of a theater were erected between the observer and the observed. A few days after Christmas 1878 Constance Gordon Cumming had watched a great fire burn through much of Hong Kong and had found the scene awful yet also wonderfully beautiful, "like a succession of pictures."[60] To Grace Fitkin, fifty years later, a nighttime fire made the river port of Wanxian "more beautiful then than ever before as the flames brought out the grotesque shapes of the hills behind in flashes of light which quickly faded only to appear again."[61] Dudley Buxton, arriving at Zhenjiang in 1922, found widespread destruction from a mutiny by the garrison the day before, though the foreign quarter and most of the "native town" had been saved. He did not think it necessary to inquire into the reasons, mentioning the event as if it were simply normal.[62] So, too, in the summer of 1937, after fighting with the Japanese had broken out at the Marco Polo Bridge, Graham Peck described foreigners gathered on the roof garden of the Hôtel de Pékin to watch the destruction of the town of Tongzhou by the Japanese, the terrible event showing only as "a squat, billowing column of black smoke."[63]

The aestheticization of misfortune usually depended on the maintenance of a certain physical and psychological distance from the scene. The observation and understanding of cruelty, however, demanded a diminished physical distance, even though the psychological distance must remain as great as ever. In 1904 an unknown photographer—probably but not certainly Western—took a picture in the Chinese city of Shanghai of a criminal being punished. It shows the prisoner standing inside a wooden cage, three bars on each side, and four on the corners, his hands bound to one of the middle bars. The cage is neck-high, or actually just a bit above neck-high, for its purpose is to have him stand on tiptoe as long as he can or as long as he cares to. Then, when the effort becomes too much for him and he must lower himself, he will strangle himself to death. His face, turned toward the street, with its eyes closed, gives no clear indication of whether he is still alive or not. The faces of eight others in the photograph are very much alive. Four of them are Chinese; one impassive, the others curious or fearful. The other four are Westerners.[64]

What is extraordinary, of course, is that these people should have chosen to have their pictures taken here. Moreover, this is by no means the only photograph of its type, and the foreigners here look for all the world like tourists, the sorts of tourists who stand on a clear summer day to be photographed by wives or children or friends, their figures dominating the foreground, while behind them rises a well-known landmark, such as the Temple of Heaven or the Tiananmen or, for that matter, the Matterhorn or El Capitan. Three look at the camera, as tourists in such settings do; one glances off to the left. None watches the prisoner. It must be summer, for three of them have on white linen trousers and wear white shoes, and all of them have white hats with dark bands around them. Two carry canes, though they seem strong enough to walk without them, and, though one looks slightly puzzled (part of his face is hidden), the others wear an air of sturdy self-confidence, of belonging in this city that is not theirs, this scene that is not theirs.

Why are they there? And why do they want to be recorded as having been there? A photograph can neutralize horror, reducing it to flat, two-dimensional manageable proportions. But this photograph is a horrifying one, and it must have been horrifying then, too. For chances are that, whatever may be the nationalities of these Westerners, their countries no longer allowed public executions. Or is that perhaps one of the reasons why they are being photographed here?

Some years earlier Isabella Bird's friend Mr. Bulkeley Johnson had stood at Shanghai's execution ground and there "saw one hundred heads fall in one morning."[65] Presumably, no one forced him to watch the bloody carnage, so he must have come there by choice. But, of course, it was a scene he could not have witnessed at home; the last public hanging in Britain took place in 1868. After that the Victorian authorities felt it their duty to cut off this particular form of public entertainment, for, while there might still be men and women drawn to such scenes, watching human beings being done to death by the state was no longer a fit attraction for a civilized society.

So, what had brought Mr. Johnson to the execution ground while the headsman went about his grisly work? Or why did our four Westerners, on that summer day of 1904 in the old city of Shanghai, choose to be photographed with a dead or dying criminal as their stage prop? Roughly two decades later Harry Franck found the body of a decapitated man in Zhengzhou, the head being gnawed on by dogs. A sight for the curious, he noted, but one that did little to disrupt the business of the nearby food stalls. "I suppose the crated heads were what any ladylike person would have called a 'gruesome sight,'" he wrote of another town where the remains of criminals were displayed, hung from the city gate, "but I fear they struck me as merely interesting. In China one quickly and unconsciously gets a sense of the cheapness of human life, so that things which would ruin a night's sleep at home are forgotten around the next corner."[66] In the early 1930s Peter Fleming, coming across two bandits trussed up by the Japanese in Manchuria before their execution, photographed them

> without compunction, but not without a vague feeling of embarrassment. They had only a few more hours to live; but the little I had seen and learnt of the effects of banditry was enough to dull all pity. Still, the conventional part of me found something queer and awkward in the thought that those two trussed bodies would be food for worms long before some chemist in a dark-room brought to light the figures they had cut on the threshold of death and dissolution. It was a situation which would have put Donne's muse on her mettle.[67]

The photographs later appeared in *One's Company,* the account of his first visit to China.

Cruelty and misfortune were part of China, real China, China where life was cheap, China land of famine, just as much as were chopsticks and pigtails. Here I am less interested in motives—the watching of forbidden sights—than in the way such sights served to validate and authenticate the traveler's experience. A photograph of a criminal dying a horrible death in the background while you stand in the foreground, looking at the camera, proves that you really have been to China, just as a photograph of the Matterhorn rising above its glaciers behind you proves that you really have been to Zermatt. And, just as the Matterhorn, with perhaps a few cows in the foreground, is typically Swiss, so the strangling criminal or the head strung up in its wicker crate, with perhaps a few curious onlookers in the foreground, is typically Chinese.

The cruelty of punishments and the public way in which they were carried out, as Sybille Fritzsche points out, became a symbol for the backwardness and cruelty of the Chinese themselves.[68] That was why Grace Thompson Seton, in the midst of a Guangzhou crowd in the early 1920s, found going through her head the

> visions of all the shocking things the Chinese do to their own when punishment is to be meted out,—beheaded human heads, hung on

trees in gay wicker baskets to warn the bandits of a like fate—the wooden cages by the roadside where prisoners are slowly strangled and starved to death and all the fiendishly ingenious methods of torture which the high intelligence and marvellous attention to detail of the Celestial has brought to a point which makes the activities of the Spanish Inquisition seem like child's play. Thoroughness is a Chinese trait. He is thoroughly kind or thoroughly horrid.[69]

Chapter 6

Journeys in the Present and Journeys to the Future

Modern China: The Treaty Ports and Hong Kong

What a revelation is Shanghai! . . . It's as cosmopolitan as Vienna! Wide European streets—in the center of town—branching off into rabbit lane byways. Chinese swarming the place. In brocaded coats—and coolie cottons . . . On we went. To the Native City. Narrower and funnier streets. Music Lane and Bird Street. Chinese flutes playing. And food stalls cooking right on the street.[1]

So goes the advertisement for a shipping line in 1930, allegedly an excerpt from a cruise passenger's diary. The images are the usual ones, almost banal from repetition: the *real* Shanghai, modern and cosmopolitan as a European capital, was the city built and dominated by foreigners. Within it, however, there still remained a quaint "native city," the term loaded with all its rich freight of meaning, where the tourist could see how the Chinese lived, following their time-honored customs in a kind of Chinatown set apart for them on their own soil.

Yet Shanghai was not China. Everyone—well, almost everyone—agreed on that. But might today's Shanghai be a vision of tomorrow's China? The prospect enchanted journalists and foreign residents of the city, as it did also, in different ways, the young modernizing technocrats of Chiang Kai-shek. But it left travelers uneasy. Their ambivalence toward the city's presence began as soon as their ships left the yellow waters of the Yangtze to steam up the Huangpu before mooring off the Bund. What were all those tall buildings along that famous waterfront doing right there in the heart of China? "Shanghai and Tientsin are white men's cities," noted Bertrand Russell; "the first sight of Shanghai makes one wonder what is the use of travelling, because there is so little change from what one is used to." "This is a horribly modern city and I'm sure we shall want to move on!" Elizabeth Enders and her husband decided when they landed in the early 1920s. Knowing it was not real China, George Kates spent no more than a night in Shanghai after disembarking from one of the Canadian Pacific Empresses in 1933, catching the train to Beijing the next day.[2] In their views of Shanghai's inauthenticity most travelers had not changed much since the days of Isabella Bird, who, as she reminded her readers, wanted to get out of the foreign concessions and settlements of the treaty ports as soon as possible.

Still, for most, Shanghai was unavoidable—or at least unavoided. "Every tourist's trip to China begins at Shanghai," Innes Jackson wrote in the mid-1930s. "Some end there. It is a city for tourists."[3] Unless you had entered China from the north or your ship had touched at Hong Kong, Shanghai was likely to be your first glimpse of the country. There it lay with its banks and business houses lining the Bund, China yet not China, at least not today's China, even if it might be tomorrow's. Forty-odd years later, in the 1960s and 1970s, travelers making the pilgrimage to the future revealed by Mao Zedong's People's Republic found much the same ambivalence in Hong Kong: a city of undeniable attractions, with the creature comforts of hot water, clean sheets, good food and drink, and yet because of these very factors inauthentic, a piece of leftover Occidental exoticism clinging to the edge of the vast land undergoing its radical transformation. If real China in those decades between the wars was the old China of George Kates or the interior China of Harry Franck, then real China in the years of the Maoist ascendancy was the rural landscape of the People's Communes or the smoky industrial cities of Manchuria with their huge Stalinist factories and steel mills. Today, of course, our views have changed. After Deng Xiaoping launched his economic reforms in the late 1970s, Hong Kong began to appear—both to the optimists in the Zhongnanhai as well as those in foreign corporate board rooms—not so much as a counterpoint to the real China as a beacon lighting the way to the future, and the gleaming new glass skyscrapers of today's Shanghai, its clean efficient subway, and its devotion to commerce are all proof of this. In People's Park, once a desert of asphalt like Tiananmen Square, suitable only for mass rallies hailing the all-powerful Leader, lawns and flowers have now been planted, and the polite reminders to keep off the grass bear the logo of Pepsi-Cola.[4]

"Nowhere else in the world," wrote Graham Peck after his first visit to Shanghai in the mid-1930s,

> could have existed such a city with its Oriental river-front of crowded wharves overshadowed by office buildings and battle-ships; its race-track ringed about by skyscrapers; its flimsy alleys and avenues lined with American filling-stations, Chinese temples, German pharmacies, English boarding-houses, Japanese brothels, French restaurants, and Russian garages; its multitudinous shops; its multigenerous cabarets and dance-halls, varying from glossy pavilions upholstered with plush, mirrors, and photo-murals, to tiny dives around whose dance-floors were curtained booths, and in the booths, beds.[5]

Here Chinese politicians living on graft from distant provinces gorged themselves on whisky and French pastries at the big hotels, Europeans knocked back their cocktails at the country clubs of the French Concession and International Settlement, as Chinese students chattered American slang to one another, and ragged little children stood begging on the street corners.

"And so at last to Shanghai, city belonging to no country," wrote Peter Fleming.

> You have all read before of the overbearing skyscrapers which line the Bund: of the Chinese City, which hardly a foreigner visits: of the meditative Sikh policemen, with their short carbines tucked under their arms, like men out shooting rabbits: of the shipping on the wide dirty river which, ranging from the sampan to the C. P. R. liner, reflects the whole history of commercial navigation: of the Shanghai Club, which has the longest bar in the world: of the unnumbered night-clubs, where the slim, slick Chinese girls are on the whole more popular than their Russian colleagues: of the rich Chinese, whose big cars are packed with guards against the kid-nappers: of the trams, and the electric lights, and the incessant noise, and the crowds forever promenading, capriciously suicidal (a traffic sense is not one of the lessons which the West has been able to teach the East): of the strange cosmopolitan atmosphere, in

which an American flavour predominates . . . You have all, I say, heard these things fully described before.

If you hear them fully described again, it will not be my fault.[6]

He was right, too. They had been described before. Never mind for the moment that Shanghai was also a place where ordinary people lived and worked and got ahead or fell behind, married and raised families, went to church, went to school; never mind that Harry Franck, arriving after his tramps through north China, found it about as exciting as a second-class American city like Omaha or Memphis.[7] That wasn't the Shanghai the world wanted to hear about. Books with titles like *Sin City* or *Shanghai: Paradise of Adventurers* or *Shanghai: City for Sale* played on the expected images, as more recently does Zhang Yimou's 1995 film, *Shanghai Triad.* It's tempting to say that, like the idealized China constructed by Voltaire and the philosophes or Margaret Mead's idyllic Samoa or Mao's progressive and egalitarian nation of the 1960s, even if it hadn't existed, this other Shanghai would have had to be invented.

But not for the same reasons. The virtues of those other imagined societies, like the virtues of More's *Utopia,* could be held up as a foil for Western vice and Western folly. Shanghai—this amoral city caught between the two worlds of "the Orient" and "the West" yet belonging to neither—served an opposite function. Its mythical role attracted the Western imagination because, among other reasons, it posited a world virtually without restrictions, a world set free from conventional bourgeois morality, a world of both financial and fleshly license, a world that offered every sort of amusement, every sort of vice that flourished east of Suez and west of San Francisco. In Shanghai, Christopher Isherwood wrote,

the tired or lustful business man will find . . . everything to gratify his desires. You can buy an electric razor, or a French dinner, or a well-cut suit. You can dance at the Tower Restaurant on the roof of the Cathay Hotel, and gossip with Freddy Kaufmann, its charming manager, about the European aristocracy or pre-Hitler Berlin. You can attend race-meetings, baseball games, football matches. You can see the latest American films. If you want girls, or boys, you can have them, at all prices, in the bath-houses and the brothels. If you want opium you can smoke it in the best company, served on a tray, like afternoon tea. Good wine is difficult to obtain in this climate, but there is enough whisky and gin to float a fleet of battle-ships. The jeweller and the antique-dealer await your orders, and their charges will make you imagine yourself back on Fifth Avenue or in Bond Street. Finally, if you ever repent, there are churches and chapels of all denominations.[8]

A seductive vision in short, holding out the promise of delights unimaginable at home. Yet a vision with dreadful warnings as well, warnings that travelers, unlike mere tourists and certainly unlike the Shanghai expatriates, were able to see and to understand. If Shanghai had earlier seemed a beacon of progress to travelers, after the May Thirtieth movement of 1925 and the troubles of 1927, to many British and Americans at home it became, as Robert Bickers puts it, a place of imperialist diehards, a place where Chinese, if they protested against their foreign overlords, were shot down in the streets.[9] Here was a hardbitten city of no rules, to some exemplifying the sins of the flesh, to others the sins of unbridled capitalism, a city of exploitation, where foreigners enjoyed luxuries unthinkable at home, where young men from Bradford or Pittsburgh learned to kick coolies out of the way, while penniless mill girls and rickshawmen starved in the streets, and where the Bund Gardens were said (mistakenly) to be guarded by a sign reading, "No Dogs or Chinese Allowed."[10] This view of foreign domination and exploitation largely reflected the image put out abroad by Chinese publicists after May Thirtieth and was used by the Chinese capitalists to demand a greater say in the running of the foreign settlements. In a different way it was also a view used against the same capitalists by the radical young activists of the Guomindang who sought unsuccessfully to take control of the municipal government of the Chinese city from the business interests after Shanghai fell to the Nationalists in 1927.[11]

Caught in Shanghai's sensual music, others might neglect monuments of unageing intellect, but travelers—real travelers—were different. They, at least, liked to think that they kept their moral and intellectual bearings, retaining the outsider's privilege of commenting on the exoticisms not only of the Chinese but of their own compatriots as well. For the traveler the foreign Shanghailanders thus became part of the cityscape, a kind of a minority people no less worthy of their own ethnography than the Miao or the Naxi of Yunnan Province. "People from whom one would run a mile at home," Peter Fleming wrote, but who in their native habitat, become, by virtue of their very limitations, fascinating subjects for study in the compounds of Cathay. To see how they adapt themselves to the subtle and exotic background against which their lives must now be led, to gauge their reactions to the charms and deceits of China, to examine their technique in exile—all these are preoccupations of the first interest. Most of the foreigners, of course, are interesting and amusing in their own right; but in a way it is the others—the transplanted nonentities—who are the most intriguing.[12]

While a band played Gilbert and Sullivan in the Municipal Park, Harold Acton met Galeazzo Ciano and his wife,

whose button eyes and massive jaw gave her a striking resemblance to her father Mussolini. She was trying to behave like royalty, surrounded by attentive myrmidons. Ciano himself had not yet developed into his father-in-law's ape. He was conspicuous as the youngest of all the foreign ministers, a very ordinary young Italian, not a whit different from the lounge-lizards who loitered in front of Doney's, criticizing the points of passing women on the Via Tornabuoni. Such a couple were appropriate to this garish setting and this horde of upstarts, all trained to make money as retrievers are trained to fetch game.[13]

The trope, once again, was that of the Pharisee and Publican, as travelers tried to put a safe intellectual and moral distance between themselves and the scene they were describing. Here precisely lay one of Shanghai's uses to travel writers. Unlike Isabella Bird or Harry Franck or Richard Dobson, they might not be off wandering the back roads and mule tracks of the interior provinces, staying in filthy inns and eating uncertain meals, hoping that their shivering did not presage the onset of malaria or worse. Under a chill winter sky the gray and buff buildings of the Bund might conjure up only dull memories of the Chicago or the Liverpool that the travelers had fled. But even as they looked on them or visited the famous fleshpots of Frenchtown or lay warm between the clean sheets of their comfortable beds in the Cathay Mansions, they could assure their readers that they knew what lay before them was not China's reality. That comforting knowledge set them apart not only from the casual tourists disembarking for a few days from the *Empress of*

Japan but also from all those old China hands who had lived in Shanghai for years, never setting foot beyond the boundaries of the foreign concessions and who, precisely because they thought themselves superior beings among an inferior race, seemed to incarnate the worst sins of dreary middle-class England or the middle western Babbitts of the American booboisie. Once more the travelers appealed to the reader's trust: having experienced China directly, they could place the treaty port expatriates accurately within the country's frame.

Like other myths, the Shanghai myth was by no means entirely wrong, and the outpouring of scholarship on the city in recent years has put flesh on some of these bones while stripping it away from others. Moreover, even in Shanghai, if you knew where to look, you could find China, or at least a particular kind of China. The Bund might be British and dignified or dull and soulless, but especially at night the streets leading off it, like Foochow Road or Nanking Road, were crowded, noisy, and colorful, with their restaurants and teahouses and singsong girls, the red and gold signboards above their shops, the banners, flags, and lanterns, the piercing sounds of gongs and flutes, the strange smells, and everywhere the sociable talk of the people thronging the streets. If that were not enough, the traveler could seek out the twisting narrow lanes of the old city, where, as Darwent wrote in his guidebook, "the odours are sometimes not good, but they are not nearly so bad or as numerous as is usually imagined, and ought not to daunt a traveler with any enterprise in him."[14]

Not real China, to be sure, but this mingling of East and West, this overload of physical and emotional sensations, of light, color, noise, food, drink, and sex, gave Shanghai its own peculiar authenticity, its sense of measuring up to its own myth. Ilona Ralf Sues, who had recently been working for the Anti-Opium Information Bureau in Geneva, found her particular variant of real Shanghai by tracking down the dreaded Du Yuesheng, one of the chief bosses of the Shanghai underworld, who by the mid-1930s had become director of the Shanghai Bureau of Opium Suppression, the better to control his drug empire. Both fascinating and repellent, she thought him,

> a gaunt, shoulderless figure, with long, aimlessly swinging arms, clad in a soiled, spotted blue cotton gown; flat feet shod in untidy old slippers; a long, egg-shaped head, short-cropped hair, receding forehead, no chin, huge, batlike ears, cold, cruel lips uncover-

ing big, yellow decayed teeth, the sickly complexion of an addict. I had never seen such eyes before. Eyes so dark that they seemed to have no pupils, blurred and dull—dead, impenetrable eyes . . . I shuddered . . . He gave me his limp, cold hand. A huge, bony hand with two-inches-long, brown, opium-stained claws.[15]

There could be no better place in these years than Shanghai to find this conventional Chinese villain, first cousin to Sax Rohmer's insidious Dr. Fu-Manchu a few decades earlier, or a few decades later to the equally wicked Dr. No, the half-Chinese, half-German creation of Peter Fleming's younger brother Ian.[16]

Yet, though Shanghai might briefly have provided a vision of what the country as a whole was going to become, in July 1937 fighting broke out between Chinese and Japanese troops at the Marco Polo Bridge (Lugouqiao) near Beijing, and by mid-August Shanghai itself was engulfed by war. The destructive battles around the city and the Japanese occupation of large parts of it called the whole Shanghai project into question. Then Graham Peck began to regret that he hadn't studied the scene more carefully, since Shanghai, that particular Shanghai, was slipping into the past. "To have seen it just before its downfall has something of the fascination that must accumulate about a visit to any place soon to be violently and permanently changed—analogous, say, to a trip to Petrograd in 1915 or '16"[17] (though, of course, it had not been Petrograd then but St. Petersburg, as it has once more become).

For a while the fighting itself became a tourist attraction. Robin Hyde took a conducted tour from her hotel, paying thirteen dollars for a car specially marked to avoid trouble from the Japanese.[18] Before long, however, the realization that the city's poverty and destitution were being made worse by war marked the fading of the old glamorous myths. Auden and Isherwood's *Journey to a War* faded out rather than ended with a picture of a city, conquered but still not yet entirely occupied, as the New Zealand activist Rewi Alley gave them a tour of mills and factories where children toiled under appalling conditions. Feeling guilty but with no remedies to suggest, as Isherwood recalled years later, they escaped from their social consciences on afternoon holidays, visiting bathouses, where they were erotically soaped and massaged by beautiful young men.[19] Richard Dobson, spending most of 1940 there after years of traveling the interior, tried at first to plunge himself into the city's undiminished night life as if nothing had changed. Then, however, the last British troops were withdrawn, going back home to join the European war. Almost every European in Shanghai turned out for the farewell ceremony at the race course, the Germans and Italians hardly less moved than the English at this scene of white retreat from Asia. "For the first time in its short vivid history Shanghai was to be without an English soldier. Few of us expected ever to see their ruddy countenances, majestic kilts and flawless khaki on Chinese soil again."[20]

If Shanghai provided an uncertain guide to Chinese reality, the other treaty ports were no better. Few travelers were attracted to gray and flat Tianjin, though Cook's 1910 guidebook had thought it the most remarkable of the modern settlements, noting with approval that "many old idolatrous temples have been transformed into up-to-date educational establishments," some of them for girls.[21] While historians favorable to the Nationalists might come to see in Guangzhou of the 1920s the city in which the new China was being born, to travelers at the time it seemed just another battleground between warlords with unpronounceable names. The energetic Grace Seton, already disenchanted by her examination of the new republic in Beijing, found herself in Hong Kong in January 1923, when she heard of a "revolution" taking place in Guangzhou. Despite friendly warnings that a woman should not undertake such a trip, she journeyed up the Pearl River at once to land in the midst of an altercation between Sun Yat-sen's sometime ally Chen Jiongming and his rivals. Browbeating the contending warlords and their deputies into granting her interviews, she was satisfied finally that she knew what was happening. "That was it. At last I had gotten to the solid meat of all this Revolutionary Nut Cracking, the reason why this particular Revolution and many another had been staged—the Re-unification of China." So she left, gratified by an overheard remark from the last general she had seen: "A woman and a foreign devil—yet 'clever'! How can this be!" Back in the British colony a few days later, she brought together (or at least took credit for doing so) A. G. Stephens, the *taipan* of the Hongkong and Shanghai Bank, and C. C. Wu (Wu Zhengting), Sun Yat-sen's representative, through her good offices, thus putting the British on the path of rapprochement with Sun's Nationalist revolution.[22]

Unfortunately for the historian, there is no evidence that this meeting did anything to improve the state of Britain's continuously troubled relations with the Guomindang. Nor did Harry Franck find much cause for hope in the luminaries of young China he found in Sun Yat-sen's

Guangzhou. Overrun with soldiers out of control, the merchants bled dry by high taxes, gambling, opium, and corruption everywhere, it seemed to him "most misgoverned city in China, if not in the world." Virtually everyone there had turned against Sun, his position now one "much as if Jeff Davis had entrenched himself at New Orleans and hung on until his death to a slice of Louisiana, intriguing now and then with the various factions of a divided North, occasionally plunging into Mississippi, but in the main by no means governing even the whole of Louisiana."[23]

Although by the 1930s Guangzhou had settled down, the city never attracted travelers as it had in the days of Isabella Bird and Constance Gordon Cumming. Peter Fleming thought it genuinely Chinese, at least compared to Shanghai, while the approach to the city, seen through the porthole of her river steamer from Hong Kong, provided Ilona Ralf Sues with her first glance of real China. Instead of the brown and pitiless land she'd imagined,

> what I saw was so unexpected, so unbelievably beautiful, that I held my breath. Here was no landscape, no earth, no depth of perspective; nothing but a gorgeous Chinese screen woven of opalescent pale rose-and-lavender mist; and painted onto it, in the most delicate water colors, were little huts with thatched roofs—tawny, dreamy, lonely little huts looking down upon the tawny, dreamy river below. Our boat was passing alongside this magic screen slowly, leaving millions of rose ripples behind . . . "*Gueidze, voici la Chine! As-tu jamais vu pareille merveille?*"[24]

Gueidze was the French-speaking cat who had accompanied her from Geneva; later she changed his name, which meant "Devil," or "Ghost," to something more appropriate. To Auden and Isherwood the junks lying off the city recalled Elizabethan galleons, but by then it was 1938, and they were depressed by the sight of a Japanese gunboat anchored in the river, its crew "self-quarantined in hatred, like sufferers from a deadly infectious disease."[25]

Guangzhou's foreign settlement, on the pretty but detached island of Shamian (Shameen), drew mixed reactions. Some admired its replication of England, while others dismissed it for its insularity. To Auden and Isherwood, coming on it after the architectural horrors of Colombo,

Singapore, and Hong Kong, it was one of the few places in the East where their countrymen had shown good taste.[26] But Harold Acton despised it and had little good to say about Guangzhou itself, with its pretensions to the modern and its lack of respect for the past, though its curio shops were more expensive than in the north. The landscape, already familiar to him from the paintings of George Chinnery and the early Victorian engravers, was "lush, and rococo, and rickety," making him yearn for the simple cleanliness of Beijing's setting.[27]

Hong Kong, being a colony, was even less connected to China than Shanghai or Guangzhou. To Victor Purcell, a civil servant in Malaya who had lived in Hong Kong in the 1920s, it was "a Chinese city with a strong Occidental tinge," a phrase that anticipated Chris Patten's description of it, on the eve of its 1997 handover, as a Chinese city with British characteristics. By the late 1930s, when he returned, the Central District had become a luxurious oasis, with acres of plate glass, massive signs, and neon lights, all dominated by the new headquarters of the Hongkong and Shanghai Bank, a "gargantuan symbol of money power," whose air conditioning staved off the oppressive heat outside by replicating the pleasant coolness of an English autumn day. Cheek by jowl, however, lay

> the same old thronged, dilapidated and squalid Chinese city, where washing flies like dirty bunting from upstairs windows, ducks squashed flat and torn intestines are draped for sale outside butchers' shops, Chinese sign-boards with their elegant, if often squiggly, characters obstruct the narrow pavements, coolies lie sleeping in the cloisters covering the sidewalk and everything is exactly as it has always been.[28]

For Purcell Hong Kong was not so much a vision of China's future as a place that was just different, neither British nor Chinese. The difference was apparent in watching the crowds on the Star Ferry, their behavior and well-modulated tones not so different from those one saw or heard in the London tube.

> In China proper there is terrific animation and confusion of talk, there is a sort of striving to silence a friend as an adversary with a torrent of words, there is a jostling and crushing at entrances and

exits. Here on the Star Ferry everyone, Chinese, Mecanese, English, negro, or half-caste, accepts the general tone of muted conversation, of precedence by time of arrival, and orderly dispatch.[29]

One country, two systems, in other words. Unlike some other travelers,
Purcell understood that New China, Young China, Awakening
China—whatever designation one preferred—had its own internal
logic, and that by no means all the country's progress could be credited
to foreign influences seeping in from places like Hong Kong and
Shanghai. Indeed, while Hong Kong might well be the great example of
Westernization in China, he realized that at the same time many of the
new ideas and institutions of the revolutionary years had passed the
colony by, leaving it in some ways behind the times.[30] His view thus
differed sharply from that of other travelers who, knowing less of contemporary history, were more apt to believe that China had two choices
before it: to continue its ageless sleep, like the country that Harry
Franck found in the interior, or to turn itself out in a modern dress cut
by the tailors of Shanghai or Hong Kong.

Foreign encounters with Hong Kong and the larger treaty ports
thus evoked a complex response. With their modern buildings, their
foreign settlements, their young men and women back from study, if
not in the United States or Europe, then at least in a local missionary
university, their Western approaches to business, such cities might well
be signaling a new China, a China that had finally broken with its past
and was pursuing a goal of progress long since defined by the West. In
one sense that was comforting, of course, testifying to a kind of domes-
tication (to use Spurr's word) of the Chinese, who now sought inclu-
sion within the confines of an all-embracing Western civilization.[31]
Chiang Kai-shek's conversion to the American Protestant faith of his
new wife provided spiritual evidence of this, and in the banks, business
houses, and busy harbors of Shanghai, Hankou, and Hong Kong might
be found the material evidence. The *mission civilisatrice* had not yet been
played out, in other words. China still had a long way to go and would
continue to depend on Western tutelage until, in the probably apoc-
ryphal phrase of Senator Kenneth Wherry, with God's help Shanghai
would be lifted up until it was just like Kansas City. And, not incidentally, as China became more like Us, it would range itself on Our side,
surrendering neither to the temptation to turn Red and evict the for-

eigners and all their works nor to make common cause with Japan in a new Asia for Asiatics alone.

All that might be comfort to the journalist, the missionary, the policy maker. But, for travelers seeking to penetrate to China's heart, the likeliness of the country's future being shanghaied was more threat than promise. Would the years to come really hold no better prospect than a country filled with these ponderous parodies of Western riverside architecture or second-class American cities like Omaha and Memphis? The picturesque, those qualities of foreignness, those differences that allowed Westerners to define China as Chinese, would be gradually eroded, as the influence of Shanghai and its look-alikes spread into the interior provinces. Why indeed, as Bertrand Russell had asked, would anyone trouble to visit a foreign land that looked just like home? After all, it was precisely the discovery of those Chinese differences—cruelty and misfortune among them—that allowed travelers to define themselves as men and women capable of penetrating behind the seductive veil of the modern (all those skyscrapers, those Miss Chens who preferred Wordsworth to Li Bo) to discern the country's reality. A China homogenized into faceless modernity could no longer be appropriated by travelers writing for their audiences back home; indeed, the travelers themselves would also become homogenized into the bland sameness of global tourists.

There was, however, another possibility: the discovery of a China that in the future would be both authentically modern and authentically Chinese.

China's Future: Nationalists and Communists

The relationship between chronology and authenticity is easy enough to see when it is the past that defines the real, as it did for a man like George Kates. Beijing was there, palpable, its links to history evident in the huge gray city walls and gates, in the fading green, gold, and red of the imperial palace and the blue-tiled roofs of the Temple of Heaven. Yet by the time Victor Purcell arrived, just as the great war between China and Japan was erupting in the summer of 1937, almost ten years had elapsed since Chiang Kai-shek's putative unification of the country and the establishment of the new capital at Nanjing in 1928. For that brief period before the outbreak of war—the so-called Nanjing decade—the Nationalists sought to build their own version of new China, harried as they were by Japanese encroachments in the north, by threats of communism in the south and west, and by the reluctance of the leading treaty powers, such as Japan, Britain, the United States, and France, to surrender their old privileges gracefully.

Innes Jackson, spending a year at the university in the new Nationalist capital, found her young contemporaries severed from the standards of their elders, however unclear they might be about the country's future. Admirable as it had once been, she wrote, the gentle and graceful erudition of the old scholar had seen its day, and now exercises in calligraphy or paintings of bamboo in the wind would have to give way to social and economic research and concern for the condition of the poor. The harmonious timelessness of the Confucian temple at Qufu in Shandong must not hide the fact that modern China blamed Confucianism for the country's stagnation and weakness. "There is more spiritual dynamite in the Sun Yat-sen mausoleum at Nanking, however much the comparison suffers aesthetically" (a glorified Standard Oil Station, Agnes Smedley called it).[32]

Trains, however uncertain their timetables, would still carry you into the old capital, where Kates and Acton lived, and highways were beginning to cut across the countryside. The road leading to the future was far less certain, however, and, though some travelers thought they knew precisely in which direction it led, others might find themselves on a voyage of exploration whose goal was by no means visible. The search for the future's reality also implied certain burdens placed on the travelers who undertook it and thus changed the nature of their accounts and the expectations of their readers. Paul Fussell, complaining of the slow death of real travel in the years before the second World War II, makes the point that by the late 1930s the travel book was giving way to the war book.[33] In China, however, even before the appearance of the war book, there was a pronounced shift toward what might be called the "whither China" book. Osbert Sitwell might be able to dismiss his publisher's request to write a book of pronounced left-wing views explaining China, preferring instead to dwell on the glories of a vanishing civilization. But in the 1930s Ada Chesterton came out to China with Fleet Street credentials, and she, like Gerald Yorke of Reuters and Peter Fleming, who had talked his way into appointment as "Special Correspondent for the *Times* in the Far East," owed their employers and their readers at least some observations on the politics and diplomacy of East Asia as well as some guesses about what the shape of the future might be.

Of course, there had never been a clear line of division between the pure travel book and the book analyzing the country's future prospects. But by the 1930s the question of China's direction grew more pressing, and the distinction between traveler and foreign correspondent became more and more difficult to draw. "China but a few short year ago was a fairyland of the Western mind, where fabulous dragons kept company with philosophic calm amid a populace devoted to rice-growing, the carving of ivories, and the development of exquisite lacquer," wrote Ada Chesterton in 1933, entirely ignoring decades of Western concern over the Sick Man of Asia. "And now, with terrifying velocity, she has shot into the forefront of European consciousness, stirring the troubled waters of discussion, commanding world attention."[34] China's position in the troubled decade of the 1930s certainly brought it a new kind of attention, particularly from the journalists and analysts of foreign affairs, who could make out unhappy parallels between what was happening there and events in Ethiopia, Spain, Austria, or Czechoslovakia. Here, however, we will be concerned particularly with the writings of those who believed that in their voyages through the wrack of war both civil and foreign they could catch a glimpse of this new and authentically Chinese future.[35]

For if Shanghai—dreary, parodistic Shanghai, looking more like Kansas City every day—might seem the future of a homogenized China, there were other possible Chinas whose dim outlines might now be becoming discernible by those with eyes to see them. One of them lay with Chiang Kai-shek's Nationalists, for, though their leader had seemed just another warlord back in the 1920s, he had now apparently come to stay. The second, for those either fed up with the Nationalists or whose ideological predilections led them in that direction, lay with the Communists.

For a brief period in the mid-1920s it had seemed that the two sides could work together. That vision came to an end when the Soviet missionary Michael Borodin and his allies sought to capture China's revolution for Stalin and the Comintern, and Chiang Kai-shek turned on the left in the savage and bloody *qingdang,* or purge, of the spring of 1927. By the time Peter Fleming entered China in 1933 those two contenders were fighting each other for control of China's destiny, while there was also emerging the not unlikely possibility that China's future would be determined not by them but by Tokyo. The new capital of Nanjing might offer some glimpse of the Nationalist vision, though it was a city whose importance came from a political act, when Chiang Kai-shek moved his government's headquarters there in 1928, leaving the old northern capital, now renamed Beiping, "Northern Peace," to dream of its vanished glory. Much of Nanjing had been destroyed by the Taiping Rebellion seventy years earlier, but by the 1930s the traveler could see that modern government office buildings were going up next to sprawls of mat huts. Meanwhile, Gerald Yorke found the main city gate spoiled

> by a huge flamboyant poster advertising a Chinese dental cream— an unfortunate sign of the growing influence of students returned from America. It has since been replaced by a vast map of the lost provinces of Manchuria. Like the Jews, the Chinese constantly remind themselves of their defeats. They celebrate days of humili- ation, when the shops close and even dancing-girls in the cabarets of Shanghai take a holiday. Confession rather than the correction of faults is a national characteristic.[36]

Yorke had already traveled with the Flood Relief Commission along the Yangtze and covered the brief uprising against Chiang Kai- shek in Fujian in 1933, before going off to study the classics in his Zhe- jiang temple. Hearing that Fleming was in the capital trying to find out more about communism, he went off to join him. The aims of the two men were modest; they simply wanted to visit the front lines and see the fighting for themselves, since they were convinced that no foreigner could reach actual Communist territory.[37] Communist territory, in those years before the Long March, meant the Soviet base in the moun- tainous borderlands between Jiangxi and Hunan, where the Red Armies had ensconced themselves after the debacle of 1927 and against which the Nationalists had launched a series of so-called extermination campaigns. Not until later, after the Communists had been driven from the region and established themselves far to the northwest, did the Soviet areas begin to become a site visited by adventurous travelers.

At Guling in the Lushan mountains—a hill station serving as retreat from the summer heat both for foreign missionaries and Nation- alist officials—Yorke and Fleming installed themselves in the Fairy Glen Hotel and went to interview Chiang Kai-shek. Impressed by him despite themselves, they sought his help in getting permission to go see the fighting in Jiangxi, for, as Fleming told him, China was the only country in the world whose armies were continually engaging the Bolsheviks, and the world should know about it.[38] Later they made their way to the provincial capital of Nanchang in Jiangxi, where they were provided with two interpreter guides, the willowy, vague, and intelligent Mr. Hsiao and the Harvard-educated Mr. Chen, the man whose Western-acquired tastes in cuisine and plumbing had led him to take refuge in the local YMCA. Still, the local authorities had received no instructions from the Generalissimo and did little to ease their passage to the front. "Few things take it out of you so much as trying to pin down a set of utterly unreliable people to a course of action to which they are rootedly opposed," wrote Fleming, sounding much like Isabella Bird some years earlier, "and when you have to do most of it through a recalcitrant interpreter, the strain is substantially increased."

Luck presented itself, however, in the form of an Irish Catholic mission, filled with refugees from the fighting, at which they stayed. It not only provided them with lots of good food and lots of cold beer but also, thanks to a general who had become a convert, lots of inside information about the Communists. "I have never known kinder hosts, or more unforgettable hospitality," wrote Fleming of the fathers. He and Yorke got more than food, drink and conversation, however. They also got, from the converted general, the coveted pass to Nanfeng near the front.[39] Even then, however, they never actually made it to the lines, though they did see parts of the countryside over which fighting had taken place and listened to stories of the depredations of the Reds, while Mr. Chen became more and more worried by reports of ambushes the closer they came to the fighting—"a Sydney Carton without the comfort of a Sydney Carton's convictions."[40]

In retrospect there's little to be said for the quality of their reporting on the Communists, which contained the usual mixture of fact and fiction then current. Communism was a foreign ideology that would never catch on in China. Life in the Red areas was literally a reign of terror, a belief confirmed by the testimony of local Catholic priests, who also pointed out that, from the point of view of the peasants, life under the government troops was every bit as bad.[41] Yet the Communists themselves seemed effective and honest in a nation in which such qualities were rare and fortunate in their leaders, the general Zhu De and his political advisor, "Mao Dsu Tung, a gifted and fanatical young man of thirty-five suffering from an incurable disease."[42] Still, when Fleming reached the end of his first trip to China, he found rather to his surprise that he and Yorke were now considered the "Greatest Living Authorities on Communism," of the Chinese variety, at least, interrogated by British officials both in Hong Kong and Shanghai, though Fleming, at least, had to suppress the sense that the two of them were "in some indefinable way rank imposters."[43]

Back in London, although he assured the Swiss traveler and journalist Ella (Kini) Maillart that it would be impossible for her to get to the Soviet Republic in south China, the two of them later joined forces to make their own Long March from the Chinese capital through Turkestan to India. Each wrote an account of the voyage, and Fleming's fame as a traveler was assured.[44] *News from Tartary* is one of the great travel works of the period, with all the ingredients of the classical adventure story, though told in the humorously ironic style that made Fleming one of the most popular travel writers of the period. Maillart's own account of the trip is rather more serious. I pass over them here simply because most of these accounts have to do with lands that, while lying within the national frontiers of China, formed part of Central Asia rather than China proper.

Nearly seventy years later Fleming's two books on China remain great fun to read not only for their descriptions but for the occasionally revealing passages about the conditions of life on the road.

> The traveller passes through many countries, but the world is too much with him; or, if not too much, at any rate all the time. All the time he is haggling or hustling or scheming: coping with contingencies or anticipating them. Everyone he meets, from the mandarin to the muleteer, he meets (to some extent) on a business footing. Either he wants something of them, or they want some of him; or both. Usually both. The muleteer wants higher pay; the traveller wants a quicker pace. The mandarin wants a public pat on the back; the traveller wants a passport in a hurry. All the time he is fighting a guerrilla war, a war of attrition. Truces are frequent; but they are clouded by the certainty that hostilities will soon be renewed. All the time—immediate or impending, acknowledged or unacknowledged—there is conflict, conflict, conflict.
>
> It is the same, of course, in other walks of life. The traveller is not the only one who seems to himself to have embarked on a petty,

inglorious Hundred Years' War, a dateless and unprofitable struggle. But, both for the traveller and in more sedentary though not less strenuous lives, there are moments when the dust evaporates and the heat is cooled—when for a brief interval one feels oneself translated to another world: truces unclouded by the coming war. On the top of a hill, or swimming in an unsuspected bay, or as often as not in far more unlikely, less spectacular surroundings the conviction suddenly descends that the world is a better place than one had supposed.[45]

Like those of earlier travelers, his writings were careful to maintain a distance between the observer and the observed. For him, however, the distance no longer came from a sense of belonging to a superior civilization but, rather, from his own self-confessed inability to make much sense out of what he was seeing. If for Fleming—or at least for the narrator of *One's Company* and *News from Tartary*—China remained something of a joke, the joke was less on the country than on the bemused traveler himself, who, as he passed through it, was always aware that his credentials as reporter promised more than he was going to be able to give.

Even so, in retrospect the humor that was so much part of Fleming's style can sometimes ring a little thin. When all was said and done, his China in many ways seemed little changed from the land depicted by the travel accounts of several decades earlier, its modern ways, modern buildings, modern armies no more than exotic growths on a country that in all likelihood was going to stay stagnant and backwards for years to come, neither Yellow Peril nor Awakening Dragon. If not perhaps the hopeless country of Elizah Scidmore, there was much about it that still had the aspect of a comic opera land whose quirks and oddities became grist for the writer rather than deserving any respect or sympathy in themselves. In this sense Fleming was far more like some contemporary travel writers than the serious-minded Victorians such as Isabella Bird.

In any case Fleming the Communist expert was about to be upstaged. In 1936 the young American journalist Edgar Snow traveled to the northwest, reaching Mao Zedong's headquarters in Baoan, where the exhausted remnant of the Red Armies had temporarily fetched up after being driven from Jiangxi by the Nationalists and after enduring hardship upon hardship during their Long March to Shaanxi.

It's no exaggeration to say that *Red Star over China,* appearing in 1938 just as China was suffering under Japan's onslaught, changed virtually overnight the views of Chinese communism held by those in the West who even knew such a thing existed, while introducing others to a phenomenon of which they'd never heard. Peter Fleming might have thought himself the first Westerner to visit the battlefront against the Reds in Jiangxi, but Snow was the first actually to go to the headquarters of the Communists, interview Mao and his colleagues, and come back to tell the tale. In doing so, he produced not only a piece of reportage, which one of his biographers calls probably the greatest book by an American foreign correspondent in the twentieth century[46] but one of the great travel books of its time as well.

For, though *Red Star* is usually read as political reportage, it had much in common with other classic narratives of travel. Snow's account was above all the tale of a quest, unfolding to the reader the story of a voyage of discovery. It was an adventure story—or, rather, two adventure stories: one about Snow and the perils through which he passed to reach Baoan; the other and greater, the heroic tale of the Long March, that modern Exodus in which Mao had led his people out of slavery into the Promised Land. The tone was set immediately in the first chapter, with its long list of questions as yet unanswered and dangers as yet unencountered, heightening the anticipation of things to come and promising the classical juxtaposition of an inner with an outer journey. *Red Star* had about it, too, a sense of certainty that set it off from the accounts we've looked at earlier. In it there were few self-deprecating and self-questioning "warnings to the reader" of the kind Fleming or Yorke had put in their books, none of the ironic self-mocking about stereotypes found in Speakman's account. Nor was there the same hesitancy the reader found in those books about China's future course. *Red Star* was thoroughly imbued with a confident optimism, and by the end of the book it was clear that Snow had reached the goal of his quest and that his passage from White into Red China had led him into a kind of Eden.

No Shangri-la or Never-never land, however, this Red utopia was very much in the world, concerned with the world's problems. Whatever else it might be, Snow's China was no mystery, unfathomable to the Western mind and unchangeable by Western means. In their aspirations, their outlooks, and their values, the Chinese—at least the *good* Chinese—were essentially little different from enlightened Westerners. Here the book set a pattern that would become common in the forthcoming years, when Britain and America found themselves China's allies against the Japanese onslaught. Beyond that, this picture of a new China, whose inhabitants seemed so much like Us, would continue among some of those who made the pilgrimage to the New China after 1949, at a time when the country, bravely facing the future, appeared to be hemmed in by a coalition led by an irrationally hostile United States.[47]

Of course, Snow was by no means the first traveler to go to China and find what he was looking for. Unlike the others, however, the tale he told on his return was a new tale, or at least new to most of his readers. "There had been perhaps no greater mystery among nations," he wrote, "no more confused an epic, than the story of Red China," for it had been isolated "by a news blockade as effective as a stone fortress," and its territory was "more inaccessible than Tibet." No one, it was thought, could possibly enter the Soviet territories and return alive; "such was the strength of years of anti-Communist propaganda in a country whose press is as rigidly censored and regimented as that of Italy or Germany."[48] Note the associations here. Germany and Italy were obvious enough analogues for the China of Chiang's Nationalist dictatorship, and the choice of Tibet could hardly have been fortuitous, with its Western-created sacred landscape, its very name carrying with it a whole freight of associations and disembodiments.[49]

> It is true there were risks involved . . . [and] I had little to cheer me on my way. Nothing, in truth, but a letter of introduction to Mao Tse-tung, chairman of the Soviet Government. All I had to do was find him. Through what adventures? I did not know. But thousands of lives had been sacrificed in these years of Kuomintang-Communist warfare. Could one foreign neck be better hazarded than in an effort to discover why? I found myself somewhat attached to the neck in question, but I concluded that the price was not too high to pay.
>
> In this melodramatic mood I set out.[50]

There is an echo of a contemporary irony, to be sure, but it was now carefully muted. *Red Star* was didactic, intentionally so as befit the most important of the "whither China" books of the period. If the work's optimism was one explanation for its enormous popularity, the appeal to the reader through the use of common stereotypes was another, for *Red Star*, while describing a phenomenon new to most of its readers, nevertheless participated fully in the hallowed traditions of travel writing and reportage out of which it came. The story embraced two Chinas and used two modes of representation. White China was the China of Chiang Kai-shek, the China of the treaty ports and foreign settlements, the China known through books and newspapers and the *National Geographic*. Yet there was another China, too, and even before his trip Snow had heard of it. For, while he and his wife had been living in Beijing, rather than restricting themselves to the placid and semi-Westernized circles bounded by the Legation Quarter's little world of whisky and soda, polo, tennis, and gossip, they had been teaching journalism and participating in the great student demonstrations of December 1935 against Japan's encroachments in northern China. Other foreigners might be pleasantly unconscious of the life going on behind the city's great walls, but Snow drew a clear line between himself and them, and it was with the departure from the old capital that the account of his journey began.[51]

It was a journey built on contrasts: first, the obvious contrast between White and Red China; and, second, the contrast in Snow's own use of two different languages in his descriptions of them. For, in writing of White China, he fell easily into the classical discourse of Orientalism. "Many of the worst rogues, scoundrels and traitors," he warned his readers, "have climbed to power under cover of respectability, the putrid hypocrisy of Confucian maxims, and the priestcraft of the Chinese classics . . . and all this is still more or less true today."[52] There were the conventional references to comic opera armies, and his scornful dismissal of traditional Chinese theater was worthy of the Shanghai mind at its best (or worst), as he praised the Red theater for having

the advantage of being emancipated from cymbal-crashing and falsetto-singing, and of dealing with living material rather than with meaningless historical intrigues that are the concern of decadent Chinese opera . . . Guests at the Red Theatre seemed actually to *listen* to what was said: a really astonishing thing in contrast with the bored opera audience, for in China opera-goers chiefly spend their time eating fruit and melon seeds, gossiping, tossing hot towels back and forth, visiting from one box to another, and only occasionally looking at the stage.[53]

One wonders, in reading such strictures, whether *Julius Caesar* or *Don Carlo* might also seem "meaningless historical intrigues." Yet such a Western view of Chinese music was commonplace, of course; Harold Acton was exceptional in his appreciation of the form.[54] Above all, when Snow talked of a China awakening now after "two milleniums of sleep," he signaled his continuing participation in that enduring representation of China going back to Hegel and Marx and echoed by countless others of a country with a long past but no history, the meaningless dramas that were the stuff of Beijing opera taking the place of the grand narrative of progress defined by the West.[55] Indeed, China's timelessness, its ahistoricity, seemed mirrored in the landscape of the northwest, a landscape where "there are few genuine mountains, only endless broken hills, hills as interminable as a sentence by James Joyce, and even more tiresome."[56]

The phrase, incidentally, was excised from later editions. Mary Louise Pratt has suggested that, when Western travelers write this way, what they really mean is that they no longer control the landscapes upon which they look and thus seek to deny them both history and variety.[57] For a man like Edgar Snow such a judgment seems unlikely, to put it mildly. Rather, his unconscious complicity with this kind of Orientalism serves to emphasize his real point: that there was another China besides this one, a China that at long last was awake, at long last distancing itself from the formless past of tradition to enter real history. In saying this, of course, he was not alone. What set him apart was his insistence that, despite all the Nationalist propaganda, all the treaty port clichés and the missionary optimism, history was going to be made not in Shanghai or Nanjing but in the Soviet areas.

There was more than a touch of Eric Ambler—particularly the Eric Ambler of Popular Front days—in Snow's description of the way he set out on his forbidden voyage. A letter arrived written in invisible ink, and a clandestine meeting in Beijing led him to a hotel room in Xi'an to wait for a man known only as "Wang." What arrangements were made remained secret.

To state precisely the manner in which, just I had hoped, I did pass the last sentry and enter no-man's-land, might incur serious difficulties for the Kuomintang adherents who assisted me on my way. Suffice it to say that my experience proved once more than anything is possible in China, if it is done in the Chinese manner. For by seven o'clock the next morning I had really left the last Kuomintang machine-gun behind, and was walking through the thin strip of territory that divided Red from White . . . It was a farewell to my last link with the White world for many weeks to come. I had crossed the Red Rubicon.[58]

By now, though, Snow's reader was still in what the map called "China," of course, the frontier had been penetrated, the act of transgression taken place and the secret crossing made. But into what? All possibilities still lay open, and the reader was still quite at liberty to believe in Guomindang propaganda about the Red bandits, though admittedly it would be a remarkably obtuse reader who did so. The division between Red and White was more than a division between two Chinas; it was a division between two entire worlds.

It was a division also between two modes of representation, and the difference was evident immediately in the shift in language that Snow employed to describe the people he met. Rather than the "rogues" and "scoundrels" who had governed China in the past and continued to govern the White China of the day, Snow met men (and sometimes women) who embodied all the sorts of qualities advanced Westerners would recognize and admire. A Red agent wearing a White uniform in Xi'an (he turned out to be Deng Fa, one of those who eased Snow's frontier passage) was a man with a pair of "intense eyes," which sparkled, a "mischievous grin" on his "bronzed face," a "grip of iron," and a "pantherish grace" with a "lithe limberness in his movements." One look at him was enough to show that "that the uniform was a disguise, that this was no sedentary bureaucrat, but an out-of-doors man of action."[59] Clearly, no official from the Confucian past or the Nationalist present would have been capable of such qualities—and, presumably, among such men it was no longer necessary to do things "in the Chinese manner."

The discoveries continued as Snow pushed farther into this new land. A young farmer, chief of the Poor People's League, was "a good-looking young man, with fine bronzed skin and good white teeth. He did not seem to belong to the race of timid peasants of China elsewhere. There was a challenge in his sparkling merry eyes and a certain bravado." Zhou Enlai, "as much a legend as a man," had about him "a kind of magnetism" and was "evidently that rarest of all creatures in China, a pure intellectual in whom action was co-ordinated with knowledge and conviction. He was a scholar turned insurrectionist." The military commander Peng Dehuai was "a gay, laughter-loving man," with "something open, forthright, and undeviating in his manner and speech"[60] (thirty years later, in the Cultural Revolution, that forthrightness would cost him his life). And, of course, there was the "gaunt, Lincolnesque" Mao Tse-tung himself, with his "lively sense of humour and a love of rustic laughter . . . He appears to be quite free from symptoms of megalomania, but he has a deep sense of personal dignity, and something about him suggests a power of ruthless decision when he deems it necessary."[61]

> Mao was a man already worthy of a book. But how to describe him?
>
> How can I select, from all the wealth of unexploited, unknown material a few hundred words to tell you about this peasant-born intellectual turned revolutionary?
>
> Do not suppose, first of all, that Mao Tse-tung could be the "saviour" of China. Nonsense. There will never be any one "saviour" of China. Yet undeniably you feel a certain force of destiny in him. It is nothing quick or flashy, but a kind of solid elemental vitality . . . Mao Tse-tung may possibly become a very great man. But I do not intend to pronounce the verdicts of history.[62]

The leaders of White China, as Snow had described them, lived with a motley assemblage of wives and concubines—though Chiang Kai-shek's divorce had been blessed by Protestant missionaries so he could marry the rich and glamorous Methodist Song Meiling.[63] Communist family values, however, were virtually indistinguishable from those of middle America, such as the readers of the *Saturday Evening Post,* for which Snow occasionally wrote. There in Baoan, Mao lived happily with his wife, the courageous He Zinian, who had been wounded as she accompanied her husband through the terrible ordeal of the Long March, and just before Snow's departure the couple become the proud parents of a baby girl. This, of course, was before the Shanghai actress Jiang Qing had arrived to enchant the Chairman and to see Mrs. Mao packed off to Moscow. As Snow sat interviewing Mao, his wife stood in an adjoining room, making a compote of wild peaches, and, though by two in the morning Snow found himself exhausted, she and her husband were both still wide awake.

> Suddenly both of them bent over and gave an exclamation of delight at a moth that had languished beside the candle. It was a really lovely thing, with wings shaded a delicate apple-green and fringed in a soft rainbow of saffron and rose. Mao opened a book and pressed this gossamer of color between its leaves.
> Could such people really be thinking seriously of war?[64]

Here in Baoan, Snow had left behind the old China of the Orientalists to enter a new land, described in admiring terms, not least because its good qualities were those his Western readers would like to recognize within themselves. Soviet China was a China marked by hard work, enthusiasm, egalitarianism, and a practical knowledge quite unlike the desiccated intellectualism of traditional Confucianism and the "priestcraft" of the classics (Confucius has been accused of many things, but priestcraft, with its particular resonances for a Protestant and secular West, is not usually one of them). Here was a "brotherhood of Chinese revolutionaries," in which there was "some force that levelled out individuals, lost them, made them really forget their own identity and yet find it somehow in the kind of fierce freedom and rigour and hardship they shared with others," a quality that was "improbable . . . if you know China."[65]

"If you know China." Red Star's Communists, in short, were attractive precisely because, unlike White China's Nationalists, they were not "Chinese." Familiarization, as we have met it before in Dingle and Bird gazing on Yunnan's Alpine landscapes or Gordon Cumming washing her face in the dews of a Zhejiang May Day, was at work again, the foreign and dangerous being brought into the safe compass of the known and the understood. The difference, of course, was that, while earlier travelers had usually done the trick with scenery, Snow, and some who followed him, did it with people, a people who no longer blocked the view over an aestheticized landscape but were a natural part of it. Snow's White China was little different from that of Eliza Scidmore or Mary Gaunt, a land lending itself to all the old stereotypes of colonial and Orientalist discourse. But Red China was represented in terms familiar to the progressive consciousness of the 1930s, and the result was to suggest that there was little dividing Us from Them or at least from the Chinese of this particular China. Just as in Beijing you could see ancient China while enjoying all modern conveniences, so in Baoan you could both go native and still keep the best of progressive Anglo-American ideas.

Red Star consequently differed from much other travel writing of the period in its irrepressibly optimistic view that, whatever the treaty port mind might believe, there was no fixed and unchangeable Chinese character, no essentialized Chinese. Others too, particularly journalists and missionaries, had discovered a new China before Snow. But for them it was to be found in the modern centers of business and commerce like Shanghai or Hankou, in the foreign run educational institutions such as St. John's or Yenching or the Peking Union Medical College, in a new China led by Chiang Kai-shek (*Time's* Man of the Year in 1937) and his charming, Wellesley-educated wife. Snow broke entirely with such easy assumptions. His view of China's future embraced no such Westernizing circles but, rather, saw the development of new kinds of people, many of them completely untouched by the West yet nevertheless, through their leaders, unconscious bearers of Western values, in one of the most backwards and desperately poor parts of the country.

Yet perhaps Snow—in a way unknown to him at the time, of course—was treading on dangerous ground in ascribing to his subjects in Baoan all those characteristics that his American and British readers would recognize and admire. For more recently some have argued that, if travelers and reporters obliterate differences that do in fact exist, perhaps ultimately—in a well-meaning but nonetheless patronizing way—they appropriate to their own cultures and their own causes those who are powerless to respond. In 1927, for example, an American missionary managed to claim China's republican revolution for his own country—"it was no Chinese who overthrew the Manchu dynasty, but three Americans—George Washington, Thomas Jefferson, and Abraham Lincoln!"[66] More recently, David Spurr has found Susan Sontag guilty of "discovering" North Vietnamese who embodied all the American virtues, claiming that her attitude betrays nothing less than the desire for a kind of imaginative colonization of Vietnam "as an outpost of classical *American* values, free from the Southern or Indian influences of the sensuous, exotic East," and thus falls into what Lévi-Strauss calls "ethnocentrism thinking itself anti-ethnocentrism." In such a reading *Red Star* participates in the tradition of Pratt's "anti-conquest narrative," using European bourgeois "strategies of representation" to secure the writer's own innocence while simultaneously asserting a Western hegemony.[67]

Perhaps. Although it does seem odd to suggest that Snow was using a bourgeois strategy of representation to engage in an imaginative colonization of China. Indeed, his enemies would later fault him precisely for the opposite reasons, claiming that he hid the communism of the Chinese to play up their supposed democratic virtues.[68] Yet, if he had insisted more strongly on the differences separating Mao and his followers from American and British progressives of the day, not only might his book have failed in its purpose, but later critics would find him guilty of perceiving a world divided by an unbridgeable opposition between the West and its Other.

Be that as it may, in Mao's Baoan, Snow had discovered a Chinese reality that was both un-"Chinese" and, while owing little to the West, was imbued with a sense of optimism and dedication that had strong Western resonances. It was a discovery, too, that helped bring to birth a new tradition. Just as early Christian travelers from the West—so Eric Leed and others have written—"manufactured" the Holy Land in the fourth and fifth centuries, editing and repackaging it as a center of philosophical travel for believers,[69] so Snow and those who came after him on the later pilgrimage to Mao's new headquarters at Yan'an sacralized it, helping make it the holy site that it would remain until after Mao's death.

Chapter 7

War Books

Conditions of Travel

Wherever may be the line that divides the territory of the travel account from reportage—the "whither China" books—the writings of the 1930s began to cross it. Snow, no doubt, thought of himself more as correspondent than traveler, and Ada Chesterton, Peter Fleming, and Gerald Yorke all carried journalists' credentials. Even *News from Tartary*, despite its disclaimer of any useful purpose, found it necessary to justify its existence by the wish to investigate reports of increased Soviet activity in far-off Xinjiang.[1] Such books had a tone different from the accounts of the 1920s, for they were written against the background both of civil war between Nationalists and Communists and the increasing threat of a Japanese domination of China. Fleming, in fact, had his first taste of fighting in watching what the Japanese called antibandit operations in their new Manchurian puppet state in 1933. Nor was he entirely unfavorable to the Japanese at that point, finding their work generally progressive, even though the atmosphere in the capital of Xinjing (Changchun) was "too thick with humbug for comfort," the Japanese laying claim to all kinds of virtues they did not have.[2]

With his two books, published in 1934 and 1936, Fleming on China had become famous. Innes Jackson read *One's Company* to learn about the country as the express carried her from Shanghai to Nanjing in 1936.[3] An exhausted Robin Hyde, given breakfast by the British consul's wife after she arrived in Hankou in April 1938, looked enviously at the empty bed in the guest room, "almost sacred because Peter Fleming had slept in it" before he had gone off to the front.[4] Auden and Isherwood met him at the British ambassador's residence with his wife, the actress Celia Johnson. "Fleming, with his drawl, his tan, his sleek, perfectly brushed hair, and lean good looks," wrote Isherwood, "is a subtly comic figure—the conscious, living parody of the pukka sahib. He is altogether too good to be true—and he knows it." Joining forces to observe the fighting in central China, they found the Fleming legend accompanying them "like a distorted shadow. Auden and I recited passages from an imaginary travel-book called 'With Fleming to the Front.'" Later Auden summed up their expedition: "'Well, we've been on a journey with Fleming in China, and now we're real travellers for ever and ever. We need never go farther than Brighton again.'"[5]

In his writing Fleming assumed the role of the accomplished amateur—a person pretending to no particular skills or specialist's knowledge, both interested and amused by what he was seeing, skeptical and self-doubting, yet making light of difficulty and danger and always capable of rising to or at least muddling through their challenges. Even the Japanese invaders, at least before their main drive into China in 1937, became figures of fun. He described, for instance, the way Père Conrad, a Belgian missionary in Manchuria, abandoned his French when he realized a Japanese agent was eavesdropping and broke into Chinese, alternately giving the Japanese the warmest praise and the most virulent abuse. "Il faut surtout les déconcerter, ces petits Japonais," he remarked after the spy had vanished. "Ce n'est pas très difficile, enfin."[6]

Yet the air of detached levity that Fleming cultivated left little room for a sense of the tragedy that was overtaking the country as war drew closer. Suppose that he had been writing about subjects closer to home, rather than the distant country of *Turandot* or *The Land of Smiles.* Would the tone have been different? Imagine *Homage to Catalonia,* for example, treating the events in Spain as somehow all part of an enormous joke. Much modern travel writing, of course, reflects the presence of what Pratt calls sentimental narrators, who place in the foreground their own identities rather than those of the lands and peoples among whom they travel. But in the face of tragedy, or even mere misfortune, such an approach too easily becomes an act of self-absorption. What was significant about the Vietnam War, for example, was what it did to the Vietnamese rather than what it did to the aesthetic sensibilities of some of those foreign visitors who wrote about it.

Before Pearl Harbor travelers from America and Europe were still officially neutral, and the war between China and Japan still undeclared, so that they could not be prevented—officially, at any rate—

from traveling in Japanese-occupied as well as unoccupied China. Furthermore, they continued to enjoy, on paper at least, the privileges of extraterritorial protection to which they were entitled under the unequal treaties. "Foreigners must be utterly exasperating to the Japanese military," wrote Joy Homer, "rather like having someone's else [*sic*] children in their home who cannot be disciplined or even ordered about. We are so annoyingly outspoken in demanding our rights, so gloriously eager to complain to Washington or London."[7] Not in Japan's puppet state of Manchukuo, however, for there, the Australian Frank Clune complained, since the United States and Britain and France had stubbornly refused to recognize the new nation, there was no such protection to be had.[8]

As the war moved inland after the late summer of 1937 and cities and rail lines came under Japanese attack, the difficulty of moving about increased, leaving the traveler more dependent than ever on chance and unscheduled trips by bus, by truck, and occasionally by aircraft. Clune himself was not particularly affected, but then he never strayed beyond occupied China. Sent by the Australian Broadcasting Commission in the spring of 1938 to visit Japan and China and prepare a series of radio talks, he wrote a book of such stunning inaccuracy (Shintoism a form of Buddhism, Confucius confused with Zhuangzi, Whampoa with the Huangpu, the dowager's marble boat somehow magically transported from the Summer Palace twelve miles east to the Forbidden City, for example) that one wonders how it ever came to be published. Perhaps, like Ilona Ralf Sues, he thought it better to keep an open mind by not reading up too much on the subject before he went. He also developed a great admiration for the way the Japanese were making the Manchurian wilderness blossom; the South Manchurian Railway, then the spearhead of Japanese economic penetration, with its smooth roadbed and luxurious passenger cars, put Australia's nineteenth-century trains to shame, while the new skyscrapers rising in the capital of Xinjing showed what a properly built Canberra might have been like.[9]

For others the dislocations of war brought changes of plans and made necessary new itineraries and new modes of entry into the country. Victor Purcell, on his way to Beijing as the fighting broke out in the summer of 1937, found his P & O liner ordered not to touch at Shanghai and so had to disembark in Hong Kong, instead. In Guangzhou he met Mr. and Mrs. "Edwards" ("I'm sure he will not mind my calling him Edwards," he said of the thin disguise he threw over I. A. Richards and his wife, Dorothea Pilley), who, driven from Beijing by the fighting, were on their way to a stretch of mountaineering in Yunnan. Together they flew to Changsha, there to be joined by the British poet "Dudley" (the critic William Empson, presumably), who had been on his way to take up a teaching position at Beijing University before the fighting started, and what had been planned as a trip to the north became instead a tour of the southern provinces. A few months later Robin Hyde, arriving from New Zealand on her way to London by the Trans-Siberian, had planned to spend no more than a day in Hong Kong, but the war delayed her ship to Kobe, and, fascinated by what she saw around her, she decided to stay. Eventually, she spent several months in China, observing the war from occupied Shanghai, from Guangzhou and Hankou, and ultimately found herself in Xuzhou when it fell to the Japanese. Joy Homer, sent by the Interdenominational Committee for China Relief, landed in Shanghai in December 1938 and boarded a Chinese ship with a German name, which would carry her through the mine-infested waters off Wenzhou, before she made her way overland behind the Japanese lines and into the interior. Returning to China on his second trip, in the spring of 1940, Graham Peck had planned to go from Hong Kong to Indochina by sea and then on to China by train. But the French, on the verge of surrender at home, suspended their shipping services, and so he joined forces with an elderly Texan missionary, who, with the help of a gang from Macao, was smuggling a cargo of Chinese virgins through the Pearl River delta by night (their families had decided they'd be safer in the interior "even though they weren't pretty").[10]

Purcell's return to China had originally grown out of his interest in the Basic English then being championed by I. A. Richards in Beijing. In southern China he and his companions found the war still no more than a distant rumble, for, while the Japanese were overrunning large parts of the northeast, that summer of 1937 they were being fought to a standstill by the Chinese defenders of Shanghai and had not yet begun their drive up the Yangtze. In Changsha his party was introduced to a vice minister—of what he never said—who was on his way in a caravan of cars down to the border of Indochina and who invited the foreigners to join him. Two of the automobiles were camouflaged, one with some skill, but the other reflected an amateur effort that "would not have deceived the youngest Japanese aviator." Still, the war had an effect on them, for, while the vice minister was in a hurry to push on to Guilin, Mr. and Mrs. Edwards insisted they take time to climb to the summit of the sacred mountain of Hengshan (Nan Yue). The vice minister accordingly arranged for the hire of chairs, only to discover that the foreigners spurned them.

> "We don't want chairs," Mrs. Edwards said. The idea that she, the conqueror of the Alps, the Pyrenees, the Rockies, the Himalayas, the Karokoram, and the Hindu Kush, should permit herself to be carried up a mole-hill of 4600 feet was insupportable to her.
> "Certainly not," echoed Edwards.
> Dudley didn't want a chair either. I said I didn't want one, though I was a bit wistful all the same.[11]

Later Purcell temporarily left the party, making his way down to Liuzhou, only to discover that, because of the bombing of Guangzhou, Chinese ships were no longer running to Hong Kong. So, there he waited, rejoining the others before crossing the frontier into Indochina, there to board a French train, which, despite its shortcomings ("the liquid soap machine that made a greasy mess, the grisly little wash-basin, the funny etceteras"), showed them that, "however much we might admire the Chinese we were, so far as flesh-pots went, still very much Europeans. And for the first time in weeks we got a cold beer."[12]

The fighting still far to the north that summer provided little more than a background color to Purcell's book, for, where there were no battlefields and no bodies shattered by Japanese shellfire or air raids, it was difficult to remember, he wrote, that one was in a country at war.[13] In some ways *Chinese Evergreen* could be seen as one of the last of the classical Chinese travel narratives, combining as it did the gently ironic tone of the twentieth century with observations on the country informed by a knowledge of many years. Other travelers, closer to the action, faced more serious dangers. The rail line from Guangzhou to Hankou had already been subjected to bombing when Auden and Isherwood traveled along it in 1938, trying to read *Framley Parsonage* and *Guy Mannering* to pass the time. Later they continued to Zhengzhou, where the gutted railway station reminded them of Ypres in 1915.[14] After leaving Hong Kong, Robin Hyde also made her way up along the same line to Hankou, sharing a sleeping compartment with a married couple and another man. Although in Hankou she found a wharfside sign that still read "To Shanghai," by then the river steamers were no longer running, and the trip could only be made by a two- or three-day train ride back down to Guangzhou, another train to Hong Kong, and then three days by ship up the coast.[15] Hyde, in fact, was to have perhaps the most extraordinary journey of all these travelers. Making her way as a journalist to Xuzhou, the crucial rail junction in northern Jiangsu, she helped with relief work as the Japanese closed in on the city and was the only journalist there when it fell to the imperial armies on 19 March 1938. Then, despite her own shock and her own injuries, she managed to make her way by foot, by mule, by wheelbarrow, and, eventually, by Japanese military train to Qingdao, where the British consulate offered an asylum long enough for her to recover before continuing her interrupted journey to London.

Two years after Purcell's visit, in a Guilin no longer spared by the war, Joy Homer watched a Japanese air raid taking place just as a munitions train was being loaded. As boxcars filled with shells began exploding, a locomotive, running the gauntlet, hooked itself up to seventeen boxcars filled with dynamite and pulled them to safety before the explosions reached them—"It takes a special kind of spine to be a railroad man in China."[16] Near the Yellow River front in 1941, Graham Peck boarded a train that included some new European *wagons-lits*, delivered just before the war.

> These immense cars might move over an uneven single track, stopping at the mud huts of village stations, but their interiors, gleaming with mirrors, tropical-wood veneers, and chromium fittings would have caused paroxysms among the foreign thing-worshipers on the South Bank of trainless Chungking. All the fine coaches were used in a deluxe "Special Fast Express" which, because of the extra weight of the imported cars, was the slowest train on the line.

If the Express stood as a metaphor for the all the contradictions of Nationalist China at war, reality returned when he had to change to another train that would carry him to Luoyang. Made up of converted cattle cars and decayed passenger coaches whose broken windows had been boarded up, while dim vegetable oil lamps provided a feeble light, this one reminded him that he had returned to the "neglected, partly dismantled outer wastes of Kuomintang China."[17]

On the other hand, it was not the war that caused Violet Cressy-Marcks to come in through Burma. Rather, because she hoped to visit the Communist areas, she thought this mode of entry might be less likely to inspire Nationalist curiosity.[18] Eileen Bigland chose the same route because she wanted to see the new Burma Road and in fact was startled to discover a Chinese official in Rangoon who assumed she had come to write about the war. Sounding as if such a thought had never occurred to her, she tried to tell him she'd always wanted to travel through China, mumbling

> disjointed phrases about Waley's translations, the picture of the "Earthly Paradise" in the British Museum, Confucsionism [*sic*] and the ceramic art of the Ming dynasty. "I suppose," I ended feebly, "I really wanted to see your people because they are so much older than any other civilized race."[19]

Not until she had crossed the border on her way to a Chongqing about to fall victim to Japanese bombardment did the reality of the fighting catch up with her.

Their War and Our War

To Paul Fussell the travel books of the late 1930s—bitter, rabidly ideological, and preachy—are a sad reflection of those that had come earlier.[20] Certainly at that point, the whither China question, though it had always formed a self-consciously utilitarian backdrop to travelers' accounts, now began to move to the foreground. Wartime travelers became of necessity reporters on China's situation, drawn into a concern with politics and China's strategic importance that earlier they might have ignored. Even when assuring their readers they had no qualifications for doing so, they nevertheless began more and more to trespass on the sphere of the journalists, drifting across vaguely demarcated professional frontiers into those lands not quite their own. Auden and Isherwood, for example, found their long shipboard voyage from wintry London to tropical Hong Kong passing almost like a dream, but, once arrived, they immediately woke into their roles as "adult, if amateur, war-correspondents," anxious not to disgrace themselves as they entered on the scene of their duties.[21]

As Dundas had warned his readers when his two volumes on China appeared in 1908, entertaining travel accounts might be all very well for placid times, but they had to give way when there were more serious matters to be examined. The crisis of war meant that readers had different questions and expected different answers. Such demands undercut the peculiar authority that travelers had always claimed. Promises to set down a direct and unmediated record of what was seen and heard were no longer enough to match the larger pictures of leaders and battles, politics and strategy, that came from the reporters, particularly in their grander and graver incarnation as foreign correspondents. Writers such as Edgar Ansel Mowrer (*China Wakes,* 1939) or Agnes Smedley (*Battle Hymn of China,* 1943) or Theodore White and Annalee Jacoby (*Thunder Out of China,* 1946), or Jack Belden (*China Shakes the World,* 1949) spoke with the gravity of experts, wise men and women analyzing and explaining the meaning of the war for a faraway West, and their voices sounded quite different from those of the travelers who had preceded them. There are, after all, very few ironic or self-doubting foreign correspondents.

Much has been written particularly of American press coverage and reporting from China during the war,[22] but here I am more concerned with how the frame of the war changed the ways in which China and China's leaders were represented in travelers' accounts. For that frame undeniably helped determine the picture that they saw or chose to see. It was not simply that the fighting turned them away from such sights as the Temple of Heaven or the Shanghai Bund or Yunnan's distant snowcapped ranges. The realization that what was happening to Them might soon be happening to Us brought the immediacy of the present to a country that for so long had seemed so far away, so disconnected from the realities of history. With it came a shift once more in the perceptions of those characteristics that had defined the country. To some, China's old traditions were now to be valued not so much for their exoticism or their seeming immunity to the modern world but because in them might be found a source of strength as certain to overcome the invading Japanese as they had earlier overcome (or at least tamed) the invading Huns, Mongols, and Manchus. To others the hardness and bitterness of war laid bare the shortcomings of those old customs and beliefs that, in Western eyes, had always held the country back. The fighting, wrote Agnes Smedley, would teach China to modernize or to perish,[23] so that out of the crucible of battle would emerge a newer and brighter nation, a nation unshadowed by history. *Dawn Watch in China,* the title Joy Homer gave the record of her own travels in 1938 and 1939, perfectly captured this spirit.

In China, at least, one way of distinguishing the travel book from the war book might come from the answer to the question: When did travelers begin to realize that Their war was becoming Our war? Fighting was nothing new in that distant land of comic opera battles staged between nameless warlords (think of Grace Seton pestering those busy generals in Guangzhou for an interview), "incidents" between Chinese and Japanese troops along the Manchurian borders, or the Japanese bombing and shelling of Zhabei, the working-class district of Shanghai, which the city's foreigners had watched from the safety of their concessions in early 1932. Five years later, in July 1937, the effects of the clash between Chinese and Japanese forces at the Marco Polo Bridge outside Beijing were only slowly apprehended and understood, and, even to foreigners in China, Their war at first seemed no more than a local inconvenience.

Graham Peck, just back in Beijing from a trip to Mongolia, first heard about the outbreak as gossip at a cocktail party, where it was dismissed simply as another incident "in the intricate opera-bouffe relations between China and Japan."[24] Even after the city fell to the conqueror with an appalling suddenness, sending most foreigners to seek refuge in the Legation Quarter, the unpleasantness was largely kept beyond Beijing's high gray walls. Hence, it was hard to see the tragedy, and the fighting became the summer's excitement, a colorful and picturesque entertainment, so that being in Beijing in 1937 seemed almost like being in Sarajevo in 1914. Within days the dances in the foreign hotels had started again, men and women trading stories about the horrors outside the city, while the breeze carried snatches of their music to the soldiers dying in the plains beyond the walls. "We foreigners were spectators to a war," wrote Peck, "to something which should under no condition have an audience. It was a puzzling and distressing situation."[25] So, too, a year later in Hankou, Auden and Isherwood stood on top of an American bank building and watched the Japanese bombers come over the city.

The searchlights criss-crossed, plotting points, like dividers; and then suddenly there they were, six of them, flying close together and high up. It was as if a microscope had brought dramatically into focus the bacilli of a fatal disease. They passed, bright, tiny, and deadly, infecting the night. The searchlights followed them right across the sky; guns smashed out; tracer-bullets bounded up towards them, falling hopelessly short, like slow-motion rockets. The concussions made you catch your breath; the watchers around us on the roof exclaimed softly, breathlessly: "Look! look! there!" It was as tremendous as Beethoven, but wrong—a cosmic offence, an insult to the whole of Nature and the entire earth. I don't know if I was frightened. Something inside me was flapping around like a fish.[26]

Before the fighting broke out, at the behest of Bennett Cerf of Random House, Faber and Faber had already commissioned a travel book from the two writers. The Japanese attack offered them, as Auden said, a war of their very own, for, though he had been briefly in Spain, Isherwood hadn't.[27] By the time they arrived in China, in early 1938, Shanghai and Nanjing had fallen, and the Japanese armies were pressing toward Hankou and Guangzhou. Yet, despite its title, *Journey to a War* was neither travel book nor war book, properly speaking. In fact, that was precisely its problem: Auden and Isherwood simply could not make up their own minds about what kind of an account they were supposed to be writing. Perhaps, too, the method of its writing got in the way, for Auden's poetry flanked Isherwood's narrative, which in turn was based on a common diary that they had kept on alternate days. In the end, generally, the travel book won out over the journalists' book. Like Fleming and others, they too confessed their ignorance about the events they were watching, reminding their readers that they had never before been east of Suez and spoke no Chinese. "Some of our informants may have been unreliable, some merely polite, some deliberately pulling our leg. We can only record, for the benefit of the reader who has never been to China, some impression of what he would be likely to hear, and of what kind of stories he would be likely to hear."[28] We are a long way not only from the nineteenth century certainties of Isabella Bird's truthful impression but from the modern certainties of the foreign correspondent as well.

We are also a long way from the seriousness of a poem such as

Auden's "Spain, 1937." Before Pearl Harbor at least, the fighting in distant Asia never captured the British or American imagination as had the war against Franco. In the sonnet sequence that ended the book Auden indeed linked China with Spain and Austria. But that was later, and at least in Isherwood's narrative much about the country they found still sounded like the far-off land of pigtails and chopsticks from which travelers brought back colorful tales. Once landed and at work, they were dogged not simply by the legend of Peter Fleming, famous Foreign Correspondent who, "in his khaki shirt and shorts, complete with golf-stockings, strong suède shoes, waterproof wrist-watch and Leica camera . . . might have stepped straight from a London tailor's window, advertising Gent's Tropical Exploration Kit,"[29] but also by the shadow of Peter Fleming, famous Travel Writer, who had visited the battle lines and made his way through Tartary to India. Hence, their air of self-mockery as they found themselves playing the role of journalists, attending press conferences, interviewing generals and politicians, watching enemy bombers above Hankou, or lying flat on the ground as Japanese aircraft swooped over them near the Yellow River, giving Auden the chance to sneak a photograph of Isherwood—"'You look wonderful,' he told me, 'with your great nose cleaving the summer air.'"[30]

Like many others, they were made uneasy by the use of human beings as beasts of burden.

> We gazed at [the chair bearers'] bulging calves and straining thighs, and rehearsed every dishonest excuse for allowing ourselves to be carried by human beings: they are used to it, it's giving them employment, they don't feel. Oh no, they don't feel—but the lump on the back of that man's neck wasn't raised by drinking champagne, and his sweat remarkably resembles my own. Never mind, my feet hurt. I'm paying him, aren't I? Three times as much, in fact, as he'd get from a Chinese. Sentimentality helps no one. Why don't you walk? I can't, I tell you. You bloody well would if you'd got no cash. But I *have* got cash. Oh, dear. I'm so heavy . . . Our coolies, unaware of these qualms seemed to bear us no ill-will however. At the road-side halts they even brought us cups of tea.[31]

What made things even worse was that Peter Fleming was making that particular journey with them but doing it on foot.

As for the subjects of their investigations, they sometimes turned into quaint Orientals, stage Chinamen. "We not wan' to fight Japan,'" Tsan Yan-fu (Zeng Yangfu), the mayor of Guangzhou, told them.

"Japan wan' to fight *us*! Ha, ha, ha! Japan velly foolish. First she wan' to be number *tree* power. Then number *two*. Then number *one*. Japan industrial country, you see. Suppose we go Japan, dlop bomb—woo-er, boom! Velly bad for Japanese, I tink? Japanese come to China. China aglicultural country. Japan dlop bomb— woo-er, boom! Only break up earth, make easier for Chinese plough land! Much people is killed of course. Velly cruel. But we have lots more, yes? Ha, ha, ha, ha!"

At this moment, we were deafeningly interrupted by the air-raid sirens. They were just outside the window. Mr. Tsang became almost unintelligible with amusement; he shook violently in his chair: "You see? The Japanese come to dlop bombs on our heads! We sit here. We smoke our cigarettes. We are not afraid! Let us have some tea!"

We both liked Mr. Tsang. If this was typical of China's attitude towards the Japanese, it was certainly an example to the West— with its dreary hymns of hate, and screams of "Baby-killer," "Hun," "sub-human fiends." This scornful, good-natured amuse- ment was, we agreed, exactly the note which a cultured, pacific country should strike in its propaganda against a brutal, upstart enemy.[32]

And the Chinese ate funny things. Face to face with the offerings of a military banquet given in their honor, Auden suddenly had to rush outside to be sick.

Throughout the meal he sat pale and shuddering, with eyes averted from a dish of small, blanched, slippery creatures which stood in the middle of the table. "It's those dreadful *efts*," he mut- tered. "I daren't look at them, or I shall do it again." The General, unaware of what was wrong, repeatedly pressed Auden to taste the "efts." Auden, with a smile of polite agony, refused to do so. He spent the rest of supper with a handkerchief stuffed into his mouth.[33]

Around many of the parts of their whole Chinese adventure lies something of an air of the schoolboy outing or at least of the self-parodying modern ironist who has somehow managed to wander into the adventurous world of G. A. Henty. Yet such a tone works better if the reader can forget that it comes against the background of a nation fighting for its life, where men and women actually were being killed. Then such encounters might be an entertainment for a Europe still wanting to believe itself insulated from events taking place on the other side of the world.

In Hankou, which had become China's temporary capital after the fall of Nanjing in December 1937, Auden and Isherwood began to make the connection between what was happening there and what soon might be happening to Europe.

> All kinds of people live in this town—Chiang Kai-shek, Agnes Smedley, Chou En-lai; generals, ambassadors, journalists, foreign naval officers, soldiers of fortune, airmen, missionaries, spies. Hidden here are all the clues which would enable an expert, if he could only find them, to predict the events of the next fifty years. History, grown weary of Shanghai, bored with Barcelona, has fixed her capricious interest upon Hankow. But where is she staying? Everybody boasts that he has met her but nobody can exactly say.[34]

Even so, when bad news came from home, it quickly reduced Hankou to its proper perspective, putting it back where it belonged, on the wrong side of the world. Returning one day in March 1938 from a visit to the headquarters of General von Falkenhausen, chief of the German military mission in the city, they heard for the first time about the Anschluss, and suddenly the China in which they found themselves seemed impossibly distant.

> As we walked home the whole weight of the news from Austria descended upon us, crushing out everything else. By this evening a European war may have broken out. And here we are, eight thousand miles away. Shall we change our plans? Shall we go back? What does China matter to us in comparison with this? Bad news of this sort has a curious psychological effect: all the guns and bombs of the Japanese seem suddenly as harmless as gnats. If

we are killed on the Yellow River front our deaths will be as provincial and meaningless as a motor-bus accident in Burton-on-Trent.[35]

Events in Europe still counted for more than those in Asia; Their war had not yet quite become Our war. Here Auden and Isherwood differed from Edgar Snow. For, even though the fighting *Red Star* described was still primarily civil war, the timing of the book's publication in 1938, a few months after the Japanese invasion, allowed its Western readers to identify the Chinese cause with their own. No doubt, a critic like Fussell would find Snow's book, with some reason, too ideological and too preachy. But then Americans, who furnished the largest national cadre of missionaries in China, were more likely to be preachy than the English and, thanks to their more methodical training in the style, better able to make the tone sound natural. Americans, remarked Ada Chesterton, had cornered the market on uplift in China.[36] Certainly, this kind of earnest didacticism, with its Protestant resonances and its overtones of smug self-righteousness, was going to become a marked aspect of the writings of certain American travelers in wartime China. Whether or not it became a disfiguring disability is a matter of taste, of course.

Two Chinas at War

Travelers, if they were sufficiently important, might meet Chiang Kai-shek themselves and, even if they were not, would hear a great deal about him. Fleming and Yorke were impressed when they ran him down in Lushan in the mid-1930s, as was Edgar Ansel Mowrer, who found in him an effective strength, no matter "how devious or ultra-Oriental" he might seem.[37] Or sometimes they met his wife. Auden and Isherwood only got a brief glimpse of the great man while they were in Hankou, but one afternoon W. H. Donald, the Generalissimo's Australian advisor, took them to tea with Madame Chiang.

She is a small, round-faced lady, exquisitely dressed, vivacious rather than pretty, and possessed of an almost terrifying charm and poise. Obviously she knows just how to deal with any conceivable type of visitor. She can become at will the cultivated, westernized woman with a knowledge of literature and art; the technical expert, discussing aeroplane-engines and machine-guns; the inspector of hospitals; the president of a mothers' union; or the simple, affectionate, clinging Chinese wife. She could be terrible, she could be gracious, she could be businesslike, she could be ruthless; it is said that she sometimes signs death-warrants with her own hand. She speaks excellent English, with an intonation which faintly recalls her American college training. Strangely enough, I have never heard anybody comment on her perfume. It is the most delicious either of us has ever smelt.

Explaining the New Life movement to them, she even made that campaign for moral regeneration sound sensible, and, though they were dubious about Chiang's willingness or ability to cooperate with the Communists, they concluded that his leadership was vital for China, and that the Madame herself was a heroic figure.[38]

If Hankou, during its brief period as capital, seemed a Chinese Madrid or Barcelona, a city of courage and hope and excitement, travelers had to look harder to discover the same qualities in Chongqing, where Chiang retreated after Hankou's fall in October 1938. Richard Dobson, awed by the sight of the great city rising on the hills above the huge swift Yangtze, saw in it the quintessence of China, convinced that, if it had been the country's capital earlier, the unequal treaties would never have been permitted.[39] He was an exception, however, for others were more apt to find a ramshackle, tumbledown collection of crowded wooden shops and houses, oozing with people, and, rising into the mists, a city of desolation and wretchedness, not all of which was caused by the war.[40]

Yet, like it or not, by the late autumn of 1938, Chongqing was the headquarters of Free China, and, at least early in the war, travelers looked hard for signs of hope amid the destruction caused by Japanese bombing and the dispiriting sight of generals riding around in big American cars and foreigners profiting enormously from the misfortunes of others. Dominating the city's ruins, its greed, misery, and death, wrote Eileen Bigland, was the figure of Chiang Kai-shek, "and once one had seen that fine gentle face one knew instinctively that this man and nobody else would lead China in the right direction. Dreamer, visionary, leader, he sat in a clean bare building and set every nerve in his wonderful brain at the service of his people."[41] Joy Homer's

Chongqing, its morale high, "on fire with something more than patriotism,"[42] sounded rather like London in the blitz, so that her reader might almost expect to find a Chinese Mrs. Miniver emerging from one of those houses set on the steep streets above the river. Then, one day when she was out riding her Tibetan pony, she saw the leader on horseback and instantly understood the city's spirit. Although he merely gave her a polite greeting,

> his presence struck me like a blow and I felt curiously abashed. Up to this moment, my young brain had decided that Chiang Kai-shek was without doubt a good deal overrated; that he had made some bad blunders in the past when dealing with the Communists; and that he was probably reaping the benefit of his wife's superior ability. Now my cherished theories collapsed in ruin. He passed me by, dressed in the uniform of the Sun Yat-sen Republic, without insignia, and accompanied by some of his associates. But he carried with him an electric and almost chilling presence, as of a personality tempered with bright steel. In no human being have I sensed such concentration of power. [Even his enemies conceded that he was] wholly selfless . . . his raison d'être was China.[43]

As Their war gradually became Our war and China's cause the world's cause, a national leader was needed who would earn the respect of those foreign nations soon to become its allies. China also needed also a people whose qualities the West could admire and for which they could feel the sympathy of kinship. The earlier *opera-bouffe* characters would no longer do. Joy Homer's account of Chiang and the Free China that he led had an almost breathlessly enthusiastic and optimistic quality to it: arriving in the country with her own preconceptions about its leadership, about the troubles between Nationalists and Communists, about the role of foreign missionaries, once there she found her skepticism being overthrown by what she saw. Guomindang officials, Communist officials, ordinary people, soldiers, generals, scholars, foreign missionaries both sacred (like her traveling companions) and secular (like Rewi Alley), all had been united by the war and by their admiration for the Generalissimo's government. Selfless Nationalists joined selfless Communists like Zhou Enlai to build a bright future. Chinese Christians were in the lead, for she found that nearly all educated people in China were Christian, and with few exceptions they were "the strongest members of their race,"[44] while students and intellectuals profited from the extraordinary freedoms they were accorded even in a time of war.[45] Homer's China, in short, was fit to be America's ally, for all that was best in this new nation being forged by conflict mirrored the qualities that best exemplified the U.S. spirit. So, too, from Robin Hyde's *Dragon Rampant* in 1939 there emerged a vision of the Chinese people fighting bravely for their lives, and her account, with appropriate changes, might almost have done for the British facing the German onslaught a year later.

Shortly after the Allied victory in 1945, Robert Payne, who spent the war working for British intelligence in Chongqing and later teaching in Kunming, wrote of the "necessary silence" that so many foreign observers in wartime China had imposed upon themselves.[46] He was referring, of course, to their readiness to fall in with the image of Chiang Kai-shek and the Nationalists, done up as leaders of a united nation, fighting for democracy's cause side by side with Churchill and Roosevelt, to say nothing of Stalin, another tyrant promoted temporarily to freedom-loving democrat by the exigencies of the period. Obviously, the time of writing and publication helped to determine the view projected by the traveler, and even the titles of Payne's two works—*Forever China* (1945) and *China Awake* (1947)—suggest two very different assessments of Chiang's rule. But all that came later. While Homer, writing in 1941, was distressed by occasional rumors of tensions between Nationalists and Communists, she managed to put such questions behind her, reassured by China's essential unity. "We believe in sacrifice for each other, and in hard work and love for all men," she was told over and over again in Communist Yan'an. "Almost it is like your Christianity."[47]

That would hardly have been a view likely to ingratiate the Communists with Agnes Smedley, who, following long-established conventions, had little good to say about either missionaries or their religion and sniffily dismissed Chinese converts as mere rice Christians—although even she, like Mary Gaunt, sometimes accepted missionary hospitality for want of a better alternative. On one occasion when she did spend a few days in a comfortable American mission house eating American food, the bed was so soft that it kept her awake half the night, a hardship that would beset her later in Hong Kong's Peninsula Hotel.[48]

Smedley had arrived in the country back in 1928, and her *Battle Hymn of China* was part autobiography, part travel memoir, and part war report. Like Edgar Snow before her and Graham Peck later, all the received images of old China, with its "medievalism" and barbarity, found their place in her writing. Like them, too, she took great pains to assure her readers of what it was that distinguished her from other foreigners in China, such as the American officials who "thought of the Chinese as 'Chinamen' who took in washing for a living,"[49] and to remind them with some frequency that she was on the side of the downtrodden rather than with the sleek businessmen of Shanghai or the fat Nationalist profiteers of Chongqing.

Battle Hymn appeared in 1943, and, though there was no question where Smedley's sympathies lay, in that year of war her criticisms of the Nationalists were also somewhat muted. Graham Peck's Two Kinds of Time, published in 1950, a year after the Communists had won control of the mainland, looked at China through spectacles almost entirely dimmed by a fog of hopelessness. It might almost be subtitled I Told You So, so suffused is it with a heavy Schadenfreude, its almost eight hundred pages of accounts of living in and traveling through the cities and countryside of wartime China shot through with condemnations of American blindness, American racism, and American stupidity, leavened only by the insights of the very few who, like Peck himself, could tell what the war was doing to China and what the shape of the future might be. Perhaps of all the war books it comes closest to that of the classical travel narrative, though interspersed with frequent analyses of the course of the fighting, the failures of the Nationalist government, and the shortsightedness of American policy. With very few exceptions—such as the New Zealander Rewi Alley—Peck's foreigners (mostly American) were either detached or patronizing (Peck despised missionaries and was as hard on them as the most relentless Old Shanghai Hand), blindly conservative (diplomats and military leaders, General Stilwell excepted), and racist (the average American soldiers and airmen who found themselves stationed in China during the war). Few have carried the convention of the traveler's distancing himself from his fellow countrymen to quite the same lengths as did Peck, and, while Two Kinds of Time remains today an extraordinary document of journeys in wartime China, its self-righteousness can sometimes be a trial to the reader. Homer's enthusiastic descriptions were designed to appeal to middle America on the eve of Pearl Harbor, drawing their images of the Orient from missionary talks and colorful magazines such as the National Geographic. Peck's China, however, was constructed for a more sophisticated audience almost a decade later—world-weary, skeptical of the shadows of the cold war, and, educated by journals such as the *Nation* and the *New Republic,* convinced that the United States had blown its chance to recruit Mao's China as its friend.

Compare, for example, the descriptions each gave of West China Union University, the institution in Chengdu formed by the Protestant colleges that had fled the Japanese occupation of the east.

> The combined American faculties of the colleges gave me an inferiority complex which has lasted to this day [wrote Homer]. Feverishly alive to the trends of the outside world, they managed to be inhumanly creative . . . A more talented and intellectually sophisticated crowd I have yet to find congregated in one city. In fact, all the university life of Chengtu was extraordinarily civilized, its social affairs gay and well dressed, its faculty *au courant,* and its tennis courts smooth. Its atmosphere failed, somehow, to blend with the antique remoteness of Chengtu. It was an atmosphere one might expect to find in an American college town that prided itself upon being very *distingué.*[50]

West China Union reminded her of Smith College, her own alma mater. She meant it as a compliment, but to Graham Peck that similarity was precisely the problem.

> While its occupants complained of wartime crowding, the campus with its big gray brick buildings, wide lawns, and rows of shade trees gave a staggering impression of American-style spaciousness, in contrast to the squalid Chinese suburbs huddled around the compound walls. The grass alone impressed me, for there were acres of it, and on it grazed a herd of imported cows belonging to Madame Chiang Kai-shek. I had been long enough in places where every fertile patch must be farmed for a common lawn to look extravagant . . .
>
> Here the American missionaries lived, usually one family to a house, with servants to take care of most of the chores of life in remote China. Outside their classrooms, they had the innocent if drowsy pleasures of life in any American college town: departmental teas, student-teacher activities, discussion groups, an occasional quiet dancing party.

What was unforgivable was that, in Peck's view, West China Union provided a second-rate education to the privileged sons and daughters of landlords and Guomindang officials, who in their luxurious American style dormitories combined high living standards with low academic standards, while the real work of education was being carried on in the South West Associated University (Lianda), the much less well-equipped coalition of non-Christian universities that had also come west to settle in Kunming.[51]

While Joy Homer's Chiang was a brilliant man selflessly devoted to China, Graham Peck's view of the country's leaders, recalled with several years of hindsight, was a good deal less flattering. His Chongqing, wrapped in fog, its steep streets greasy with filth, with all its corruption, its Chinese-hating foreigners, encapsulated everything that was going wrong with China under the Nationalists. The wartime capital had become a city of death whose inhabitants, fed up with Chiang Kai-shek and his ways, could only wait for his decease or deposition. For them, as for Peck himself, the Generalissimo, far from being a selfless patriot, stood revealed as an emperor with no clothes or, even worse, a traitor trying to make secret deals with the Japanese puppet Wang Jingwei, while his wife became greedier and more spoiled than ever after the adulation given her during a wartime trip to the United States.[52] "The Kuomintang's misleading propaganda might be patterned after 'The Big Lie' of Western fascism but this government itself was 'The Enormous Practical Joke.'"[53]

Their war might indeed be Our war, but for writers like Peck and Smedley not all of Them were worthy to be Our allies, for among Them could be found scoundrels undeserving of our emotional or material attachments. Nor was the point made simply in denunciations of Chiang Kai-shek and his Nationalist henchmen. Rather, as we have already seen with Snow, their writing was packed with the unflattering images of old China made familiar by earlier travelers. Filthy inns, primitive transport, an uncertain attitude toward the truth, the grinding poverty of peasant villages whose inhabitants were held back by idolatry, superstition, and the bonds of custom—there they all were, every bit as evident to Agnes Smedley and Graham Peck as they had been four or five decades earlier to Eliza Scidmore and Edwin Dingle. Smedley, on her first crossing from the Soviet Union into China back in 1928, had "turned to face—the Middle Ages," [54] and her descriptions a decade later of the squalor, disease, and poverty of China's wartime villages were as graphic as those of any nineteenth-century traveler. Like earlier travelers, Smedley marveled at the beauty of the countryside and the picturesque human dwellings framed by nature.

> In the afternoon we stood on the crest of a high mountain range and looked down on glory. Below us lay a natural basin of gold with a long azure lake reflecting the azure sky. Fields of ripe grain gleamed like liquid gold. A few small white villages, set in green foliage, sparkled like jewels, and above and about this vision towered black volcanic peaks.

Yet, as with earlier travelers, such a distant view aestheticized the harsh reality of those settlements, with their appalling destitution, dirt, and poverty, their stagnant green slime bubbling in open gutters, their disease and death.

> From earth's grandeur we would descend into squalid valley villages where poverty bred sickness and suffering. Here was cause and effect in graphic simplicity: the villages rose directly in the shadows of the landlords' mansion—indeed, they were its shadows. High walls, with watchtowers, pierced by loop-holes, protected the mansion. The landlords had fled, leaving agents behind to collect the rents.[55]

Like Harry Franck and others before him, Peck deplored the superstition that wasted good farmland on grave sites, noting that Rewi Alley put the blame on priests, wizards, and geomancers.[56] Like Harry Franck, too, he nudged his reader heavily in the ribs with his disbelieving references to the celibacy of Buddhist priests and monks, his allusions freighted with the scornful trappings of a traditional Western anticlericalism.[57] "Decades of deepening poverty," he wrote of peasant resistance to and distrust of Alley's cooperative movement, "had created such superstitious timidity and conservatism—you might say such stupidity—that they suspected anything new, even when it was to their benefit," so that the hangovers from a "huge black past of ignorance and fear" slowed the work of the reformers.[58] Traveling into the hill villages beyond Chengdu in the early 1940s, he found that the picturesque colored papers on the houses, the fresh incense and tapers for the approaching Chinese New Year—still observed at its traditional time outside Chungking—were pathetic signs of superstition, an expensive and hopeless way of coping with uncomprehended troubles. The bold mottoes painted on the public buildings—which I assumed were war slogans—more often advised local obedience than national resistance: OBEY THE LEADER AND RECONSTRUCT THE COUNTRY, OBEY THE LEADER AND OBSERVE THE THREE PEOPLE'S PRINCIPLES.[59]

In such passages the reader can sense an almost perverse delight found by the writers in these retellings of old tales, these redrawings of venerable images culled from so many past imaginings of old China. Here they all were, in Peck and Smedley and Snow, those failings and shortcomings that progressive Westerners had so long inveighed against: dirt, poverty, cruelty, illiteracy, backwardness, superstition, a readiness to profit from the misfortune of others, and, above all, an inability to break out of age-old habits of thought and action. Such "Chinese characteristics" in the 1940s remained seemingly as frustrating and as soul destroying as they had been back in the days of Eliza Scidmore and her contemporaries. "Students of colonial discourse," says the critic Mary Louise Pratt, "will recognize here the language of the civilizing mission, with which North Europeans produce other peoples (for themselves) as 'natives,' reductive, incomplete beings suffering from the inability to have become what Europeans already are, or to have made themselves into what Europeans intend them to be."[60]

Her context is somewhat different (she is writing of Latin America in that particular passage), and her examples, she claims, reflected the way "the capitalist vanguard read themselves into the futures of those they sought to exploit, as a kind of moral and historical inevitability." Yet mutatis mutandis, the diagnosis fits here too. Of course, Smedley and Snow would hardly have been pleased to be numbered among the agents of the "capitalist vanguard"; still, we can note that the use of this kind of colonial discourse, this kind of production of China and the Chinese with all their alterity and consequent need to be civilized, was by no means to be found only in the world of the travelers Pratt analyzes so carefully. Nineteenth-century European bourgeois capitalism, after all, has not been the only framework that has conceived of itself as participating in a moral and historical inevitability. Marx and his disciples have seen to that.

For such writers as these, there were two Chinas: China of the present, Nationalist China, still mired in the web of its unfortunate past; and China to come, the China most visible from the Communist base in Yan'an. What separated them was not only their attitude toward past and future or the cartographic line dividing the lands patrolled by Chiang's weary and defeated troops, on one side, and the optimistic young recruits of Mao's Eighth Route Army, on the other. It was also the discursive frontier plotted by the writings of Western observers. As we have already seen, Snow had constructed these two different entities through the use of two different discourses, and the same technique can be found in the accounts of, say, Agnes Smedley or Graham Peck and some others. The insistence on poverty, dirt, disease, superstition, and the like seems at first glance a kind of Orientalist strategy, drawing on those familiar and persistent images—China, Land of Famine—in which the country had been presented to the Western mind. Yet the purpose of this Orientalism was no longer the justification of a European and American cultural and political hegemony over semicolonial China; rather, it sought to subvert that hegemony by showing how badly it had failed. Chiang Kai-shek and his American friends, such as Henry Luce with his journalistic empire, the missionaries attracted by his Protestantism, investors attracted by his firm stand against communism, and so forth, had done little for China, and what the Marxists termed its "feudal" characteristics continued to testify that nothing significant had taken place in Nationalist China to jolt the country awake after its millenia of sleep.

Yet there was a difference. For now the blame for China's misfortunes no longer lay with the Chinese people themselves or even with the closely woven and unchanging net of Confucian tradition that had bound them into a sterile changelessness, condemning them forever to lag behind a progressive West. Rather, the people themselves were the victims of a system—"the shadow of a decaying landlord-merchant economy [which] hovered over the land," Smedley called it.[61] Even more were they the victims of a particular regime: Chiang Kai-shek and his Nationalists, those who, according to Smedley, were turning Chongqing into a bastion of reaction, sending dissidents off to prison camps, and who were outspoken in their admiration for the Germans after the fall of Paris.[62]

Neo-Orientalism, as one might call this approach, had its own particular aims and its own particular techniques. China, with all its failings, was no longer the hopeless land that travelers had discovered only a few decades earlier. The war itself was not only dissolving those ancient traditions of "Confucian priestcraft" but also overthrowing their modern legacies evident in the corruption and despotism of Chiang's regime. These writers found hope in the Chinese themselves, at least the good Chinese who seemingly shared many of the same qualities enlightened Westerners found in themselves. While Joy Homer might be encouraged by the leadership shown by Chinese Christians, so Smedley, admiring a parade of the Manchurian troops who had kidnapped Chiang Kai-shek near Xi'an in December 1936, reported that with their fur caps they "looked much like pictures of Daniel Boone . . . as tall and strong as Americans."[63]

For Smedley, of course, the future of new China lay with Marxism, with its optimistic unilinear trajectory of progressive development and its objective laws, which, though discovered in Europe, were every bit as valid for China as they were for the West. The communism Snow found in Baoan in 1936 was just as hopeful, though he was implicitly at least less willing than Smedley to grant the Soviet Union a commanding role in setting China's future direction. Such differences, however, were unimportant. To such writers, and to others who visited Yan'an in those years, even though Japan might at first appear to be winning the war, even though Nationalist power appeared to be collapsing internally as well as in the face of the enemy, a new China was being forged. When it emerged from the purifying fires of struggle at last, it would be a country far more familiar to the West than old China ever had been, and no tears need be shed for the latter's passing. For the inhabitants of this admirable new China, whether rulers or ruled, were so much more like Us than Them.

The Roads to Yan'an

Some thirty-odd years after the war, as the Great Proletarian Cultural Revolution was being played out, the term *Yan'an syndrome* or *Yan'an complex* came to be used by writers such as Mark Gayn, Benjamin Schwartz, and Robert Lifton to describe the psychotic effects growing out of the Communists' idealization of a particular moment in their own past.[64] That town, set among barren hills of the northwest, came to embody the memory of a small group of men and women standing shoulder to shoulder in a resistance against Japanese imperialism and Nationalist reaction, determined to conquer the future for their people. There they created a mythicized heroic age of Chinese communism, just as the Minutemen of Lexington and Concord had created a mythicized heroic age of America's own struggle for freedom. Moreover, whatever its effects on the later disasters of the Cultural Revolution, during those wartime years the Yan'an vision was also being configured for Western consumption. Not only by travelers, of course, for, after Edgar Snow's pioneering journey to Baoan, many other foreigners, including journalists, observers of various sorts, and even the American military men of the Dixie Mission in 1944, made their way to the Yan'an Soviet and reported on what they saw there.

Granted that by then the distinction between travelers and other observers had begun to become blurred, perhaps even artificial. Yet even in this period travelers' accounts continued to appeal to the kind of veracity that grew out of direct experience, experiences different from those of the journalist, who might fly in and out to do a particular story, or the members of Dixie, whose main purpose was to learn more about Communist operations against Japan. Here I want to examine the ways in which several of them helped to give shape to a highly unfamiliar phenomenon—Chinese communism—and ordered their observations so that they both made sense in the context of their Chinese travels and became comprehensible for Western readers.

Snow's journey was unique in the sense that from the start his goal had been the discovery of Red China, and, in writing of it, he shaped his account in a way that allowed him to take advantage of the range of structures and metaphors of the classic travel adventure story. No other account came close to the excitement of Snow's book. Not only was he the first to make it to the Communist headquarters, but at Baoan the Reds were still on the move, their society still under construction, so to speak, unlike the relatively settled Yan'an of later years. Moreover, for travelers after Snow, the voyage to Yan'an was only one episode, even if the climactic one, in a larger encounter with China. Some saw the Communist base simply as another part of China, and they applied to it essentially the same criteria they used in judging the rest of the country. For others, however, Yan'an was qualitatively different not simply from the rest of wartime China but from any other China the

West thought it had known. Accordingly, as Snow had already done, they produced a Yan'an that was distinguished precisely because it was *not* "Chinese" in the sense implied by the familiar constellation of images drawn from the past. "Journalists never returned from the Red Army," Agnes Smedley remarked, "without feeling that they had been among modern men, men much like themselves."[65] The generalization was by no means true only of journalists.

In mid-1938 Isherwood and Auden turned down an offer from Bo Gu, the Communist representative in Hankou, to visit the Yan'an Soviet and the Eighth Route Army, on the grounds that there had already been sufficient coverage of the Reds.[66] A missed opportunity, of course, but the reason they gave was an indication of the Communists' growing prominence after Snow's trip. Well before *Red Star* appeared that year, his accounts of his discoveries had appeared in both the British and American press, and by the time of Bo Gu's offer other foreigners had made their way to Yan'an as well. Agnes Smedley, Owen Lattimore, Victor Keen of the *New York Herald Tribune,* the New Zealand journalist James Bertram, and Nym Wales (Helen Foster Snow, Edgar Snow's wife) were among the dozen or so who breached the Nationalist blockade to reach the Soviet.[67]

A few years earlier, by the banks of the Oxus, the British traveler Violet Cressy-Marcks had talked to a man who had

> fought and lived with Mao Tse-tung, who knew Lin Piao well and a half a dozen other notable red leaders. Up till then I had known where Chiang Kai-shek and a number of Chinese war lords were and what they were doing, but the Reds were nearly a closed book to me. I realized that I knew only one side and the other had still to speak.[68]

Hence her own trip to China, and when she reached Yan'an in early 1938 she seems to have been convinced she was the first Westerner to have gone there.[69] Undeterred by the hair-raising warnings from friends who assured her that no foreigner had ever visited the Reds and that she was likely to be killed as a capitalist, she persisted, reaching Xi'an in February 1938. There she met Lin Boqu, the same Long March veteran who had eased Snow's passage to Baoan almost two years earlier. From Xi'an a ramshackle and overcrowded bus carried her and Frank Fisher—she called him simply her companion, though in fact he was her husband—through the wintry Shaanxi countryside on the two day trip to Yan'an, which by now had become the Communist head-quarters.[70]

Although Cressy-Marcks might never have heard of her predecessors, both her reception and her observations were very close to theirs, suggesting either that by then Mao and his colleagues had decided on a routine for the treatment of foreign visitors or that she, like Snow, had already decided what it was she would find. Like his Baoan, her Yan'an was a town with no beggars or robbers, whose people lived a hardy simple life, motivated by an idealism not found elsewhere in the country.[71] Like him, too, she visited academies and training schools and hospitals, including the one run by the Christian Dr. Nelson Fu (she was surprised to find so many Christians in Yan'an). She admired the work being done both by and for women, though she strongly opposed their ever being sent into battle, since their chief duty to their countries was to bear children, and they should be kept from the bestiality of fighting.[72] As it had Snow, the Red theater impressed her, though the American journalist would have been appalled by the parallel she drew between it and the *Kraft durch Freude* movement in Germany. Like Snow, too, she provided her readers with brief biographies of Mao and his general Zhu De as well as a description of what she called the Great March. She visited Zhang Guotao, another of the Long March leaders, in his cave a few months before he fled Yan'an to seek refuge with the Nationalists. Finally, though she never met him, she heard much about Lin Biao,[73] who, after being wounded earlier, was in Yan'an as head of Kangda, the Communists' National Resistance University.

Far from being Snow's "gaunt, Lincolnesque" figure, her Mao Zedong was a short man whose "ears were different from any man's I have ever seen—quite flat on top," with thin fingers and nicely shaped hands and a surprisingly quiet manner and voice. Carried on through four interpreters, their interview got off to a difficult start when in response to his question she repeated some of the horror stories she had heard about the Reds. Then, however, he gave her a sudden smile and said, "'No, I don't eat babies for tiffin,' and the ice was broken." A five-hour conversation followed, which must have covered much of the same ground he had earlier gone over with Snow: the movement's history, the nature of the army, the war with Japan, and its place in the global struggle against imperialism.[74] Hearing him speak to a meeting a few days later, she found him the only orator I have ever seen who made no gesture whatsoever. He kept his hands clasped behind him and he spoke for three hours. He had no notes and just looked at the audience . . . On and on he went. He spoke quietly but clearly, and completely dispassionately. There is no doubt whatsoever that these people all worshipped him. He was their leader, to whom they looked up, and they took unquestioningly his advice and doctrine. While Mao Tse-tung lives he will have complete control of the Communist Party in China.[75]

"[A] strange city," she concluded of Yan'an when the time came to leave, "but a live one: no dictator could have raised higher hopes in human beings or infuse them more than had been done in that place." Perhaps, she mused, dictators, who were the "forerunners of mass psychology," might give way to "something better," influencing many countries instead of one, "and then, after the inevitable clash, it will not be so many countries ranged on one side and so many on the other, but one doctrine or train of thought against another, and thereby, in any future war, all humans would be brought in, and at last that ghastly nightmare, 'war,' would be no more."[76] Precisely what all that was supposed to mean remains unclear, at least to this reader. But her experience in Yan'an allowed her to break free of the generalizations of earlier writers like Fleming and Yorke, who had seen communism running dead against the Chinese character.

> If so-called Communism spreads over China, it will be different again from that of Russia . . . Communism should work well in the East, where all souls are born into a world gaining comfort in philosophy, and have more time and a better rendering of it than we have in the West; but in the East their philosophy has usually been in practice for thousands of years, has stood the test of time, and that, perhaps, is the secret.

The secret of what, again one is not quite sure. The view from Yan'an, however, allowed her to envision with equanimity an England turned Communist, for, by the time such a conversion took place, few people would object, even though she did allow herself to question whether the cradle-to-grave security promised by communism was quite what the Maker had intended.[77]

Ironically enough, while Cressy-Marcks seems to have had no knowledge of other Western visitors to Yan'an before her, the standard accounts of Yan'an's dealings with the outside world seem also to have entirely ignored her own visit there. Of course, compared to the palpable excitement of Snow's account, there is no question that her description of the Communist headquarters is pallid, even drab. *Red Star* remains immensely readable today, but few would say the same of *Journey into China*. Despite the similarity of their experiences and observations, Cressy-Marcks maintained toward Yan'an the same dispassionate, even unreflective, view that she adopted toward the rest of the country, and, unlike Snow and some of the others who followed him, she made little attempt to contrast the failures of White China with the promises of Red China. Her Yan'an might be China's future—a "so-called communism" with Chinese characteristics—but then again it might not. She made no predictions.

Nor did Joy Homer, for that matter, who showed up in Yan'an a year later, in 1939. Like Cressy-Marcks, she too refused to draw sharp distinctions between Red and White China, but that was because of her determination to give her readers a China selflessly united in a great cause. She had arrived in the Soviet more gradually, first reaching Xi'an in March 1939 (a city of a "queer, stubborn, courage") before going on to the Yellow River front, through Luoyang to a Zhengzhou badly damaged by Japanese bombing and shelling.[78] Even before entering Yan'an, she was impressed by both the non-Communist guerrillas and the regulars she met in Shanxi and Shaanxi, and her description of them bore more than a passing resemblance to Snow's discoveries in Baoan. They, too, had their resistance universities (modeled on those of Yan'an, the warlord Yan Xishan told her), the theatrical groups mixing entertainment with political education, the little industries inspired by Rewi Alley's cooperatives, all run by men and women fired with a patriotic determination to unify and better their country.[79]

Yan'an itself was the first city she'd seen in China that was entirely destroyed, a ghost city by day, though by night it came alive, rebuilding itself in the loess caves nearby. Put up in a cave hotel and given a welcoming dinner with her companions, she admired the cooperation she found between Nationalists and Communists, discovering to her surprise that Chiang was furnishing the Communists with a monthly financial subsidy.[80] Although she confessed her inability to explain Chinese communism, she did become convinced that it had nothing to do with Soviet communism, a point drummed into her daily by those she talked to, who also emphasized the similarity of their ethic to that of her own Christianity.[81]

Indeed, though Mao Zedong admitted to her that his forces had been guilty of atrocities against Christians in the past, his Party now welcomed them if not as members, then as allies. "We consider your way of life and thought closer to our own than any other single philosophy," he told her. He seemed a genius to her and, save for Chiang Kai-shek, probably the brightest man in the country. Humorous, happily boyish looking and witty, he had a mind "sharp and flexible as steel." And, though it was obvious to her that communism would never gain ground among the Chinese, "to whom personal freedom and individuality is a religion," the Communists might be useful after the war as "a good, nagging minority" who would energize the Nationalist government. Yet, while the Nationalists themselves were "astonishingly democratic in spirit," Homer came away from Yan'an vaguely disquieted by reports of tension between the two parties, though she dismissed the fears of the American press that the country was on the verge of civil war by reassuring herself that such fallings-out were no more than the result of clashes between individual leaders.[82]

If Cressy-Marcks observed Yan'an dispassionately and Homer chose those aspects that undergirded her view of a united and democratic China, there were others who, like Snow, discovered in the Chinese variant of communism a promising future finally broken away from all the long-held conventional images of the traveler's China. Agnes Smedley had been in Xi'an when Chiang was kidnaped by his Manchurian troops in December 1936, and shortly thereafter, fearing pursuit by Nationalist assassins, she had made her way to the Communist base. She was there when the fighting between Japan and China broke out in July 1937 and tried to bring in other foreign journalists up there from Shanghai, only to be upset when she discovered that everyone wanted to be first. "I had not reckoned, however, with the journalistic practice of seeking 'scoops' . . . I held such practices in contempt, for I did not consider great national movements publicity stunts." In fact, she'd been infuriated that Snow, her friend and rival, had beaten her to the northwestern Soviet and had carried away the palm gathered from the first encounter with this particular New World.[83]

In the end Smedley reported on Yan'an more as journalist than traveler, interviewing some of its leaders such as Zhu De, whose biography she would later write, and the always attractive Zhou Enlai. Mao, on the other hand, clearly put her off in their first meeting—she found his face sinister and inscrutable, his womanly lips giving him an air of aestheticism that repelled her. It was not long, however, before she discovered how wrong she'd been, and a "precious friendship" followed, the sinister quality she had first observed proving to be no more than the mark of a spiritual isolation.[84] Still, for all the virtues she found there, for all her developing friendship with Mao, who would come to her cave to dine and talk with her, the Yan'an Soviet that emerged from her writing was less fresh and compelling than Snow's Baoan had been a year earlier. The real vitality of her book as travel account came from her far longer descriptions of her journeys with the New Fourth Army, the large Communist detachment, half-regular, half-guerrilla, that operated behind the Japanese lines in the lower Yangtze region in the years before the Nationalists turned on it and cut it to pieces in January 1941.

She had joined them both as medical helper and as reporter for the *Manchester Guardian* after the fall of Hankou in October 1938, moving with them between occupied and unoccupied China, between regions where the Red influence was strong and those still in the hands of the Nationalists or the "feudal" warlords of the south and west. From those travels there emerged a sense of life and excitement rare among wartime accounts. Perhaps because Snow had beaten her to the punch, Yan'an by then had become old news, or, as Dean MacCannell might say, the kind of back region made up or altered for visitors to make them think they were confronting the real thing.[85] The New Fourth Army, on the other hand, was untouched, a genuine back region. Best of all, she had it all to herself and didn't have to share it with Snow or the beautiful Nym Wales or the other visitors who began to come trickling into the northwest. No doubt, too, like Isabella Bird, there was a touch of the savage about Smedley, and she preferred being on the move with guerrillas who were doing real fighting to staying confined in the relatively placid and staid New Jerusalem of Mao's Yan'an Soviet.

Throughout her travels the spirit of the Communist soldiers contrasted sharply with the hopelessness, poverty, and destitution of the countryside through which they moved. Like Snow, she emphasized the distinction between the Communists and their rivals, noting in the faces of the Red Army soldiers "something of the vital awareness that had been so pronounced in the great Lu Hsun," rather than the depressed, empty, and hopeless expressions of so many ordinary troops.[86] Passing from Red China back into White China was like breaking out of a charmed circle

> and into an ocean of darkness, poverty, and oppression. Along the highway I had found none of those slogans by which the Chinese express their hopes, no songs of conviction, no activity of the people. Sick and diseased people surrounded me everywhere, pleading for help—babies that had congenital syphilis—skin diseases—scabby heads—pus-filled eyes—ulcerous legs! . . .
>
> "What destitution, dirt, and disease!" I wrote. "I have used up half of my medicine, but there is no end. Only a gigantic transformation could end this misery!"[87]

Although the difficulties and dangers of that transformation were evident (it would be like going through "darkest Africa," the Communist commander Ye Ting had warned her),[88] there was a solid practicality and earthiness about Smedley's accounts of communism that stood in contrast both to that of Snow, who preceded her, and Ilona Ralf Sues, who followed her.

Unlike Violet Cressy-Marcks, Sues knew that others had been to Yan'an before her but stayed true to her earlier determination not to have her mind warped by reading their opinions before she went to see for herself. Later, however, she admitted it had been a mistake not to look at *Red Star* first.[89] Doing French and English broadcasts for the United Front from Hankou before that city fell to the Japanese in October 1938, she'd become disillusioned with the Nationalists and had been on the verge of quitting to return to Geneva. Then she met Anna Louise Strong, whose stories of the Communists made her decide she could not leave China without a visit to the Soviet. Ultimately, in the company of several others, Sues made it through to Shaanxi, where Peng Dehuai, whom she'd met in Hankou, came all the way to Fenglingtu on the Yellow River to meet them, "which was sweet of him and put us all into a wonderful humor."[90]

Like Snow and Smedley, she found the people in the Soviet impressive because of their difference from other Chinese she had known. Luo Ruiqing, the head of the Anti-Japanese University in Yan'an, was "a tall, lanky man in his thirties, with a small, intelligent face almost too gentle for the director of a military academy." She was charmed by Zhu De, "the little muscular man, with his ready, jovial smile and hearty cordiality," a generalissimo so different from Chiang Kai-shek, who was, with his "superb remoteness and seclusion, unapproachable to common mortals." Sues and her companions spent several mornings interviewing Zhu, who gave uncomplicated practical answers to their questions. "We sat and listened like school children to his frank, simple replies which opened a new world to us—the Chinese People's China. It was all common sense, sound economics, human understanding. No tutelage, no compulsion. No witchcraft either." Even the variety of the northwest landscape fascinated her—nine mountain ranges there were on the way to Xi'an, and every one of them different[91] (perhaps, unlike Snow, she'd never tried to grapple with James Joyce).

At a mass meeting Sues was reprimanded for shouting "Da dao Riben" (Down with Japan). It was Japanese imperialism, not the Japanese people, that was their enemy, she was reminded; the proper slogan was "Dadao Riben diguozhuyi" (Down with Japanese imperialism).[92] At another gathering, held to denounce two Chinese traitors, she was asked to speak but found herself stunned into silence. Fortunately, Charley Higgins, one of her missionary companions, saved the day by making an impassioned speech to remind his hearers that the two men before them were not alone in their treason. "Every Chinese capitalist who makes his millions out of the sweat and blood of the people, and places his ill-gotten gain in American and British banks, is a traitor whose judgment you must demand." Ma Haide (the American doctor George Hatem), sitting next to her, was impressed. " 'That lad is wonderful,' he murmured; *'c'est bien dommage de vouloir en faire un prêtre.' "*[93] Much to her surprise, Zhu De invited her to attend a Catholic mass said by Vincent Lebbe (Lei Mingyuan), the Belgian priest who had become a Chinese citizen. He was doing medical and educational work in the anti-Japanese resistance and seemed to Sues a wonderful example of how Christians and patriots worked together. Two years later, in 1940, Lebbe would die after interrogation and torture at the hands of the Communists.[94]

The climax of Sues's visit came late one night when, after days and days of waiting for the invitation, she and her companions finally met Mao himself.

Our guide opened the door. Mao stood in the middle of the room to welcome us—tall, broad-shouldered, placid, in a disheveled

padded uniform, with a zigzagging mane that clamored for a hair-
cut, and over the crumpled, unbuttoned collar the most wonderful
face I had ever seen. I had looked forward to seeing a man—a great
revolutionary, but a man just the same. I had not expected to find
myself face to face with the Chinese nation incarnate.

Mao Tse-tung combined all the characteristics of the Chinese
people: their wisdom, in his high, square forehead; their patience
and untold suffering in those sparse, painfully knitted brows; their
dreams and their keenness, their shrewdness and irony, in his
large black eyes, under those heavy eyelids that one lowers when
it becomes necessary to put a wall of impassivity between one's
own and the outer world; their energy and pride in his strong,
high-bridged nose; their determination, in his high cheekbones;
their epicurean tastes, in his pale, mat, delicate complexion; their
sensuality in his full lips; their sensitiveness to beauty in those nervous, finely shaped ears; their tolerant mellow kindness in the soft
curve of his chin; and their sense of humor in the corners of his
eyes and mouth.

There are moments when life unexpectedly gives us a fleeting
glimpse of eternity. That is what I felt at the first sight of this
imposing, timeless, erect figure. Peasant, poet, philosopher, revolutionary, and statesman in one—rooted in a legend, grown out of
China's history of sorrow and glory, matured in our days into a
living part of China's destiny, and leading his people out of
bondage into freedom, into the future.[95]

"The Chinese nation incarnate." It is difficult to read such a statement today without having it refracted through our knowledge of what
would become of China and, more particularly, what would become of
Mao. All the more so since thirty-odd years after Sues's meeting, in the
great days of the Cultural Revolution, when the cult of the personality
had reached its height, such sentiments would become commonplace.
The point here, obviously, is not to find Sues guilty of an early instance
of the sort of Mao worship, with all its consequent traffic in relics and
miracles, that China would become much too familiar with later.
Rather, it is that her reading of Mao must be put in the context of the
same search for authenticity that had motivated other travelers in the
country. They might have discovered reality in the signs of an
unchanging China, evident in the gray walls and gates or the crimson

and gold temples and palaces that defined Beijing, the canals and gardens of Suzhou, the mountains and rivers that looked as if they had come straight out of a Northern Song landscape or even the "medieval" barbarities of its customs. Sues, however, had found it in a single man, a Leader who linked the burdens of China's long and sorrowful history with all the promises of the future.

James Buzard's analysis is to the point here: while "tourists" are incapable of grasping the authentic, integrative concept of a place or a people, "travelers" reach for symbols that stand for and express the essence of the whole, coming to believe that they have made a meaningful contact with what those places are.[96] Sues's symbol (or her back region) came in a man who looked "Chinese" in an essential sense, rather than a monument or a landscape. But for her, too, it was a way of taming the enormous size and diversity of the land, a way to say, "There, I have found it—this is the real China." All the same, reading of this vision of a single man incarnating the Chinese nation brings back the uncomfortable memory of Eliza Scidmore's decidedly unflattering picture of hundreds of millions of Chinese, from one end of the empire to the other, as alike as peas in a pod.

Sues's Mao, moreover, was cosmopolitan in a way that other Chinese were not, a man who from his Shaanxi cave kept in touch with the world while finding time to read ancient Greek as well as modern European and American philosophers. Because of her Polish background, he quizzed her about Joseph Beck and his reactionary Cabinet of Colonels who were selling out to Hitler and then turned to Higgins to ask him about the American labor movement.[97] Oddly enough, the Soviet Union seems not to have been a subject of discussion, or, if it was, Sues made no mention of it. Perhaps it would have been tactless, in a book published in 1944, to have to remind her readers that roughly a year after Mao asked his question it would not be Joseph Beck and his Polish colonels but, rather, Joseph Stalin and his Soviet Communists who ultimately would sell Poland out to the Nazis. Smedley, faced with the same problem, accepted the Soviet-Nazi Pact as a "temporary expedient" for which she blamed Britain and France, though she remained discreetly silent about Stalin's later treaty with Tokyo in April 1941.[98]

"Our trip had taught us an astonishing thing," Sues wrote later; "notwithstanding all statements to the contrary, the Chinese people were ripe for democracy. Given a chance, they understood and practised it. In the Borderland, each citizen, man and woman, over eighteen, had the right to vote, and to elect most of the public functionaries." All people participated in the government and were equal before the law; there was freedom of religion, freedom of speech and the press, freedom of assembly. Free education brought an increase in literacy; free medical treatment brought better public health. "Every step we made brought us proof that democracy worked. It worked to the point of a miracle: *Not one person died of famine.*"[99]

If British and Americans, ever since John Stuart Mill and others in the mid-nineteenth century, had assumed that China's advance would come only if it were able to insinuate itself into a narrative of progress already written by Europe and America, these wartime travelers were no exception. The faith in the civilizing mission continued to burn as strongly as ever, even though that mission might no longer lie in the hands of Christianity (though it still did for Homer, of course) or in the examples of modern capitalism visible in Shanghai or Hong Kong. New China would be made up of modern men, men who were much like ourselves, as Agnes Smedley called them. Even for these admiring visitors to Yan'an, therefore, the need to reshape China according to norms devised in the West was unchanged. So was the old assumption that such norms, whether stemming from Adam Smith or Karl Marx, were the characteristics of universal history. Thus, Westerners must remain the judges, using the rules of their home playing fields, of what was and what was not feudal or modern or progressive, even what was and what was not Chinese. In the end it was the West that would remain, as Edward Said has complained, as much in control of Oriental time and history as ever.

In this way the advent of war did not so much stop the quest for authenticity as bring to it a new focus. By the time writers such as Homer, Bigland, Sues, Smedley, and Graham Peck published their books, old China—whether one saw it as hopelessly backward or a haven of exotic difference in an increasingly homogenized world—was now taking second place to the emerging new China with which the democratic nations of the West could make common cause against a common enemy. Real China was as much as ever the object of the traveler's search, but the reality was now one to be glimpsed in the future. Purified and made stronger by its resistance to the invader, China would become a new nation worthy of the sufferings of those who were helping to build it and worthy to range itself as an ally of the democracies that linked themselves to it. Nor did it really make much difference whether this was to be Homer's Christian nation, Sues's democratic nation, or Smedley and Snow's socialist nation. For in the Chinese context, when seen through spectacles colored by the great united front against Japan and the fascists, such words simply seemed different ways of expressing the same thing.

There in Yan'an travelers could most easily glimpse this new China. Yet, ironically enough, what made it new and what made it real was precisely the absence from Yan'an of all the old Chinese characteristics that for so long had hobbled the people. Gazing down on China from the northwestern Soviet, the view was simple and clear, untroubled by all those excrescences that seemed to pop up with such disturbing frequency elsewhere—corruption, poverty, famine, mind-crushing superstition, rumors of underhanded dealings between the Nationalists and the Japanese or their puppets such as Wang Jingwei.

All the more was this true as the simple early optimism of a Joy Homer or an Eileen Bigland about Chiang Kai-shek's regime became more and more difficult to sustain as the war dragged on. Growing clashes between Nationalist and Communist forces, such as the New Fourth Army incident of January 1941, exposed the hollowness of the United Front. Then it was that Chongqing and Yan'an became metaphors for the opposing sides. The former was a filthy miasmal city of defeat, threatening to slide down the steep and slimy fog-hung riverbanks to which it clung, a medieval city thrust uncomprehendingly into the twentieth century, fearful under the ever-present threat of Japanese bombers, its streets filled with the poor and scabrous, the sleek profiteers and opportunists. Yan'an was a city of poverty too, but under its bright clear northern skies travelers found there the inspiriting poverty of modern democratic equality rather than the traditional, age-old wretchedness and exploitation of its southwestern counterpart.

It was no accident then that Graham Peck's *Two Kinds of Time* exuded such a sense of hopelessness. Peck, after all, never made the trip to Yan'an or traveled with Smedley's New Fourth Army guerrillas. His Nationalist China was old China unvarnished, with all its familiar vices, cruelties, and superstitions, old China collapsing into nothingness. Not until after the war, in the spring of 1946, did he make a brief foray into one of the Communist regions in the north, and, though he came away mildly encouraged, he was too wary to make any predictions about the future.[100] Just as well, perhaps, for his analyses of the war, and of his fellow countrymen in the war, seem rather beside the point today, and his often self-righteous reactions to American missionaries and soldiers and officials seem to tell us more about the author than about his subjects.

What today still gives Peck's book its life and its staying power are the descriptions of his travels as he moved about a country that was tired and losing hope, a country whose leaders were waiting for others to win the war for them. No one ever would take his writing as disinterested reporting, even without the analyses of everything the Americans and their Nationalist allies were doing wrong. Yet in its travel sections *Two Kinds of Time* still reflects an extraordinary sense of historical authenticity that the other accounts lack: reading it today and knowing what the years would bring, one thinks, yes, this is what it must have been like in those years—a partial view, no doubt, but a view that captured something important about China during the war. Peck kept his eyes and his ears wide open. If the credibility of the traveler, as opposed to that of the journalist or the expert, lies in the record of what was seen and heard, his account holds up in a way that today no longer seems quite as true of Sues or Homer or even of Edgar Snow himself. And that, at least, is no small accomplishment.

Chapter 8

Conclusion

As the travel books evolved into the journalistic and war books of the late 1930s and 1940s, there was one important way in which they differed from their predecessors. For in them the Chinese—a few Chinese, at least—began to take shape as individuals, emerging as distinct entities separated out from those faceless masses whose appalling sameness from Cochin China to Siberia had so upset Eliza Scidmore. Although earlier travelers such as Isabella Bird or Harry Franck might on occasion mention particular names, they were still apt to deal with the Chinese if not as a whole, then as members of classes or groups. The bearers of these names were less individuals than essentialized types, so that even if you could not generalize about "the Chinese," you could at least say, "Peasants believe this" or "Mandarins behave like that." The military official who told Isabella Bird of the vortex that had swallowed up three foreign navies encapsulated the overweening pride and ignorance of outside matters common to his class, as the grave dignity of others who emerge in her pages represented their good qualities. The dirty and corrupt priests of Harry Franck and Graham Peck typified all that was wrong with Chinese religious superstition. The educated young women in whom Grace Seton found such signs of hope spoke for all young educated Chinese women, despite their unfortunate preference for Wordsworth over Du Fu, while her Cantonese warlords stood for all the faceless and eminently forgettable gray-uniformed generals who marched and countermarched their troops across the face of China in the 1920s. If it was no longer possible as the twentieth century went on to say quite so easily that "the Chinese do this, the Chinese believe that," and think that you were speaking for every human being from Heilongjiang to Yunnan, it was still at least possible to talk about Chinese generals or returned students from America or

Hunan farmers or scholarly university professors or Shanghai busi-nessmen in a way that swept them all together, as if the importance lay in their similarities rather than in whatever differences might lie between them.

As the war closed in, however, changing the frame through which travelers saw China, out of the faceless masses there began to come into focus at least a few individuals with recognizable features. Most impor-tant were the leaders, Nationalist and Communist, whose new person-alities stood in marked contrast to the essentialized Chinese of earlier writings. Yet it is one of the conventions of travel writing that authen-ticity is to be found among the people rather than among their leaders (look at Sues's desire to be "the eyes and the ears of the man-in-the-street"), and the discovery of China's leaders as appropriate objects of description was one of the signs of the further breakdown of the divide between travel writing and journalism. Ada Chesterton, with her some-what skeptical view of Chiang Kai-shek, Joy Homer and Eileen Bigland describing the selfless and inspiring Nationalist leader tirelessly devoted to the advancement of his people, all participated in this new approach. So did Edgar Snow, Nym Wales, and Ilona Ralf Sues as well as those others who found in Mao Zedong, Zhu De, Zhou Enlai, and other Communist leaders a new breed of Chinese. Names and even physical features, described in some detail, set such individuals apart from the ordinary mass of their countrymen, as the repulsive charac-teristics of Sues's gangster Du Yuesheng also did. Whether Mao was gaunt and Lincolnesque (Snow) or short with squared-off ears (Cressy-Marcks) or round cheeked and boyish looking (Homer) or tall and broad shouldered with uncut hair (Sues) or dark and inscrutable with an aesthete's unattractive feminine mouth (Smedley) is not the point. Rather, it is that his appearance was worth describing, because no longer did all Chinese look alike. And if we were going to fight side by side with China, we needed not only a new China that was becoming modern like us but also a China with leaders whose features we could recognize as easily as those of the other democratic leaders we knew: Franklin Roosevelt, Winston Churchill, Charles de Gaulle, Joseph Stalin. Henry Luce's choice of Chiang Kai-shek as *Time*'s Man of the Year for 1937 made the same point: Their war was becoming Our war, and, even before China became the formal ally of Britain and the United States after Pearl Harbor, it had already become an emotional, even ideological ally.[1]

Still, such individuals remained exceptional. The old modes of representation did not suddenly disappear, and, as we've seen, some writers, particularly those on the Left, lapsed into the traditional discursive formations of Orientalism for those generalized aspects of China they liked or, more often, disliked. Below the ranks of the leaders, boatmen, and chair coolies, whatever Lu Xun might have wished, remained tireless and good natured, the young girls of Shanghai and Beijing were slender as spring willows, diners in restaurants either had exquisite manners or spat on the floor, young men and women who had studied abroad were either using their foreign learning for the good of their people or wasting their substance on the fleshpots of the cities, military officers were staunch defenders of their country or men who sacrificed their rank-and-file soldiers purely for selfish purposes.

Thus, the wife of the unnamed banker in wartime Hankou who, reminded of all those who were starving beyond her banquet table, remarked to Ralf Sues, "Who cares for coolies? They're better off dead than alive, anyway,"[2] was less an individual than a type, her callousness standing for everything that was wrong with Chiang's government and its values. So were the scheming, immoral, and incompetent Nationalist officials of Snow's *Red Star*, while Isherwood's mayor of Guangzhou, with his "woo-er boom" descriptions of the war, remained, however admirable his approach, a stage Chinese. Graham Peck's people—suffering and superstitious peasants, crafty priests, corrupt officials and the like—remained almost as essentialized as ever, even when their characteristics took his fancy. But then Peck never hobnobbed with Chiang or Mao or their colleagues, and, as we have seen, his foreigners, such as American missionaries, diplomats, and soldiers, were equally essentialized, uncomprehending at best and racist at worst, and, save for an occasional exception such as Rewi Alley, having as little individuality as did the Chinese. Even Sues's Mao Zedong, while on the one hand very much an individual, on the other was also the incarnation of the entire Chinese race, and one wonders whether she would so easily have found in, say, Charles de Gaulle, an incarnation of the entire French race.

It all depended on what kind of a China you wanted to produce for your audience at home. Still, by the war the reporters had gained the upper hand over the travelers, for the obvious reason that no one traveled for enjoyment or enlightenment in the China of the 1940s. China, which had been an object for Western improvement in the years prior to World War I, turned into an object lesson for the West in some of the writing just after that war and by the late 1930s had become an object of concern. What was then happening to China, just as what was happening to Spain, began slowly to seem a warning about what might soon happen to Britain and America. Auden made the connection in the verses he wrote on his return to Europe.

> While in an international and undamaged quarter,
> Casting our European shadows on Shanghai,
> Walking unhurt among the banks, apparently immune
>
> Below the monuments of an acquisitive society,
> With friends and books and money and the traveller's freedom,
> We are compelled to realize that our refuge is a sham.
>
> For this material contest that has made Hongkew
> A terror and a silence, and Chapei a howling desert,
> Is but the local variant of a struggle in which all
> . . . .
> In all their living are profoundly implicated.[3]

After Pearl Harbor the question for policy makers was how to keep China in the war as a useful strategic instrument in the Allied campaigns against Japan; still later, with the return of peace, the question was how to keep China a useful diplomatic instrument in the West's postwar Asia. Then, after 1949, of course, the question was how to keep this new Soviet satellite, as the popular American mind saw it, from carrying Stalin's Cold War to the East.

Travel writers, like others, reflected such changes. By the late 1930s, whether you liked or disliked China, if you took China at all, you had to take it seriously. Perhaps the travelers of the period, anxious to make China seem familiar, recognizable enough to be accepted as a worthy member of the great Allied cause, had done their jobs too well, so that their readers were unprepared for the disillusionment that would follow 1945. Perhaps that's also why their audiences either wanted to forget the country or wanted to turn to *real* experts to tell them what was going to happen: foreign correspondents like Theodore White, Annalee Jacoby, Jack Belden, and others who promised to reveal the meaning behind the appearances or scholars like Doak Barnett, in *China on the Eve of the Communist Takeover*, or John King Fairbank, whose first edition of *The United States and China* appeared in 1948. No longer were the travelers, who simply recorded their impressions of what they saw and heard, sufficiently authoritative.

During those years prior to the Communist victory occasionally a book appeared that harked back to the older style. Derk Bodde's fascinating *Peking Diary,* though not really a travel book, chronicled the period that saw the collapse of the Nationalists in the north and the entry of the Red Armies into the old capital. It thus forms a useful counterpoint to the earlier writings of George Kates and Harold Acton, for Bodde too was a man who knew and loved Beijing, who had immersed himself in both its popular and high culture. As Acton and Kates had watched the Japanese invaders come into their city, so Bodde watched the Communist victors of the civil war march in. Ten or fifteen years after Kates and Acton, he understood the changes that the war had brought. Like many other foreigners at the time, he believed that under the Nationalists, at least as they were then constituted, little of the old could be saved, noting the filth and debris that littered the grounds of the Temple of Heaven, while the magnificent ancient cypresses there and at the Confucian temple were being cut down. To him, as undoubtedly to many Chinese, the Communist victory was less a cause for rejoicing than a relief, simply because it might at least bring some stability and tranquillity to a land so long torn by war.

As it did, of course, at least for a few years before Mao and his colleagues unleashed the unprecedented catastrophes of the Great Leap Forward and the Great Proletarian Cultural Revolution. Events such as those played their own role in the accounts of Western travelers, both those who chose to see in China no more than a Soviet satellite or an empire of the blue ants and the others for whom it now became the new Jerusalem, since after Khruschev's denunciation of Stalin in 1956 only a tiny remnant of Old Believers continued to look toward Moscow for salvation. Indeed, it is tempting, reading the accounts of journeys to Mao's China after 1949, to say that in that period the travelers once again recaptured their earlier ground. For during those decades before Mao's death the China-watching scholars and journalists, unable to enter the country, congregated in the universities of America and Europe or in Hong Kong and Taiwan and had to depend on interviews with refugees, on the tightly controlled Chinese press and radio, and on rumor for news of happenings in the People's Republic. Their inability to agree on whether or not there was starvation in China during the greatest famine in the history of the world, from 1959 to 1961, was simply one example of the inadequacy of such approaches.[4] But the few travelers who were fortunate enough to hold the right kind of passport and to be favored with the right kind of entry visa were able to cross the border, and the reports of what they saw and heard (or chose to see and hear or were allowed to see and hear) seemed once again to carry a kind of veracity denied to the China watchers who, for all their research grants, were shut out of the Middle Kingdom. That, however, is a subject that runs well beyond the purview of this study and is best left to others.

Notes

Chapter 1

1. Isabella Bird (Mrs. J. F. Bishop), *The Yangtze Valley and Beyond: An Account of Journeys in China, Chiefly in the Province of Sze Chuan and among the Man-Tze of the Somo Territory* (London, 1899), 1. Although she signed herself by her married name, she had begun publishing under her maiden name, and for the sake of convenience I will refer to her henceforth as Isabella Bird.

2. Harold R. Isaacs, *Scratches on our Minds: American Images of China and India* (New York, 1958); Raymond Dawson, *The Chinese Chameleon: An Analysis of European Conceptions of Chinese Civilization* (London, 1967); Jonathan Spence, *The Chan's Great Continent: China in Western Minds* (New York: W. W. Norton, 1998). One of the earliest surveys was Adolf Reichwein, *China and Europe: Intellectual and Artistic Contacts in the Eighteenth Century,* trans. J. C. Powell (London, 1925).

3. Here I share many of the misgivings of John MacKenzie's trenchant dismantling of such approaches, and in particular his concern with their ahistoricism; see his book *Orientalism: History, Theory and the Arts* (Manchester, 1995), 20–39.

4. See Anne-Marie Brady, "West Meets East: Rewi Alley and Changing Attitudes towards Homosexuality in China," *East Asian History,* no. 9 (June 1995): 97–120. I am indebted to the author for sending me her article.

5. Peter Bishop, *The Myth of Shangri-La: Tibet, Travel Writing and the Western Creation of Sacred Landscape* (Berkeley, 1989), 3.

6. Dennis Porter, *Haunted Journeys: Desire and Transgression in European Travel Writing* (Princeton, 1991), 19–20, 304–5.

7. Michael Kowaleski, ed., *Temperamental Journeys: Essays on the Modern Literature of Travel* (Athens, Ga., 1992), 8.

8. Paul Fussell, *Abroad: British Literary Traveling between the Wars* (New York, 1980).

9. Eliza Ruhamah Scidmore, *China: The Long-Lived Empire* (New York, 1900), 456.

10. Victor Purcell, *Chinese Evergreen* (London: Michael Joseph, Ltd., 1938), 264.

11. Kowaleski, *Temperamental Journeys*, 14.

12. Mary Louise Pratt, *Imperial Eyes: Travel Writing and Transculturation* (London and New York, 1992), 34, 39, 57.

13. Eric Leed, *The Mind of the Traveler: From Gilgamesh to Global Tourism* (New York, 1991), 13, 50–51.

14. Chris Taylor et al., *China: A Lonely Planet Travel Survival Kit* (Hawthorn, Australia, 1996), 109.

15. Leed, *Mind*, 276–78; Sara Mills, *Discourses of Difference: An Analysis of Women's Travel Writing and Colonialism* (London and New York, 1991), 12, 111.

16. Archibald John Little, *Through the Yang-tse Gorges; or Trade and Travel in Western China*, 3d ed. (1887; rpt., Taipei, 1972), vii; Violet Cressy-Marcks, *Journey into China* (London, 1940), 1–2.

17. Mills, *Discourses*, 85, 103.

18. Paul Cohen, *Discovering History in China: American Historical Writing on the Recent Chinese Past* (New York, 1984) chap. 4; David Spurr, *The Rhetoric of Empire: Colonial Discourse in Journalism, Travel Writing, and Imperial Administration* (Durham, N.C., 1993), chap. 12; Porter, *Haunted Journeys*, 4–5. In fairness to Said it might be argued that his interest lies in the dissection of Orientalist texts and their discursive formations and "*not* with the[ir] correctness of the representation nor [their] fidelity to some great original" (*Orientalism* [New York, 1978], 21). Still, if one grants his suppositions, it would seem difficult, if not impossible, to judge the correctness of the representation.

19. Bird, *Yangtze Valley*, vii–viii.

20. Henry James, *Italian Hours*, ed. John Auchard (New York, 1995), 106.

21. Spurr, *Rhetoric*, 3; Porter, *Haunted Journeys*, 3.

22. Roland Barthes, *Empire of Signs*, trans. Richard Howard (New York, 1982), 7.

23. Spurr, *Rhetoric*, 46.

24. Porter, *Haunted Journeys*, 302.

25. Wilde, "The Decay of Lying," in *Oscar Wilde*, ed. Isobel Murray (Oxford and New York, 1989), 235. I am indebted to John Bertolini for pointing me to Wilde's passage.

26. Said, *Orientalism*, 3.

27. Edward Said, *Culture and Imperialism* (New York, 1993), 100. One might argue that Japanese imperialism was no more than an aping of Western forms of power—but, of course, such a statement would be thoroughly Orientalist.

28. To take two examples: in the index to Patrick Williams and Laura Chrisman's *Colonial Discourse and Post-Colonial Theory: A Reader* (New York, 1994) there is a single reference to China and none to Japan. Said himself (in *Orientalism*, 73) appears to believe that the Portuguese dominated Japan in the sixteenth and seventeenth centuries and stands the Shimabara Rebellion of 1637 on its head by seeing it directed not (as in fact it was) by Christian peasants against a fiercely anti-Christian *daimyo*, but against the Portuguese themselves.

29. Dawson, *Chinese Chameleon*, 59. Though Said makes a passing mention of this kind of Orientalism (in Mozart's *Entführung*, for instance), for the most part he leaves it unstudied. The subject forms a large part of Reichwein's *China and Europe*

and has been examined most recently by Spence in *The Chan's Great Continent*, especially chaps. 2 and 4.

30. Pratt, *Imperial Eyes*, 140–53.

31. Granted, there were a few exceptions. Mount Everest was one, if it's considered to be in China; so was Mount Morrison (Yushan), the highest peak in Taiwan (or Formosa, as it used to be called in the West).

32. Mills, *Discourses*, 12.

33. Porter, *Haunted Journeys*, 19; Pratt, *Imperial Eyes*, 31–32.

34. James Buzard, *The Beaten Track: European Tourism, Literature, and the Ways to Culture, 1800–1918* (New York, 1993), 31–40, 97.

35. Quoted in Buzard, *Beaten Track*, 85, 323.

36. Anthony Trollope, *The Duke's Children* (1880; rpt., London, 1973), 332.

37. Morrison, *An Australian in China; Being the narrative of a quiet journey across China to British Burma* (1895; rpt., London and Sydney, 1972), 1.

38. Archibald R. Colquhoun, *Overland to China* (New York and London, 1900), x–xi.

39. Archibald Little, *Through the Yang-tse Gorges*, 51, viii.

40. Scidmore, *China*, 8.

41. Elizah Ruhamah Scidmore, *Westward to the Far East: A Guide to the Principal Cities of China and Japan, with a Note on Korea*, 5th ed. (Montreal[?], 1894); John Henry Gray, *Walks in the City of Canton* (Victoria, Hong Kong, 1875); Alicia Little (Mrs. Archibald Little), *Guide to Peking* (Tientsin, 1904); *Cook's Handbook for Tourists to Peking, Tientsin, Shan-hai-kwan, Mukden, Dalny, Port Arthur, and Seoul* (London, 1910).

42. Bird, *Yangtze Valley*, 15.

43. Elizabeth Kendall, *A Wayfarer in China: Impressions of a Trip across West China and Mongolia* (Boston and New York, 1913), vii–viii.

44. Harold Acton, *Memoirs of an Aesthete* (1948; rpt., London, 1984), 294; George Kates, *The Years That Were Fat: Peking, 1933–1940* (New York, 1952), 8.

45. Owen Lattimore, *The Inner Asian Frontiers of China* (New York, 1951); Jean Heffer, *Les États-Unis et le Pacifique: histoire d'une frontière* (Paris, 1995), 11.

Chapter 2

1. Sybille C. Fritzsche, *Narrating China: Western Travelers in the Middle Kingdom after the Opium War* (Ann Arbor, 1995), 13.

2. Said, *Orientalism*, 206–7. For the place of race thinking in Darwin and the Darwinians, see Nancy Stepan, *The Idea of Race in Science: Great Britain, 1800–1960* (Hamden, Conn., 1982), chap. 3.

3. George W. Stocking Jr., *Race, Culture, and Evolution: Essays in the History of Anthropology* (New York, 1968), 119.

4. *Primitive Culture*, quoted in Stocking, *Race, Culture, and Evolution*, 81; A. H. Keane, *Ethnology*, 2d ed. (Cambridge, 1896), 322.

5. Reginald F. Johnston, *From Peking to Mandalay: A Journey from North China to*

Burma through Tibetan Ssuch'uan and Yunnan (1908; rpt., Taipei, 1972), 366–67. Of course, not all Europeans or all Orientals were the same; as late as 1919, Edward M. East of Harvard and Donald F. Jones, in *Inbreeding and Outbreeding,* could assert that the Irish were "principally the product of the intermingling of two savage Mongolian tribes" (cited in Elazar Barkan, *The Retreat of Scientific Racism: Changing Concepts of Race in Britain and the United States between the World Wars* [Cambridge, 1992], 227).

6. James Harrison Wilson, *China Travels and Investigations in the "Middle Kingdom": A Study of Its Civilization and Possibilities, with a Glance at Japan* (1887; rpt., Wilmington, Del., 1972), 22; see also Edwin J. Dingle, *Across China on Foot: Life in the Interior and the Reform Movement* (New York, 1911), 295.

7. Bishop, *Shangri-La,* 141, 159, 181–85; Porter, *Haunted Journeys,* 169; see also Said, *Orientalism,* 208.

8. Patrick Brantlinger, "Victorians and Africans: The Genealogy of the Myth of the Dark Continent," in Henry Louis Gates Jr., ed., *"Race," Writing, and Difference* (Chicago, 1986), 185–222; see particularly 201–6 for scientific racism; Robert H. Macdonald, *The Language of Empire: Myths and Metaphors of Popular Imperialism, 1880–1918* (Manchester, 1994), 32–36.

9. Richard Dobson, *China Cycle* (London, 1946), 41.

10. Wilson, *China,* 308, 82.

11. Wilson, *China,* x; Mrs. Archibald Little [Alicia Little], *Round about My Peking Garden* (London and Philadelphia, 1905), 39; Mary Gaunt, *A Woman in China* (London, n.d. [1914?]), 383.

12. Mills, *Discourses,* 190.

13. Said, *Orientalism,* 86.

14. For a fascinating discussion of the appropriation by the Orient of "Orientalist" categories, see Chen Xiaomei, "Occidentalism as Counterdiscourse: 'He Shang' in Post-Mao China," *Critical Inquiry* 18, no. 4 (Summer 1992): 686–712.

15. Scidmore, *China,* 1. The opening chapter, from which these words are taken, is called, appropriately enough, "The Degenerate Empire."

16. Gaunt, *Woman in China,* 38, 346.

17. Pratt, *Imperial Eyes,* 4.

18. James Buzard, "Victorian Women and the Implications of Empire," *Victorian Studies* 36, no. 4 (Summer 1993): 443–53.

19. Mills, *Discourses,* 95, 34–35. See also Dorothy Middleton, *Victorian Lady Travellers* (1965; rpt., Chicago, 1982), especially the introduction. Susan Morgan, noting this same phenomenon, suggests that we have exaggerated the constraints on Victorian women in order to congratulate ourselves on our modernity; see her book *Place Matters: Gendered Geography in Victorian Women's Travel Books about Southeast Asia* (New Brunswick, N.J., 1996), 19–20.

20. Mills, *Discourses,* 12, 81.

21. Middleton, *Lady Travellers,* 5.

22. Pratt, *Imperial Eyes,* 64, 75.

23. Mills, *Discourses,* 196.

24. Mills, *Discourses,* 4, 29–30, 196. In "Victorian Women," 450–51, James Buzard, as an exercise, takes an outrageously racist text and, by reading it ironically

as a critic might, manages to turn it into a piece of anti-imperialism, thus suggesting "that critics can complicate even the most seemingly univocal text."

25. Mary Gaunt, *A Broken Journey: Wanderings from the Hoang-ho to the Island of Saghalien and the Upper Reaches of the Amur River* (London, n.d. [1919?]), 146; Scidmore, *China*, 456–57.

26. Dea Birkett, *Spinsters Abroad: Victorian Lady Explorers* (Oxford, 1989), 137, 167.

27. Morgan, *Place Matters*, esp. chap. 1; see also Susan Schoenbauer Thurin, *Victorian Travelers and the Opening of China, 1842–107* (Athens, Ohio, 1999).

28. Archibald Little, *Through the Yang-tse Gorges*, xxi–xxiv; see also Nathan A. Pelcovits, *Old China Hands and the Foreign Office* (New York, 1948), 242–43.

29. Bird, *Yangtze Valley*, 29, 478.

30. Isabella L. Bird, *The Golden Chersonese and the Way Thither* (1883; rpt., Kuala Lumpur, 1967), 92.

31. Birkett, *Spinsters Abroad*, 242.

32. Archibald R. Colquhoun, *Across Chrysê: Being the Narrative of a Journey of Exploration through the South China Borderlands from Canton to Mandalay*, 2 vols. (New York, 1883), 1:vii, 1; 2:189–240.

33. Colquhoun, *Across Chrysê*, 1:248–49.

34. William Spencer Percival, *The Land of the Dragon: My Boating and Shooting Excursions to the Gorges of the Upper Yangtze* (London, 1889), 31.

35. Dingle, *Across China*, viii.

36. Johnston, *Peking to Mandalay*, 1, 265–92.

37. Gaunt, *Broken Journey*, 2.

38. Philip Wilson Pitcher, *In and about Amoy: Some Historical and Other Facts Connected with One of the First Open Ports in China* (Shanghai and Foochow, 1909), 89.

39. Archibald Little, *Through the Yang-tse Gorges*, ix.

40. Pitcher, *Amoy*, 90–91.

41. Bird, *Yangtze Valley*, 202, 205.

42. Dundas, Lawrence John Lumley, Earl of Ronaldshay, *A Wandering Student in the Far East*, 2 vols. (Edinburgh and London, 1908), 1:120.

43. Spurr examines the gaze in *Rhetoric*, chap. 1; see also Pratt, *Imperial Eyes*, 205; Fritzsche, *Narrating China*, 121, 171–73.

44. Bird, *Yangtze Valley*, 348, 250.

45. Dingle, *Across China*, 90.

46. Dingle, *Across China*, 21–22.

47. Dingle, *Across China*, 24–25.

48. Scidmore, *China*, 307, 316.

49. Constance Frederica Gordon Cumming, *Wanderings in China* (Edinburgh and London, 1880), 287–88, 315.

50. Colquhoun, *Across Chrysê*, 1:32, 36, 51.

51. R. Margary, *The Journey of Augustus Raymond Margary, from Shanghae to Bhamo, and Back to Manwyne. From His Journals and Letters, with a Brief Biographical Preface: To Which is Added a Concluding Chapter by Sir Rutherford Alcock, K. C. B.*, 2d ed. (London, 1876), 106.

52. Dingle, *Across China*, 172–73.

53. Eileen Bigland, *Into China* (London: Collins, 1940), 189.

54. Kendall, *Wayfarer*, 61.

55. Pratt, *Imperial Eyes*, 205.

56. Fritzsche, *Narrating China*, 12; see also 203; Leed, *Mind*, 68.

57. Dingle, *Across China*, 274–75.

58. Gaunt, *Broken Journey*, 37.

59. See L. Carrington Goodrich and Nigel Cameron, eds., *The Face of China as Seen by Photographers and Travelers, 1860–1912* (Millerton, N.Y., 1978); and Clark Worswick and Jonathan Spence, *Imperial China: Photographs, 1850–1912* (New York, 1978); Ernst Boerschmann, *Picturesque China, Architecture and Landscape: A Journey through Twelve Provinces* (New York, n.d. [1923?]); Eliot Porter, *All under Heaven: The Chinese World* (New York, 1983).

60. Colquhoun, *Across Chrysê*, 2:21.

61. Buzard, *Beaten Track*, 188.

62. Archibald Little, *Through the Yang-tse Gorges*, 167.

63. Bird, *Yangtze Valley*, 231.

64. Fritzsche, *Narrating China*, 12.

65. Colquhoun, *Across Chrysê*, 1:177.

66. Pitcher, *Amoy*, 32.

67. Gordon Cumming, *Wanderings*, 174–75.

68. Gordon Cumming, *Wanderings*, 28, 34.

69. Bird, *Chersonese*, 44, 51.

70. Gordon Cumming, *Wanderings*, 2, 372, 452; Bird, *Chersonese*, 64.

71. Gordon Cumming, *Wanderings*, 366, 371.

72. Wilson, *China*, 161.

73. Scidmore, *China* 183, 60–61.

74. Gordon Cumming, *Wanderings*, 388.

75. Little, *Round about My Peking Garden*, 15–18.

76. Gordon Cumming, *Wanderings*, 455.

77. Arthur Waldron, *The Great Wall of China: From History to Myth* (Cambridge, 1990), esp. chap. 11.

78. Scidmore, *China* 248. In the 1920s Adam Warwick made the more modest (and common) assertion that it could be seen from the moon (Adam Warwick, "A Thousand Miles along the Great Wall of China," *National Geographic* 43, no. 2 (February 1923): 123. For the history of this kind of statement, which continues to be repeated today, see Waldron, *Great Wall*, 1–2, 203–14.

79. Scidmore, *China*, 36–37.

80. Wilson, *China*, 219–20; Gaunt, *Woman in China*, 117–18, 127.

81. Kendall, *Wayfarer*, 234.

82. Dingle, *Across China*, 276.

83. Scidmore, *China*, 458–59.

84. Mills, *Discourses*, 90; Pratt, *Transculturation*, 153; see also Spurr, *Rhetoric*, on "Debasement: Filth and Defilement," 76–91.

85. Buzard, *Beaten Track*, 189–90, 207.

86. Morrison, *Australian*, 99.

87. Dingle, *Across China*, 250–51, 80–81. See also Archibald Little, *Through the Yang-tse Gorges*, 158; and Arthur H. Smith, *Chinese Characteristics* (Boston and Chicago, 1894), 271.

88. Bird, *Yangtze Valley*, 194.

89. Agnes Smedley, *Battle Hymn of China* (New York, 1943), 196; Colquhoun, *Across Chrysê*, 2:47; Morrison, *Australian*, 141; also Dundas, *Student in China*, 1:167.

90. Bird, *Chersonese*, 67–76, 83–85. The morbid fascination with such scenes lives on; see "Mainland's Final Site for the Condemned," *South China Morning Post* (Hong Kong), 30 October 1998.

91. Bird, *Yangtze Valley*, 217.

92. Morrison, *Australian*, 103–4, 139.

93. Archibald Little, *Through the Yang-tse Gorges*, 168.

94. Little, *Round about My Peking Garden*, 143. For Mrs. Little's stand on footbinding, see Thurin, *Victorian Travelers*, 182–87.

95. Gaunt, *Broken Journey*, 82.

96. Larissa N. Heinrich, "Handmaids to the Gospel: Lam Qua's Medical Portraiture," in *Tokens of Exchange: The Problem of Translation in Global Circulations*, ed. Lydia Liu (Durham, N.C., 1999), 269–70.

97. Little, *Round about My Peking Garden*, 194.

Chapter 3

1. Leed, *Mind*, 172.

2. Scidmore, *China*, 4.

3. Johnston, *Peking to Mandalay*, 370–71.

4. See, for instance, R. Bin Wong, *China Transformed: Historical Change and the Limits of European Experience* (Ithaca, N.Y., 1997); and Andre Gunder Frank, *ReOrient: Global Economy in the Asian Age* (Berkeley, 1998). The reasons for China's decline have been much debated. Two good starting points, besides the books of Wong and Frank, are Ping-ti Ho, *Studies on the Population of China, 1368–1953* (Cambridge, Mass., 1959); and Mark Elvin, *The Pattern of the Chinese Past* (Stanford, 1973).

5. The distinction between *civilization* and *Civilization* draws on a similar distinction between *history* and *History* (as the Enlightenment defined it) used by Prasenjit Duara in *Rescuing History from the Nation: Questioning Narratives of Modern China* (Chicago, 1995). For some of the recent debates in China on *wenming* and *wenhua*, with their overtones of distinction between *civilization* and *culture*, see Ann Anagnost, *National Past-Times: Narrative, Representation, and Power in Modern China* (Durham, N.C., 1997), 75–97.

6. MacKenzie, *Orientalism*, 214.

7. Gaunt, *Woman in China*, 38.

8. MacDonald, *Language of Empire*, 43, 75–76, 168.

9. David Starr Jordan, *The Human Harvest: A Study of the Decay of Races through the Survival of the Unfit* (Boston, 1907).

10. Reichwein, *China and Europe*, 77.

11. Gordon Cumming, *Wanderings*, 127, 403.

12. Wilson, *China*, 309.

13. Dingle, *Across China*, 174.

14. Bird, *Yangtze Valley*, 367, 177–78.

15. Scidmore, *China*, 279; Dundas, *Student in China*, 1:71.

16. Scidmore, *China*, 336.

17. Scidmore, *China*, 5–6.

18. Bird, *Yangtze Valley*, chap. 17; Gaunt, *Woman in China*, 144–49.

19. Bird, *Yangtze Valley*, 11–12; Little, *Round about My Peking Garden*, 176.

20. Bird, *Yangtze Valley*, 11, 276; Little, *Round about My Peking Garden*, 238, referring to the *juren*, the degree granted at the provincial level of the civil service examinations, and often translated as *master's degree*.

21. Scidmore, *China*, 23, 57, 279, 456–57.

22. Gaunt, *Broken Journey*, 146.

23. Bird, *Yangtze Valley*, 544.

24. Scidmore, *China*, 154.

25. Wilson, *China*, 20–22.

26. Scidmore, *China*, 281, 285–86.

27. Gaunt, *Woman in China*, 233.

28. Kendall, *Wayfarer*, 85.

29. Bird, *Yangtze Valley*, 20–21, 64–65; Dingle, *Across China*, 44–47.

30. Gaunt, *Woman*, 251.

31. Gaunt, *Woman in China*, 139; Bird, *Yangtze Valley*, 523. Wilson made the same point (*China*, 348).

32. Little, *Round about My Peking Garden*, 216–18.

33. For an interesting discussion of the imagined similarities of Catholicism and what Westerners called "lamaism" (Tibetan and Mongol Buddhism), see Donald S. Lopez, *Prisoners of Shangri-la: Tibetan Buddhism and the West* (Chicago, 1998), 21–40.

34. Gaunt, *Broken Journey*, 75–76; *Woman in China*, 139.

35. Archibald Little, *Through the Yang-tse Gorges*, 214.

36. Wilson, *China*, 348; Gaunt, *Woman in China*, 387; J. A. Hobson, *Imperialism: A Study*, 3d rev. ed. (1938; rpt., Ann Arbor, 1965), 202. Hobson's book appeared originally in 1902.

37. Kendall, *Wayfarer*, 211.

38. Archibald Little, *Through the Yang-tse Gorges*, 174; Kendall, *Wayfarer*, 157.

39. Bird, *Yangtze Valley*, 101–2; Wilson, *China*, 286–88.

40. Gaunt, *Woman in China*, 387.

41. Patrick Brantlinger, *Rule of Darkness: British Literature and Imperialism, 1830–1924* (Ithaca, N.Y., 1988), 194–95.

42. Gaunt, *Broken Journey*, 50–51.

43. Arnold, *A Handbook to the West River, Being a Short Description of the Chief Places of Interest between Canton and Wuchow*, 2d rev. ed. (Hong Kong, 1909), 52.

44. Dingle, *Across China*, 72, 430.

45. Bird, *Yangtze Valley*, 291.

46. Bird, *Yangtze Valley*, 521.

47. Scidmore, *China*, 287.

48. Scidmore, *China*, 115; Wilson, *China*, 107, 158; the later references to Li can be found in the third edition of his work (New York, 1901), xiii, 101, 150.

49. Gaunt, *Woman in China*, 70. The reference to murder presumably has to do with the killing of the Nationalist Party leader Song Jiaoren by Yuan Shikai's gunmen in March 1913.

50. Dundas, *Student in China*, 1:162.

51. Dingle, *Across China*, 113–14, 68, 215–16; Kendall, *Wayfarer*, 28.

52. Scidmore, *China*, 456–57.

53. Archibald Little, *Through the Yang-tse Gorges*, 117.

54. For examples from Feng, Li, Guo, and Ma, see the excerpts in J. K. Fairbank and S. Y. Teng, *China's Response to the West* (Cambridge, Mass., 1961), 53, 57, 95–97, 100–101; for the impact of social Darwinism, see James Pusey, *China and Charles Darwin* (Cambridge, Mass., 1983). Frank Dikötter, however, objects to the use of the term for China; see his book *The Discourse of Race in Modern China* (Stanford, 1992), 100–101.

55. Ban Wang, *The Sublime Figure of History: Aesthetics and Politics in Twentieth Century China* (Stanford, 1997), 57–59.

56. Smedley, *Battle Hymn*, 59. For the Feetham report, see Nicholas Clifford, *Spoilt Children of Empire: Westerners in Shanghai and the Chinese Revolution of the 1920s* (Hanover, N.H., 1991), 271–72.

57. Qiu Jin (Ch'iu Chin), "An Address to Two Hundred Million Fellow Countrywomen," in *Chinese Civilization and Society: A Sourcebook*, ed. Patricia Ebrey (New York, 1981), 247–48.

58. Pratt, *Imperial Eyes*, 7–8; Arif Dirlik, "Chinese History and the Question of Orientalism," *History and Theory* 35, no. 4 (December 1996): 96–119.

59. Scidmore, *China*, 4.

60. Gaunt, *Woman in China*, 18–19, 383.

61. Dingle, *Wayfarer*, 283–84.

62. Bird, *Yangtze Valley*, 13.

Chapter 4

1. Elizabeth Crump Enders, *Swinging Lanterns* (New York, 1923), 170–71.

2. Florence Ayscough, *A Chinese Mirror: Being Reflections of the Reality behind Appearance* (Boston and New York, n.d.[1925?]), 334.

3. In a sequel to *Swinging Lanterns*, however, Enders passed a harsher judgment on footbinding (*Temple Bells and Silver Sails* [New York, 1925], 257–58).

4. Among the representative journalistic and scholarly writings of the period were: Thomas F. Millard, *China: Where It Is Today and Why* (New York, 1928); Putnam Weale (Bertram Lennox Simpson), *Why China Sees Red* (New York, 1925); P. T. Etherton, *The Crisis in China* (Boston, 1927); Harley Farnsworth MacNair, *China in Revolution: An Analysis of Politics and Militarism under the Republic* (Chicago, 1931);

Lionel Curtis, *The Capital Question of China* (London, 1932); Hallett Abend and Anthony Billingham, *Can China Survive?* (New York, 1936); and Edgar Ansel Mowrer, *The Dragon Wakes: A Report from China* (New York, 1939).

5. Bertrand Russell, *The Problem of China* (London, 1922), 16.

6. Russell, *Problem,* 17, 65.

7. For the use of the term *warlord,* which both Chinese and foreigners saw as central to an understanding of China in the 1920s, see Arthur Waldron, "The Warlord: Twentieth-Century Chinese Understandings of Violence, Militarism, and Imperialism," *American Historical Review* 96, no. 4 (October 1991): 1073–1100.

8. Lothrop Stoddard, *The Rising Tide of Color against White World-Supremacy* (New York, 1922), 180–96.

9. Pratt, *Imperial Eyes,* 74.

10. Russell, *Problem,* 16. In his fear of "negro armies" Russell was joined by the American race writer Lothrop Stoddard (*Rising Tide,* 208–11) as well as progressives such as G. Lowes Dickinson, who warned that the black troops being raised in the French colonies might overwhelm Europe (Philip Darby, *Three Faces of Imperialism: British and American Approaches to Asia and Africa, 1870–1970* [New Haven, 1987], 104), while E. D. Morel protested against the "primitive African barbarians" in the French army of occupation in the Rhineland (Barkan, *Retreat,* 24).

11. Russell, *Problem,* 167.

12. See, for instance, Upton Close [Josef W. Hall], "The Dove in Chinese War: The Ultimate Appeal to Reason in the Comic Madhouse of Martial China," *Asia* 25, no. 3 (March 1925); 1:233–37, 246–48 see also Close's *In the Land of the Laughing Buddha: The Adventures of an American Barbarian in China* (New York and London, 1924).

13. Russell, *Problem,* 193.

14. Graham Peck, *Through China's Wall* (Boston, 1940), 272–73.

15. Jackson Lears, *No Place of Grace: Antimodernism and the Transformation of American Culture, 1880–1920* (Chicago, 1994), 175.

16. For Pound's and Buck's contributions to American visions of China, see Spence, *Continent,* 168–74,and 180–83.

17. The title of chap. 6 of *The Chinese Chameleon.*

18. Noel Annan, *Our Age: English Intellectuals between the World Wars—a Group Portrait* (New York, 1990), 79.

19. On the other hand, as late as 1925, Putnam Weale was capable of writing "that the nervous energy of the educated Chinese is 0.24 of the white man and that of the laborer 0.18," the scientific precision of his figures explaining why it would never do to employ Chinese in the place of individual foreigners (*Why China Sees Red,* 282). Particularly in the United States this period brought a new interest in eugenics. Madison Grant's book *The Passing of the Great Race* was published in 1916, for example; for its effect and the work of the American eugenics societies, see Barkan, *Retreat,* 69–76.

20. See Stoddard, *Rising Tide,* 27–31, 236–98. Chinese immigration had been effectively prohibited after 1882; by 1904, when a Sino-American treaty of 1894 expired, an exclusion act had already been passed without a terminal date. On 17 December 1943 an annual quota of 105 immigrants from China was to be allowed.

Elazar Barkan cites a study of the children of mixed English and Chinese parentage done in Liverpool in the late 1920s under the sponsorship of the Eugenics Society. It concluded that, even though such children were in no way inferior to their peers, "the continuation of the birth of numbers of these children in our midst is a serious social danger" (Barkan, *Retreat*, 63).

21. Martin Green, *Dreams of Adventure, Deeds of Empire* (New York, 1979), 321–23.

22. John M. MacKenzie, *Propaganda and Empire: The Manipulation of British Public Opinion, 1880–1960* (Manchester, 1984), 10, 252.

23. Dobson, *China Cycle*, 1.

24. Robin Hyde, *Dragon Rampant* (London, n.d. [1939?]), 38.

25. Gerald Yorke, *China Changes* (New York, 1936), 19.

26. Peter Fleming, *One's Company: A Journey to China* (New York, 1934), foreword. In earlier years this kind of humorous disclaimer had generally been more typically found in women's travel accounts (see Mills, *Discourses*, 77–78).

27. Speakman, *Beyond Shanghai* (New York, 1922), 12.

28. Harry Franck, *Roving through Southern China* (New York, 1925), vii–viii.

29. Osbert Sitwell, *Escape with Me: An Oriental Sketch-Book* (New York, 1940), xiii–xv.

30. Ilona Ralf Sues, *Shark's Fins and Millet* (Boston, 1944), 8.

31. Barthes, *Empire*, 9.

32. Acton, *Memoirs*, 275–76.

33. Kates, *Years That Were Fat*, 11–12; see also Acton, *Memoirs*, 327.

34. Acton, *Memoirs*, 371.

35. Eric Teichman, *Travels of a Consular Officer in North-West China* (Cambridge, 1921), 86.

36. Purcell, *Chinese Evergreen*, 41.

37. Owen Lattimore, *The Desert Road to Turkestan* (1929; rpt., New York, 1995), 16.

38. *China Weekly Review* (Shanghai), 39, no. 11 (12 February 1927): 290.

39. *China Year Book, 1938*, ed. H. G. W. Woodhead (Shanghai, 1938), 570.

40. E. Darwent, *Shanghai: A Handbook for Travellers and Residents to the Chief Objects of Interest In and Around the Foreign Settlements and Native City*, 2d ed. (Shanghai, 1920); *All about Shanghai and Environs: A Standard Guidebook* (1934–35; rpt., Hong Kong, 1983); *Guide to China, with Land and Sea Routes between the American and European Continents*, 2d rev. ed. (Tokyo, 1924); *Peking and the Overland Route*, 3d ed. (London, 1917); *Peking, North China, South Manchuria and Korea*, 5th ed. (London, 1924); Carl Crow, *Handbook for China (including Hongkong)*, 4th ed. (New York, 1926).

41. Peck, *Through China's Wall*, 9.

42. Purcell, *Chinese Evergreen*, 149.

43. Dobson, *China Cycle*, 117.

44. Fleming, *One's Company*, 232–33.

45. Enders, *Temple Bells*, 329–32.

46. *China Year Book, 1938*, 246–47.

47. Denton Welch, *Maiden Voyage* (1943; rpt., Harmondsworth, 1983), 127.

48. Mrs. Cecil Chesterton (Ada Elizabeth Chesterton), *Young China and New Japan* (Philadelphia, n.d. [1933?], 117.

49. Purcell, *Chinese Evergreen*, 52.

50. Fleming, *One's Company*, 93.

51. Cressy-Marcks, *Journey*, 84; Bigland, *Into China*, 273.

52. Fleming, *One's Company*, 288–89; Peck, *Through China's Wall*, 250.

53. See, for instance, Mabel Croft Deering, "Ho for the Soochow Ho," *National Geographic* 51, no. 6 (June 1927): 623–49, for a description of a trip to the "Venice of China."

54. Franck, *Wandering in Northern China* (New York, 1923), 289.

55. Graham Peck, *Two Kinds of Time* (Boston, 1950), 28.

56. Chesterton, *Young China*, 116, 174.

57. John Dewey and Alice Chipman Dewey, *Letters from China and Japan*, ed. Evelyn Dewey (New York, 1920), 262.

58. Scidmore, *China*, 61.

59. Franck, *Southern China*, ix.

60. Porter, *Haunted Journeys*, 164.

61. Dean McCannell, *The Tourist: A New Theory of the Leisure Class* (New York, 1976, issued with new introduction in 1989), 10. "Self-contempt and a sense of fraudulence distinguish the attitude of contemporary, self-conscious travelers," writes Eric Leed. "There is a touching desperation in the attempts of professional tourists, well-funded anthropologists, and recording travelers, to distinguish themselves from the traveling masses and run-of-the-mill adventurers" (*Mind*, 286–87). But the sentiment is still with us. "China: Be a traveler, not a tourist," runs an advertisement in *Harvard Magazine* of October 1998 from Marco Polo and Company, complete with toll-free telephone number and website address.

62. Spurr, *Rhetoric*, 49.

63. Buzard, *Beaten Track*, 5–6; Fussell, *Abroad*, 47.

64. Speakman, *Beyond Shanghai*, 17.

65. Bird, *Yangtze Valley*, 195.

66. Arthur Ransome, *The Chinese Puzzle* (London, 1927), 28–32; Nicholas R. Clifford, "A Revolution Is Not a Tea Party: The Shanghai Mind(s) Reconsidered," *Pacific Historical Review* 59, no. 4 (November 1990): 501–26.

Chapter 5

1. Renato Rosaldo, "Imperialist Nostalgia," *Representations* 26 (Spring 1989): 107–8.

2. James, "Autumn in Florence" (1873), *Italian Hours*, 239.

3. Langdon Warner, *The Long Old Road in China* (Garden City, N.Y., 1926), 157.

4. Robert Bickers, *Britain in China: Community, Culture and Colonialism, 1900–1949* (Manchester, 1999), 29–30.

5. Lu Xun, "Some Notions Jotted Down by Lamp-light" (29 April 1925), *Selected Works* (Beijing, 1964), 2:140.

6. Russell, *Problem of China*, 201.

7. Emily Lucy de Burgh Daly, *An Irishwoman in China* (London, 1915), 72.

8. Pratt, *Imperial Eyes*, 7.

9. Smedley, *Battle Hymn*, 52.

10. Innes Jackson, *China Only Yesterday* (London, 1938), 46.

11. Acton, *Memoirs*, 276.

12. Grace Thompson Seton, *Chinese Lanterns* (New York, 1924), 106.

13. Fleming, *One's Company*, 238–39.

14. Enders, *Swinging Lanterns*, 37–38.

15. Speakman, *Beyond Shanghai*, 30, 33.

16. Speakman, *Beyond Shanghai*, 49, 68.

17. Sitwell, *Escape*, xiii.

18. Buzard, *Beaten Track*, 209.

19. Ayscough, *Chinese Mirror*, 148, 155, 195.

20. Yorke, *China Changes*, 145–46.

21. Yorke, *China Changes*, 147.

22. Yorke, *China Changes*, 163.

23. Seton, *Chinese Lanterns*, 44.

24. Peck, *Through China's Wall*, 5, 7.

25. *Peking and the Overland Route*, 1.

26. Warwick, "Along the Great Wall of China," 137.

27. Harold Acton, *Peonies and Ponies* (1941; rpt., Hong Kong, 1983), 299.

28. Enders, *Swinging Lanterns*, 83.

29. L. C. Arlington and William Lewisohn, *In Search of Old Peking* (1935; rpt., Hong Kong, 1991), v–vi.

30. Mrs. Alec-Tweedie (Ethel Brillana Tweedie), *An Adventurous Journey: Russia-Siberia-China*, 2d ed. (London, 1929), 116; Franck, *Northern China*, 201, 435.

31. Sitwell, *Escape*, xx.

32. Kates, *Years*, 25, 49.

33. Acton, *Memoirs*, 276.

34. Acton, *Memoirs*, 328.

35. Peck, *Through China's Wall*, 17–19.

36. Sitwell, *Escape*, 161–63, xvi–xvii.

37. Peck, *Through China's Wall*, 26–27; Acton, *Memoirs*, 327–28.

38. L. H. Dudley Buxton, *The Eastern Road* (London, 1924), 214; Acton, *Memoirs*, 327–31, 380.

39. Acton, *Memoirs*, 355; Cressy-Marcks, *Into China*, 135. Some sixty years earlier Archibald Colquhoun had also found Chinese music "Wagnerian," in that it appeared to some to consist of "simple noise" (*Across Chrysê*, 1:14).

40. Sitwell, *Escape*, 302.

41. James, *Italian Hours*, 239.

42. Acton, *Memoirs*, 404.

43. Enders, *Temple Bells*, chap. 16.

44. McCannell, *Tourist*, 91–102. McCannell's analysis distinguishes between various kinds of "backs," some more real than others.

45. Dundas, *Student in China*, 1:39.
46. Franck, *Southern China*, viii.
47. Jackson, *China Only Yesterday*, 43.
48. Peck, *Through China's Wall*, 56.
49. Peck, *Through China's Wall*, 158–60.
50. Enders, *Temple Bells*, 288.
51. Franck, *Southern China*, vii–viii.
52. Franck, *Northern China*, viii.
53. Russell, *Problem*, 160. Russell was by no means alone in holding such a belief; various others, English and French, shared the view.
54. Franck, *Northern China*, 308.
55. Franck, *Northern China*, 143–45, 150; *Southern China*, 129–30.
56. For the comparisons to Rome, see Franck, *Northern China*, 150; *Southern China*, 591.
57. Franck, *Southern China*, 401.
58. Franck, *Southern China*, 6–7.
59. Walter H. Mallory, *China: Land of Famine* (1926; rpt., Freeport, N.Y., 1972).
60. Gordon Cumming, *Wanderings*, 15.
61. Gretchen Mae Fitkin, *The Great River: The Story of a Voyage on the Yangtze Kiang* (Shanghai, 1922), 128.
62. Buxton, *Eastern Road*, 214–15.
63. Peck, *Through China's Wall*, 320–21.
64. Goodrich and Cameron, *Face of China*, 89.
65. Bird, *Chersonese*, 67–76, 83–84.
66. Franck, *Northern China*, 333, 362–63.
67. Fleming, *One's Company*, 170.
68. Fritzsche, "Narrating China," 116.
69. Seton, *Chinese Lanterns*, 153.

Chapter 6

1. Advertisement for the American Mail and Dollar Lines, *Asia* 30, no. 3 (March 1930): 220.
2. Russell, *Problem*, 75; Enders, *Swinging Lanterns*, 7; Kates, *Years That Were Fat*, 8.
3. Jackson, *China Only Yesterday*, 24.
4. Marie-Claire Bergère discusses Shanghai's relationship to the "real China" in "'The Other China': Shanghai from 1919 to 1949," in *Shanghai: Revolution and Development in an Asian Metropolis*, ed. Christopher Howe (Cambridge, 1981), 1–35.
5. Peck, *Wall*, 133.
6. Fleming, *One's Company*, 177–78.
7. Franck, *Southern China*, 1.
8. W. H. Auden and Christopher Isherwood, *Journey to a War* (London, 1939), 237–38.

9. Bickers, *Britain in China*, 87.

10. Robert Bickers and Jeffrey Wasserstrom, "Shanghai's 'Dogs and Chinese Not Admitted' Sign: Legend, History and Contemporary Symbol," *China Quarterly* 142 (June 1995): 444–466, give the fullest account of the supposed existence of this sign.

11. Christian Henriot, *Shanghai: élites locales et modernisation dans la Chine Nationaliste* (Paris, 1991), 56–69.

12. Fleming, *One's Company*, 87.

13. Acton, *Memoirs*, 289.

14. Darwent, *Shanghai*, 84–85.

15. Sues, *Shark's Fins*, 89–90.

16. Fu-Manchu also had an "amazing skull," "clawish hand," eyes sometimes "horribly filmed," and "his emotionless face [was] a mask of incredible evil." Sax Rohmer's 1916 description of his creation is quoted in Spence, *Continent*, 140.

17. Peck, *Through China's Wall*, 134.

18. Hyde, *Dragon Rampant*, 89.

19. Auden and Isherwood, *Journey*, 243–52; Christopher Isherwood, *Christopher and His Kind, 1929–1939* (New York, 1976), 308.

20. Dobson, *China Cycle*, 206.

21. *Cook's Handbook for Tourists*, 68.

22. Seton, *Chinese Lanterns*, 163, 165–66.

23. Franck, *Southern China*, 266–69.

24. Fleming, *One's Company*, 300; Sues, *Shark's Fins*, 22.

25. Auden and Isherwood, *Journey*, 29.

26. Scidmore, *China*, 432; Franck, *Southern China*, 225; Auden and Isherwood, *Journey*, 30.

27. Acton, *Memoirs*, 294–95.

28. Purcell, *Chinese Evergreen*, 12–13.

29. Purcell, *Chinese Evergreen*, 38.

30. Purcell, *Chinese Evergreen*, 13.

31. Spurr, *Rhetoric*, 32–36.

32. Jackson, *Only Yesterday*, 285–86, 276–78, 156; Smedley, *Battle Hymn*, 58. It had been designed by the Cornell-trained architect Y. C. Lu (Lu Yuanzh).

33. Fussell, *Abroad*, 216.

34. Chesterton, *Young China*, 9.

35. American reporting on China has been examined in various studies; two of the most recent are Janice R. and Stephen R. MacKinnon, *China Reporting* (Berkeley, 1987); and Peter Rand, *China Hands: The Adventures and Ordeals of the American Journalists Who Joined Forces with the Great Chinese Revolution* (New York, 1995).

36. Yorke, *China Changes*, 51, 55; Fleming, *One's Company*, 203–4.

37. Yorke, *China Changes*, 245.

38. Yorke, *China Changes*, 177; Fleming, *One's Company*, 221, 227.

39. Fleming, *One's Company*, 237, 251, 258–60.

40. Fleming, *One's Company*, 267.

41. Fleming, *One's Company*, 188, 190, 243.

42. Fleming, *One's Company*, 185.

43. Fleming, *One's Company*, 300–301.

44. Peter Fleming, *News from Tartary* (1936; rpt., London, 1980). Ella K. Maillart, *Forbidden Journey: From Peking to Kashmir*, trans. Thomas McGreevy (New York, 1937), gives her side of the trip.

45. Fleming, *One's Company*, 257–58.

46. John Maxwell Hamilton, *Edgar Snow: A Biography* (Bloomington, Ind., 1988), 90. The following analysis of *Red Star* draws heavily on my essay "White China, Red China: Lighting Out for the Territory with Edgar Snow," *New England Review* 18, no. 2 (Spring 1997): 103–11.

47. See, for example, Felix Greene, *Awakened China: The Country Americans Don't Know* (New York, 1961). Both this book and the documentary film made from it were remarkable in showing how similar the Chinese were to Americans, a view that in those days could hardly have been flattering to Mao and his colleagues, whatever Greene's intentions. The film had a charming scene of a little girl showing her aging granny how she was learning to write; what it neglected to say was that the characters shown on screen read, "Mao zhuxi wansui!" (Long live Chairman Mao!).

48. Edgar Snow, *Red Star over China* (New York, 1938), 3, 8.

49. Peter Bishop, *Shangri-La*; and Donald Lopez, *Prisoners of Shangri-La*, both address this aspect of the West's Tibet.

50. Snow, *Red Star*, 8.

51. Snow, *Red Star*, 9.

52. Snow, *Red Star*, 13.

53. Snow, *Red Star*, 101.

54. Acton, *Memoirs*, 354–55.

55. Snow, *Red Star*, 280, 106.

56. Snow, *Red Star*, 57.

57. Pratt, *Imperial Eyes*, 220. She makes the point about Paul Theroux on Patagonia and Alberto Moravia on Africa, but the idea is the same.

58. Snow, *Red Star*, 17, 29, 31. Snow, for reasons of his companion's safety, made no mention of George Hatem (Ma Haide), the American doctor who accompanied him across the frontier (Hamilton, *Edgar Snow*, 70).

59. Snow, *Red Star*, 23.

60. Snow, *Red Star*, 30, 45, 263.

61. Snow, *Red Star*, 66, 69–70.

62. Snow, *Red Star*, 71.

63. Snow, *Red Star*, 13.

64. Snow, *Red Star*, 68, 84, 92–93.

65. Snow, *Red Star*, 51.

66. *North China Herald* (Shanghai), 7 May 1927, 243.

67. Spurr, *Rhetoric of Empire*, 41; Pratt, *Imperial Eyes*, 3, 7, and chaps. 3 and 4.

68. See, for instance, Kenneth Shewmaker, *Americans and Chinese Communists, 1927–1945: A Persuading Encounter* (Ithaca, N.Y., 1971), 257–58; Tang Tsou, *America's Failure in China, 1941–1950* (Chicago, 1963), 231–33.

69. Leed, *Mind*, 142–44.

Chapter 7

1. Fleming, *News from Tartary*, 11–12.
2. Fleming, *One's Company*, 78, 131.
3. Jackson, *China Only Yesterday*, 42.
4. Hyde, *Dragon Rampant*, 162.
5. Auden and Isherwood, *Journey*, 156, 214, 232.
6. Fleming, *One's Company*, 126–27.
7. Joy Homer, *Dawn Watch in China* (Boston, 1941), 285.
8. Frank Clune, *Sky High to Shanghai: An Account of My Oriental Travels in the Spring of 1938, with Side Glances at the History, Geography and Politics of the Asiatic Littoral, Written with Charity to All and Malice to None* (Sydney and London, 1939), 202.
9. Clune, *Sky High*, 173, 177.
10. Peck, *Two Kinds of Time*, 11–20.
11. Purcell, *Chinese Evergreen*, 124–25.
12. Purcell, *Chinese Evergreen*, 258.
13. Purcell, *Chinese Evergreen*, 160.
14. Auden and Isherwood, *Journey*, 45–46, 74.
15. Hyde, *Dragon Rampant*, 172.
16. Homer, *Dawn Watch*, 65–66.
17. Peck, *Two Kinds of Time*, 235, 238–39.
18. Cressy-Marcks, *Journey*, 35–36, 84.
19. Bigland, *Into China*, 14–15, 164–65.
20. Fussell, *Abroad*, 19.
21. Auden and Isherwood, *Journey to a War*, 29, 34.
22. Some examples are: Harold Isaacs, *Scratches on Our Minds*; Shewmaker, *Persuading Encounter*; Tang Tsou, *America's Failure*, esp. chap. 6, "The American Image of Chinese Communism"; T. Christopher Jespersen, *American Images of China, 1931–1949* (Stanford, 1996); Rand, *China Hands*.
23. Smedley, *Battle Hymn*, 285.
24. Peck, *Through China's Wall*, 288.
25. Peck, *Through China's Wall*, 294–95, 320–23.
26. Auden and Isherwood, *Journey to a War*, 71.
27. Brian Finney, *Christopher Isherwood: A Critical Biography* (New York, 1979), 168.
28. Auden and Isherwood, *Journey to a War*, 13.
29. Auden and Isherwood, *Journey to a War*, 207.
30. Auden and Isherwood, *Journey to a War*, 115.
31. Auden and Isherwood, *Journey to a War*, 226.
32. Auden and Isherwood, *Journey to a War*, 35–36.
33. Auden and Isherwood, *Journey to a War*, 216.
34. Auden and Isherwood, *Journey to a War*, 49–50.
35. Auden and Isherwood, *Journey to a War*, 59.
36. Chesterton, *Young China*, 127.
37. Mowrer, *Dragon Wakes*, 82.
38. Auden and Isherwood, *Journey to a War*, 65, 69.

39. Dobson, *China Cycle,* 111–12.

40. Cressy-Marcks, *Journey,* 86; Homer, *Dawn Watch,* 70, 85; Bigland, *Into China,* 274–76.

41. Bigland, *Into China,* 282.

42. Homer, *Dawn Watch,* 76, 256–57.

43. Homer, *Dawn Watch,* 77–78.

44. Homer, *Dawn Watch,* 180, 161.

45. Homer, *Dawn Watch,* 270–71.

46. Robert Payne, *China Awake* (New York, 1947), viii.

47. Homer, *Dawn Watch,* 227.

48. Smedley, *Battle Hymn,* 380–81, 511–12.

49. Smedley, *Battle Hymn,* 197.

50. Homer, *Dawn Watch,* 121.

51. Peck, *Two Kinds of Time,* 363–65. For the Chinese university, see John Israel, *Lianda: A Chinese University in War and Revolution* (Stanford, 1998).

52. Peck, *Two Kinds of Time,* 308–9, 580–81, 476–79.

53. Peck, *Two Kinds of Time,* 99.

54. Smedley, *Battle Hymn,* 31.

55. Smedley, *Battle Hymn,* 329–30, 372–73.

56. Peck, *Two Kinds of Time,* 157, 202, 205.

57. Peck, *Two Kinds of Time,* 47–48, 250.

58. Peck, *Two Kinds of Time,* 179.

59. Peck, *Two Kinds of Time,* 154–55.

60. Pratt, *Imperial Eyes,* 152–53.

61. Smedley, *Battle Hymn,* 249; see also 372–73.

62. Smedley, *Battle Hymn,* 500–503.

63. Smedley, *Battle Hymn,* 150.

64. Robert J. Lifton, *Revolutionary Immortality* (New York, 1968), 6, and endnote, 163–64, examines the uses of the term and its meaning.

65. Smedley, *Battle Hymn,* 181.

66. Auden and Isherwood, *Journey to a War,* 61.

67. Shewmaker, *Persuading Encounter,* 72–85.

68. Cressy-Marcks, *Journey,* 162.

69. Cressy-Marcks, unfortunately, was very sparing in her use of dates, and, though Sir Percy Sykes, who wrote the introduction to her book, says her trip took place in 1938, in fact it appears to have begun early in 1937, for she referred to being in China for New Year's on 11 February, the date on which that festival fell in 1937. That may explain her apparent ignorance of earlier trips by others to Yan'an. The date of her arrival in Xi'an, in any case, is firm.

70. Cressy-Marcks, *Journey,* 143, 153–54.

71. Cressy-Marcks, *Journey,* 171, 183.

72. Cressy-Marcks, *Journey,* 184–86, 238.

73. Cressy-Marcks, *Journey,* 172, 176–80.

74. Cressy-Marcks, *Journey,* 163–64.

75. Cressy-Marcks, *Journey,* 188.

76. Cressy-Marcks, *Journey*, 193.

77. Cressy-Marcks, *Journey*, 194.

78. Homer, *Dawn Watch*, 151, 156–57.

79. Homer, *Dawn Watch*, 186–94, 203–12, 219.

80. Homer, *Dawn Watch*, 223. For the subsidy—probably about $600,000 a month—which lasted from 1937 until about early 1941, see Mark Selden, *The Yenan Way in Revolutionary China* (Cambridge, Mass., 1971), 139, 180.

81. Homer, *Dawn Watch*, 227.

82. Homer, *Dawn Watch*, 236–39, 269, 237.

83. Smedley, *Battle Hymn*, 178; Shewmaker, *Persuading Encounter*, 73.

84. Smedley, *Battle Hymn*, 169.

85. McCannell, *Tourist*, 101–2.

86. Smedley, *Battle Hymn*, 152.

87. Smedley, *Battle Hymn*, 378–79.

88. Smedley, *Battle Hymn*, 299.

89. Sues, *Shark's Fins*, 192.

90. Sues, *Shark's Fins*, 226.

91. Sues, *Shark's Fins*, 231–36, 276, 255.

92. Sues, *Shark's Fins*, 234.

93. Sues, *Shark's Fins*, 279–81.

94. Sues, *Shark's Fins*, 248–49. For Lebbe's death, see Maochun Yu, *OSS in China: Prelude to Cold War* (New Haven, 1997), 218–19.

95. Sues, *Shark's Fins*, 283–84.

96. Buzard, *Beaten Track*, 10. For some later versions of the Western view of Mao as somehow incarnating China, see Paul Hollander, *Political Pilgrims: Travels of Western Intellectuals to the Soviet Union, China, and Cuba, 1928–1978* (1981; rpt., Lanham, Md., 1990), 325–31.

97. Sues, *Shark's Fins*, 285.

98. Smedley, *Battle Hymn*, 300.

99. Sues, *Shark's Fins*, 287–88. According to a recent study, the literacy campaigns of the Yan'an years were generally restricted to the army, and their purpose was less literacy than political mobilization. See Glen Peterson, *The Power of Words: Literacy and Revolution in South China, 1949–95* (Vancouver, 1997), 40–41.

100. Peck, *Two Kinds of Time*, 708–11.

Chapter 8

1. Jespersen, *American Images*, 24–44, examines *Time*'s treatment of Chiang.

2. Sues, *Shark's Fins*, 294.

3. Auden, "Commentary" to the sonnet sequence, "In Time of War," from *Journey to a War*, 291–92.

4. See Jasper Becker, *Hungry Ghosts: Mao's Secret Famine* (New York, 1997), esp. 287–304; Roderick MacFarquahar, *The Origins of the Cultural Revolution*, vol. 3: *The Coming of the Cataclysm, 1951–1966* (New York, 1997), 1–8.

Bibliography

Primary Sources

Acton, Harold. *Memoirs of an Aesthete.* 1948. Reprint. London: Hamish Hamilton, 1984.

———. *Peonies and Ponies.* 1941. Reprint. Hong Kong: Oxford University Press, 1983.

Alec-Tweedie, Mrs. (Ethel Brillana Tweedie). *An Adventurous Journey: Russia-Siberia-China.* 1926. Reprint. London: Thornton Butterworth, 1929.

All about Shanghai and Environs: A Standard Guidebook. 1934. Reprint. Hong Kong: Oxford University Press, 1983.

Alsop, Gulielma F. *My Chinese Days.* Boston: Little, Brown, 1918.

Arlington, L. C., and William Lewisohn. *In Search of Old Peking.* 1935. Reprint. Hong Kong: Oxford University Press, 1991.

Arnold, J. *A Handbook to the West River, Being a Short Description of the Chief Places of Interest between Canton and Wuchow-fu,* 2d rev. ed. Hong Kong: Hong Kong, Canton and Macao Steamboat Co.; China Navigation Co. Indo-China Steam Navigation Co., 1909.

Auden, W. H. *Prose and Travel Books in Prose and Verse,* vol. 1: *1926–1938,* ed. Edward Mendelson. Princeton: Princeton University Press, 1996.

Auden, W. H., and Christopher Isherwood. *Journey to a War.* London: Faber and Faber, 1939.

Ayscough, Florence. *A Chinese Mirror: Being Reflections of the Reality behind Appearance.* Boston and New York: Houghton Mifflin, n.d. [1926?].

Barnett, A. Doak. *China on the Eve of Communist Takeover.* New York: Frederick A. Praeger, 1963.

Bigland, Eileen. *Into China.* London: Collins, 1940.

Bird, Isabella. *The Golden Chersonese and the Way Thither.* 1883. Reprint. Kuala Lumpur: Oxford University Press, 1967.

——— (Mrs. J. F. Bishop). *The Yangtze Valley and Beyond: An Account of Journeys in China, Chiefly in the Province of Sze Chuan and among the Man-Tse of the Somo Territory.* London: John Murray, 1899.

Bland, J. O. P. *Houseboat Days in China.* London: Edward Arnold, 1909.

Bodde, Derk. *Peking Diary, 1948–1949: A Year of Revolution.* 1950. Reprint. Greenwich, Conn.: Fawcett Publications, 1967.

Boerschmann, Ernst. *Picturesque China, Architecture and Landscape: A Journey through Twelve Provinces.* New York: Brentano, n.d.

Buxton, L. J. Dudley. *The Eastern Road.* London: Kegan Paul, Trench, Trubner and Co., 1924.

Carlson, Evans F. *Twin Stars of China: A Behind-the-Scenes Story of China's Valiant Struggle for Existence by a U.S. Marine Who Lived & Moved with the People.* 1940. Reprint. Westport, Conn.: Hyperion Press, 1975.

Chesterton, Ada Elizabeth (Mrs. Cecil Chesterton). *Young China and New Japan.* Philadelphia: J. B. Lippincott Co., n.d. [1933?].

China Year Book, 1938, ed. H. G. W. Woodhead. Shanghai: North China Daily News and Herald, 1938.

Colquhoun, Archibald R. *Across Chrysê: Being the Narrative of a Journey of Exploration through the South China Borderlands from Canton to Mandalay,* 2 vols. New York: Scribner, Welford and Co., 1883.

———. *Overland to China.* New York and London: Harper and Bros., 1900.

Cook's Handbook for Tourists to Peking, Tientsin, Shan-hai-kwan, Mukden, Dalny, Port Arthur, and Seoul. London: Simpkin, Marshall, Hamilton, Kent and Co., 1910.

Close, Upton [Josef W. Hall]. *In the Land of the Laughing Buddha: The Adventures of an American Barbarian in China.* New York and London: G. P. Putnam's Sons, 1924.

———. "The Dove in China War: The Ultimate Appeal to Reason in the Comic Chinese Madhouse of Martial China." *Asia* 25, no. 3 (March 1925): 233–37, 246–48.

Clune, Frank. *Sky High to Shanghai: An Account of My Oriental Travels in the Spring of 1938, with Side Glances at the History, Geography and Politics of the Asiatic Littoral, Written with Charity to All and Malice to None.* Sydney and London: Angus and Robertson, 1939.

Cressy-Marcks, Violet. *Journey into China.* London: Hodder and Stoughton, 1940.

Daly, Emily Lucy French (Mrs. de Burgh Daly). *An Irishwoman in China.* London: T. Werner Laurie, 1915.

Darwent, C. E. *Shanghai: A Handbook for Travellers and Residents to the Chief Objects of Interest in and around the Foreign Settlements and Native City.* Shanghai: Kelly and Walsh, 1920.

Deering, Mabel Croft. "Ho for the Soochow Ho." *National Geographic* 51, no. 6 (June 1927): 623–49.

Dewey, John, and Alice Chipman Dewey, *Letters from China and Japan,* ed. Evelyn Dewey. New York: E. P. Dutton and Co., 1920.

Digby, George. *Down Wind.* New York: E. P. Dutton and Co., 1939.

Dingle, Edwin J. *Across China on Foot: Life in the Interior and the Reform Movement.* New York: Henry Holt, 1911.

Dobson, Richard P. *China Cycle.* London: Macmillan and Co., 1946.

Dundas, Lawrence John Lumley, Earl of Ronaldshay. *A Wandering Student in the Far East,* 2 vols. Edinburgh and London: William Blackwood and Sons, 1908.

Enders, Elizabeth Crump. *Swinging Lanterns.* New York: D. Appleton and Co., 1923.

———. *Temple Bells and Silver Sails.* New York: D. Appleton and Co., 1925.

Fitkin, Gretchen Mae. *The Great River: The Story of a Voyage on the Yangtze Kiang.* Shanghai: North China Daily News, and Kelly and Walsh, 1922.

Fleming, Peter. *News from Tartary: A Journey from Peking to Kashmir.* 1936. Reprint. London and Sydney: Futura Macdonald and Co., 1983.

———. *One's Company: A Journey to China.* New York: Charles Scribner's Sons, 1934.

Franck, Harry A. *Roving through Southern China.* New York: Century Co., 1925.

———. *Wandering in Northern China.* New York: Century Co., 1923.

Gaunt, Mary. *A Broken Journey: Wanderings from the Hoang-ho to the Island of Saghalien and the Upper Reaches of the Amur River.* London: T. Werner Laurie, n.d. [1919?].

———. *A Woman in China.* London: T. Werner Laurie, n.d. [1914?].

Geil, William Edgar. *A Yankee on the Yangtze: Being a Narrative of a Journey from Shanghai through the Central Kingdom to Burma.* New York: A. C. Armstrong and Son, 1904

Goodrich, L. Carrington, and Nigel Cameron, eds. *The Face of China as Seen by Photographers and Travelers, 1860–1912.* Millerton, N.Y: Aperture, Inc., 1978.

Gordon Cumming, C. F. (Constance Frederica). *Wanderings in China.* Edinburgh and London:William Blackwood, 1880.

Gray, John Henry. *Walks in the City of Canton.* Victoria, Hong Kong: De Souza and Co.,1975.

Guide to China with Land and Sea Routes between the American and European Continents. 2d ed. Tokyo: Japanese Government Railways, 1924.

Hahn, Emily. *China to Me: A Partial Autobiography.* Philadelphia: Blakiston Co., 1944.

Homer, Joy. *Dawn Watch in China.* Boston: Houghton Mifflin Co., 1941.

Hyde, Robin (Iris Wilkinson). *Dragon Rampant.* London: Hurst and Blackett, 1939[?].

Isherwood, Christopher. *Christopher and His Kind, 1929–1939.* New York: Farrar Straus Giroux, 1976.

Jackson, Innes. *China Only Yesterday.* London: Faber and Faber, 1938.

James, Henry. *Italian Hours,* ed. John Auchard. 1909. Reprint. New York: Penguin Books, 1995.

Johnston, R. F. *From Peking to Mandalay: A Journey from North China to Burma through Tibetan Ssuch'uan and Yunnan.* 1908. Reprint. Taipei: Ch'eng Wen, 1972.

Kates, George. *The Years That Were Fat: Peking, 1933–1940.* New York: Harper and Brothers, 1952.

Kendall, Elizabeth. *A Wayfarer in China: Impressions of a Trip across West China and Mongolia.* Boston and New York: Houghton Mifflin, 1913.

Kerby, Philip. *Beyond the Bund.* New York: Payson and Clarke, 1927.

Lattimore, Owen. *The Desert Road to Turkestan.* 1929. Reprint. New York: Kodansha America, 1995.

Little, Archibald John. *Through the Yang-tse Gorges: or Trade and Travel in Western China.* 1898. Reprint. Taipei: Ch'eng Wen, 1972.

———. *Across Yunnan: A Journey of Surprises, Including an Account of the Remarkable French Railway Line Now Completed to Yunnan-fu,* ed. by Mrs. Archibald Little. London: Sampson Low, Marston and Co., 1910.

Little, Alicia (Mrs. Archibald Little). *Guide to Peking.* Tientsin: Tientsin Press, 1904.

———. *Round about My Peking Garden*. London: T. Fisher Unwin; and Philadelphia: J. B. Lippincott, 1905.

Lu Hsun (Zhou Shuren). "Some Notions Jotted Down by Lamp-Light." *Selected Works of Lu Hsun*, 2:131–41. Beijing: Foreign Languages Press, 1964.

MacGowan, J. *Pictures of Southern China*. London: Religious Tract Societies, 1897.

Mackenzie-Grieve, Averil. *A Race of Green Ginger*. London: Putnam, 1959.

Maillart, Ella K. *Forbidden Journey: From Peking to Kashmir*, trans. Thomas McGreevy. New York Henry Holt, 1937.

Margary, Augustus R. *The Journey of Augustus Raymond Margary, from Shanghae to Bhamo, and Back to Manwyne. From His Journals and Letters, with a Brief Biographical Preface: To which is added a Concluding Chapter by Sir Rutherford Alcock, K. C. B.* 2d ed. London: Macmillan and Co., 1876.

Mayers, William F., N. B. Dennys, and Charles King. *The Treaty Ports of China and Japan: A Complete Guide to the Open Ports of Those Countries, Together with Peking, Yedo, Hongkong and Macao, Forming a Guidebook and Vade Mecum for Travellers, Merchants, and Residents in General*. London: Trübner and Co., 1867.

McMahon, Thomas J. *The Orient I Found*. London: Duckworth, 1926.

Morcom, Col. R. K. [?]. *Eastward Ho! A Private Diary of a Public Excursion, 1930–31*. Bromsgrove: Messenger Co., n.d.

Morrison, G. E. *An Australian in China: Being the Narrative of a Quiet Journey across China to British Burma*. 1895. Reprint. London and Sydney: Angus and Robertson, 1972.

Morrison, Hedda. *A Photographer in Old Peking*. Hong Kong: Oxford University Press, 1985.

———. *Travels of a Photographer in China, 1933–1946*. Hong Kong: Oxford University Press, 1987.

Mowrer, Edgar Ansel. *The Dragon Wakes: A Report from China*. New York: William Morrow and Co., 1939.

Parker, E. H. *Up the Yang-tse*. Hong Kong: Printed at the *China Mail* Office, 1891.

Payne, Robert. *China Awake*. New York: Dodd, Mead and Co., 1947

———. *Forever China*. New York: Dodd, Mead and Co., 1945.

Peck, Graham. *Through China's Wall*. Boston: Houghton Mifflin Co., 1940.

———. *Two Kinds of Time*. Boston: Houghton Mifflin Co., 1950.

Peking and the Overland Route. 3d ed. London: Thomas Cook and Son, 1917.

Percival, William Spencer. *The Land of the Dragon: My Boating and Shooting Excursions to the Gorges of the Upper Yangtze*. London: Hurst and Blackett, 1889.

Pitcher, Philip Wilson. *In and about Amoy: Some Historical and Other Facts Connected with One of the First Open Ports in China*. Shanghai and Foochow: Methodist Publishing House in China, 1909.

Porter, Eliot. *All Under Heaven: The Chinese World*. New York: Pantheon, 1983.

Purcell, Victor. *Chinese Evergreen*. London: Michael Joseph, 1938.

Qi Fang and Qi Jiran, eds., *Old Peking, The City and Its People*. Hong Kong: Hai Feng Publishing House, 1993.

Ransome, Arthur. *The Chinese Puzzle*. London: G. Allen and Unwin, 1927.

Russell, Bertrand. *The Problem of China*. London: G. Allen Unwin, 1922.

Scidmore, Eliza Ruhamah. *China: The Long-Lived Empire.* New York: Century Co, 1900.

———. *Westward to the Far East: A Guide to the Principal Cities of China and Japan, with a Note on Korea.* 5th ed. Montreal[?]: Canadian Pacific Railway, 1894.

Seton, Grace Thompson. *Chinese Lanterns.* New York: Dodd, Mead and Co., 1924.

Shanghai of To-day: A Souvenir Album of Fifty Vanduke Gravure Prints of "The Model Settlement." 3d rev. ed. Shanghai: Kelly and Walsh, 1930.

Shor, Jean Bowie. *After You, Marco Polo.* New York: McGraw-Hill, 1955.

Sitwell, Osbert. *Escape with Me! An Oriental Sketch-Book.* New York: Harrison-Hilton Books, 1940.

Smedley, Agnes. *Battle Hymn of China.* New York: Alfred A. Knopf, 1943.

Smith, Arthur H. *Chinese Characteristics.* Boston and Chicago: United Society for Christian Endeavor, 1894.

Snow, Edgar. *Red Star over China.* New York: Random House, 1938.

Snow, Helen Foster (Nym Wales). *Inside Red China.* 1932. Reprint. New York: Da Capo Press, 1977.

Speakman, Harold. *Beyond Shanghai,* New York: Abingdon Press, 1922.

Stoddard, Lothrop. *The Rising Tide of Color against White World-Supremacy.* New York: Charles Scribner's Sons, 1922.

Sues, Ilona Ralf. *Shark's Fins and Millet.* Boston: Little, Brown and Co., 1944.

Teichman, Eric. *Travels of a Consular Officer in North-West China.* Cambridge: Cambridge University Press, 1921.

Thomson, John. *Through China with a Camera.* London and New York: Harper and Bros., 1899.

Warner, Langdon. *The Long Old Road in China.* Garden City, N.Y.: Doubleday, Page and Co., 1926.

Warwick, Adam. "A Thousand Miles along the Great Wall of China." *National Geographic* 43, no. 2 (February 1923): 113–43.

Welch, Denton. *Maiden Voyage.* 1943. Reprint. Harmondsworth: Penguin Books, 1983.

White, Theodore, and Annalee Jacoby. *Thunder Out of China.* New York: William Sloane Associates, Inc., 1946.

Wilson, James Harrison. *China Travels and Investigations in the "Middle Kingdom": A Study of Its Civilization and Possibilities, with a Glance at Japan.* 2d ed. 1887. Reprint. New York: D. Appleton and Co., 1901.

Wingate, A. W. S. *A Cavalier in China.* London: Grayson and Grayson, 1940.

Worswick, Clark, and Jonathan Spence. *Imperial China: Photographs, 1850–1912.* New York: Pennwick, 1978.

Yorke, Gerald. *China Changes.* New York: Charles Scribner's Sons, 1936.

Secondary Works

Anagnost, Ann. *National Past-Times: Narrative, Power, and Representation in Modern China.* Durham, N.C.: Duke University Press 1997.

Annan, Noel. *Our Age: English Intellectuals between the World Wars—a Group Portrait.* New York: Random House, 1990.

Avineri, Shlomo. *Karl Marx on Colonialism and Modernization*. New York: Doubleday and Co., Inc., 1968.

Barkan, Elazar. *The Retreat of Scientific Racism: Changing Concepts of Race in Britain and the United States between the World Wars*. Cambridge: Cambridge University Press, 1992.

Barr, Pat. *A Curious Life for a Lady: The Story of Isabella Bird*. 1970. Reprint. London: Penguin Books, 1985.

Barthes, Roland. *Empire of Signs*, trans. Richard Howard. New York: Hill and Wang, 1970.

Becker, Jasper. *Hungry Ghosts: Mao's Secret Famine*. New York: Free Press, 1997.

Bergère, Marie-Claire. "'The Other China': Shanghai from 1919 to 1949." In *Shanghai: Revolution and Development in an Asian Metropolis*, ed. Christopher Howe. Cambridge: Cambridge University Press, 1981.

———. *L'age d'or de la bourgeoisie chinoise, 1911–1937*. Paris: Flammarion, 1986.

Bickers, Robert. *Britain in China: Community, Culture and Colonialism, 1900–1930*. Manchester: Manchester University Press, 1999.

Bickers, Robert, and Jeffrey Wasserstrom. "Shanghai's 'Dogs and Chinese Not Admitted' Sign: Legend, History, and Contemporary Symbol." *China Quarterly* 142 (June 1995): 444–66.

Birkett, Dea. *Spinsters Abroad: Victorian Lady Travellers*. Oxford: Basil Blackwell, 1989.

Bishop, Peter. *The Myth of Shangri-La: Tibet, Travel Writing and the Western Creation of Sacred Landscape*. Berkeley: University of California Press, 1989.

Brantlinger, Patrick. *Rule of Darkness: British Literature and Imperialism, 1830–1914*. Ithaca: Cornell University Press, 1988.

———. "Victorians and Africans: The Genealogy of the Myth of the Dark Continent." In *"Race," Writing, and Difference*, ed. Henry Louis Gates Jr. et al. Chicago: University of Chicago Press, 1986.

Buzard, James. *The Beaten Track: European Tourism, Literature, and the Ways to Culture, 1800–1918*. New York and London: Oxford University Press, 1993.

———. "Victorian Women and the Implications of Empire." *Victorian Studies* 36, no. 4 (Summer 1993): 443–53.

Chen Xiaomei. "Occidentalism as Counterdiscourse: 'He Shang' in Post-Mao China." *Critical Inquiry* 18, no. 4 (Summer 1992): 686–712.

———. *Occidentalism: A Theory of Counter-Discourse in Post-Mao China*. London and New York: Oxford University Press, 1995.

Chen, Jerome. *China and the West: Society and Culture, 1815–1937*. Bloomington: Indiana University Press, 1979.

Cheyfitz, Eric. *The Poetics of Imperialism: Translation and Colonization from* The Tempest *to* Tarzan. New York: Oxford University Press, 1991.

Clifford, James, and George Marcus, eds. *Writing Culture: The Poetics and Politics of Ethnography*. Berkeley: University of California Press, 1986.

Clifford, Nicholas R. "A Revolution Is Not a Tea Party: The 'Shanghai Minds' Reconsidered." *Pacific Historical Review* 59, no. 4 (November 1990): 501–26.

———. "White China, Red China: Lighting Out for the Territory with Edgar Snow." *New England Review* 18, no. 2 (Spring 1997): 103–11.

————. *Spoilt Children of Empire: Westerners in Shanghai and the Chinese Revolution of the 1920s.* Hanover, N.H.: University Press of New England, 1991.

Cohen, Paul. *Discovering History in China: American Historical Writing on the Recent Chinese Past.* New York: Columbia University Press, 1984.

————. *History in Three Keys: The Boxers as Event, Experience, and Myth.* New York: Columbia University Press, 1997.

Darby, Phillip. *Three Faces of Imperialism: British and American Approaches to Asia and Africa, 1870–1970.* New Haven: Yale University Press, 1987.

Dawson, Raymond. *The Chinese Chameleon: An Analysis of European Conceptions of Chinese Civilisation.* London: Oxford University Press, 1967.

Dikötter, Frank. *The Discourse of Race in Modern China.* Stanford: Stanford University Press, 1992

Dirlik, Arif. "Chinese History and the Question of Orientalism." *History and Theory* 35, no. 4 (Dec. 1996): 96–119.

Duara, Prasenjit. *Rescuing History from the Nation: Questioning Narratives of Modern China.* Chicago: Chicago University Press, 1995.

Duncan, James, and Derek Gregory, eds. *Writes of Passage: Reading Travel Writing.* London and New York: Routledge, 1999.

Ebrey, Patricia. *Chinese Civilization and Society: A Sourcebook.* New York: Free Press, 1981.

Fairbank, John K., and S. Y. Teng. *China's Response to the West.* Cambridge, Mass.: Harvard University Press, 1961.

Fritzsche, Sybille. *Narrating China: Western Travelers in the Middle Kingdom after the Opium War.* Ann Arbor: University Microfilms, 1995.

Fussell, Paul. *Abroad: British Literary Traveling between the Wars.* New York: Oxford University Press, 1980.

Green, Martin. *Dreams of Adventure, Deeds of Empire.* New York: Basic Books, 1979.

Heffer, Jean. *Les États-Unis et le Pacifique: histoire d'une frontière.* Paris: Albin Michel, 1995.

Heinrich, Larissa N. "Handmaids to the Gospel: Lam Qua's Medical Portraiture." In *Tokens of Exchange: The Problem of Translation in Global Circulations,* ed. Lydia Liu, 239–75. Durham, N.C: Duke University Press, 1999.

Hobson, J. A. *Imperialism: A Study.* 1938. Reprint. Ann Arbor: University of Michigan Press, 1965.

Hollander, Paul. *Political Pilgrims: Travels of Western Intellectuals to the Soviet Union, China, and Cuba, 1928–1978.* 1981. Reprint. Lanham, Md.: University Press of America, 1990.

Hudson, G. F. *Europe and China: A Survey of their Relations from the Earliest Times to 1800.* London: Edward Arnold and Co., 1931.

Isaacs, Harold. *Scratches on Our Minds.* New York: John Day, 1958.

Jesperson, T. Christopher. *American Images of China, 1931–1949.* Palo Alto: Stanford University Press, 1996.

Jordan, David Starr. *The Human Harvest: A Study of the Decay of Races through the Survival of the Unfit.* Boston: American Unitarian Association, 1907.

Kaplan, Caren. *Questions of Travel: Postmodern Discourses of Displacement.* Durham, N.C.: Duke University Press, 1996.

Keane, A. H. *Ethnology*. 2d ed. Cambridge: Cambridge University Press, 1896.

Kowaleski, Michael, ed. *Temperamental Journeys: Essays on the Modern Literature of Travel*. Athens: University of Georgia Press, 1992.

LaCapra, Dominick. "History, Language, and Reading: Waiting for Crillon." *American Historical Review* 100, no. 3 (June 1995): 799–828.

Lears, Jackson. *No Place of Grace: Antimodernism and the Transformation of American Culture, 1880–1920*. Chicago: University of Chicago Press, 1994.

Leed, Eric. *The Mind of the Traveler: From Gilgamesh to Global Tourism*. New York: Basic Books, 1991.

Lifton, Robert J. *Revolutionary Immortality*. New York: Random House, 1968.

Lopez, Donald S. *Prisoners of Shangri-la: Tibetan Buddhism and the West*. Chicago: University of Chicago Press, 1998.

MacDonald, Robert H. *The Language of Empire: Myths and Metaphors of Popular Imperialism, 1880–1918*. Manchester: Manchester University Press, 1994.

MacFarquahar, Roderick. *The Origins of the Cultural Revolution*, vol. 3: *The Coming of the Cataclysm, 1951–1966*. New York: Columbia University Press, 1997.

MacKenzie, John M. *Propaganda and Empire: The Manipulation of British Public Opinion, 1880–1960*. Manchester: Manchester University Press, 1984.

———. *Orientalism: History, Theory and the Arts*. Manchester: Manchester University Press, 1995.

Mackinnon, Janice R., and Stephen R. Mackinnon. *Agnes Smedley: The Life and Times of an American Radical*. Berkeley: University of California Press, 1988.

———. *China Reporting*. Berkeley: University of California Press, 1987.

Mao Zedong. "The Chinese Revolution and the Chinese Communist Party." *Selected Works of Mao Tse-tung*, 3:305–34. Beijing: Foreign Languages Press.

McCannell, Dean. *The Tourist: A New Theory of the Leisure Class*. New York: Schocken Books, 1976 (issued with new introduction in 1989).

Middleton, Dorothy. *Victorian Lady Travelers*. 1965. Reprint. Chicago: Academy Chicago, 1982.

Mills, Sara. *Discourses of Difference: An Analysis of Women's Travel Writing and Colonialism*. London and New York: Routledge and Kegan Paul, 1991.

Ming Xie. "The Postmodern as the Postcolonial: Re-cognizing Chinese Modernity." *Ariel: A Review of International English Literature* 28, no. 4 (Oct. 1997): 11–32.

Morgan, Susan. *Place Matters: Gendered Geography in Victorian Women's Travel Books about Southeast Asia*. New Brunswick: Rutgers University Press, 1996.

Pelcovits, Nathan A. *Old China Hands and the Foreign Office*. New York: King's Crown Press, 1948.

Porter, Dennis. *Haunted Journeys: Desire and Transgression in European Travel Writing*. Princeton: Princeton University Press, 1991.

———. "Orientalism and Its Problems." In *Colonial Discourse and Post-colonial Theory: A Reader*, ed. Patrick Williams and Laura Chrisman, 150–61. New York: Columbia University Press, 1994.

Pratt, Mary Louise. *Imperial Eyes: Travel Writing and Transculturation*. London and New York: Routledge and Kegan Paul, 1992.

Pusey, James. *China and Charles Darwin*. Cambridge, Mass.: Council on East Asian Studies, Harvard University, 1983.

Rand, Peter. *China Hands: The Adventures and Ordeals of the American Journalists Who Joined Forces with the Great Chinese Revolution.* New York: Simon and Schuster, 1995.

Reichwein, Adolf. *China and Europe: Intellectual and Artistic Contacts in the Eighteenth Century,* trans. J. C. Powell. London: Kegan Paul, Trench, Trubner and Co., 1925.

Rosaldo, Renato. "Imperialist Nostalgia." *Representations* 26 (Spring 1989): 107–22.

Said, Edward. *Orientalism.* New York: Random House, 1978.

———. *Culture and Imperialism.* New York: Alfred A. Knopf, 1993.

Selden, Mark. *The Yenan Way in Revolutionary China.* Cambridge, Mass.: Harvard University Press, 1971.

Shewmaker, Kenneth. *Americans and Chinese Communists, 1927–1945: A Persuading Encounter.* Ithaca: Cornell University Press, 1971.

Smith, Arthur H. *Chinese Characteristics.* Boston and Chicago: United Society Christian Endeavor, 1894.

Spence, Jonathan. *The Chan's Great Continent: China in Western Minds.* New York: W. W. Norton and Co., 1998.

Spurr, David. *The Rhetoric of Empire: Colonial Discourse in Journalism, Travel Writing, and Imperial Administration.* Durham, N.C.: Duke University Press, 1993.

Stepan, Nancy. *The Idea of Race in Science: Great Britain, 1800–1960.* Hamden, Conn.: Archon Press, 1982.

Stocking, George W., Jr. *Race, Culture, and Evolution: Essays on the History of Anthropology.* New York: Free Press, 1968.

———. *Victorian Anthropology.* New York: Free Press, 1987.

Thurin, Susan Schoenbauer. *Victorian Travelers and the Opening of China, 1842–1907.* Athens: Ohio University Press, 1999.

Tinling, Marion. *Women into the Unknown: A Sourcebook on Women Explorers and Travelers.* Westport, Conn.: Greenwood Press, 1989.

Tsou, Tang. *America's Failure in China, 1941–1950.* Chicago: Chicago University Press, 1963.

Waldron, Arthur. *The Great Wall of China: From History to Myth.* New York: Cambridge University Press, 1990.

———. "The Warlord: Twentieth-Century Chinese Understandings of Violence, Militarism, and Imperialism." *American Historical Review* 96, no. 4 (Oct. 1991): 1073–1100.

Wang Ning. "Postcolonial Theory and the 'Decolonization' of Chinese Culture." *Ariel: A Review of International English Literature* 28, (Oct. 1997): 33–47.

Wang, Ban. *The Sublime Figure of History: Aesthetics and Politics in Twentieth Century China.* Stanford: Stanford University Press, 1997.

Wolfe, Patrick. "History and Imperialism: A Century of Theory, from Marx to Postcolonialism." *American Historical Review* (April 1997): 388–420.

Wood, Frances. *No Dogs and Not Many Chinese: Treaty Port Life in China, 1843–1943.* London: John Murray, 1998.

Wong, R. Bin. *China Transformed: Historical Change and the Limits of European Experience.* Ithaca: Cornell University Press, 1997.

Wright, Mary, ed. *China in Revolution: The First Phase, 1900–1913*. New Haven: Yale University Press, 1968.

Yu, Beongcheon. *The Great Circle: American Writers and the Orient*. Detroit: Wayne State University Press, 1983.

Xi, Lian. *The Conversion of Missionaries: Liberalism in American Protestant Missions in China, 1907–1932*. University Park: Pennsylvania State University Press, 1997.

Zhang Longxi. "The Myth of the Other: China in the Eyes of the West." *Critical Inquiry* 15, no. 1 (Autumn 1988): 108–31.

Index

Chinese names of cities and people are indexed under their pinyin spelling; thus Amoy is to be found as Xiamen, Canton as Guangzhou, and Li Hung-chang as Li Hongzhang. See pp. xiii–xiv, "Note on Romanization."